Gamal al-Ghitani (1945–2015) was an Egyptian novelist, literary editor, political commentator, and public intellectual. He published over a dozen novels, including *Zayni Barakat* (AUC Press, 2004) and *The Zafarani Files* (AUC Press, 2009), as well as several collections of short stories. He was also founding editor of the literary magazine, *Akhbar al-adab* (1993–2011). He was awarded the Egyptian State Prize for the Novel (1980), the Chevalier de l'Ordre des Arts et des Lettres from France (1987), and the Egyptian State Prize for Literature (2007). In 2015, he received the Nile Award in Literature, Egypt's highest literary honor.

Nader K. Uthman is associate professor in the department of Middle Eastern and Islamic Studies at New York University.

T0352460

TRACES

a memoir

Composition Books – No. 5

Gamal al-Ghitani

Translated by
Nader K. Uthman

The American University in Cairo Press
Cairo New York

First published in 2020 by
The American University in Cairo Press
113 Sharia Kasr el Aini, Cairo, Egypt
One Rockefeller Plaza, New York, NY 10020
www.aucpress.com

Dar el Kutub No. 10990/19
ISBN 978 977 416 953 3

Dar el Kutub Cataloging-in-Publication Data

Al-Ghitani, Gamal.
        Traces: A Memoir / Gamal al-Ghitani.—Cairo: The American University in Cairo Press,
    2020.
            p. cm.
            ISBN 978 977 416 9533
            1. Al-Ghitani, Gamal, 1945–2015—Diaries
            920

1 2 3 4 5   24 23 22 21 20

Designed by Adam el-Sehemy
Printed in the United Kingdom

"As if life were a memory . . . "
—Fuad Haddad

Getting ready to leave

The extension rings; it's her voice—optimistic, always suggestive of the moment of sunrise, the beginning of a new day. Since I first joined thirty-six years ago, we've talked once or twice a year, exchanging inquiries about children and health and touching briefly, sometimes, on things having to do with work. In the past year, she's always taken the initiative, showing a generous affection, perhaps because we've known each other for so long—our instinctive understanding, our parallel circumstances, the children moving from one phase in life to another, questions about the future, engagement, marriage. She's not a grandmother yet, nor am I a grandfather. Just hearing her voice fills me with a kind of happy anticipation.

"Did you notice the raise this month?" she asks brightly.

I tell her it was the bursar who'd drawn my attention to it. I'd lost any sense of my salary years ago, when the fall in the value of the Egyptian pound meant that it covered only the very basic needs.

"Nothing is enough anymore," she agrees, "whether it's a little or a lot. But this raise is significant."

"I expected a performance bonus," I say.

"The performance bonuses will be paid next month, but this raise is in recognition of those who've reached the beginning of their last year of service," she says.

Smiling, I reply, "So that's what those fifty pounds are?"

She says she wanted to tell me so that I wouldn't be too puzzled. Then she adds that ours has been a lifelong friendship and that the difference between us is just one year. She will retire the year after me, in the same month. Warmly, I wish her good health and peace of mind.

After the call is over, I look up at the office walls—the photos in their frames, the paintings and prints that I always look at, the books in the bookcase facing me.

I must start clearing all of this out so that I don't suddenly find myself having to empty out the place in just a few days. It's no surprise that I've reached my last year, that I'll arrive at the point of retirement this time next year. I've been thinking about it for a while, but this is the first time I've been faced with the practicality of it. Everything is proceeding according to a precise system that's been in place for a long time. I'm still surprised by that bonus, which nobody had mentioned before. I think about the procedures that accompany the end of service: settling my pension, confirming that I've completed my years of service, finalizing the necessary documents, determining the benefits I'll receive from social insurance, the savings pool at work, and the union. A week ago, an old friend visited me. He retired two years ago. I asked him what he'd gone through: the administrative procedures that were weighing on my mind, the documents that had to be completed, and the total amount of the severance payment that I would deposit in the bank and whose interest I would use to make up for the drop in my income after I left service.

Leaving service?

Retirement?

Why should I feel so astonished, taken by surprise, confused, like someone who's lost his bearings, even though, for some time now, I've been looking back at what was, rather than looking forward to what will be?

Why is my sense of time suddenly heightened, as if I've been caught unawares, even though the facts have been clear—and for quite a while?

And so I'm living through a critical period, a stage between two different states. I'm not fully alert, only receiving signals that could be either a sharp jab or a gentle touch. Is it possible that her voice over the phone should have alerted me to such decisive moments?

I stare at an indeterminate point, semiconscious, as if floating on brief moments from the past, not knowing whether they're passing me by or I'm passing by them. Those days, months, years; those seconds and minutes—why the tears in my eyes, why am I on the verge of shedding tears without tears, while all of this has been so expected?

Is it her voice announcing the start of the procedures, the preparing of the documents, the thud of the ink stamps, the closing of files? That bonus she mentions is a gentle reminder to be ready, a signal to pack the suitcases for departure, a faint beam that alerts the traveler that he's arriving at his destination. How quickly time passes!

I see myself through the eyes of a bird circling at a great height as I once crossed that road to the old administration building. The particular day or month escapes me, yet I see the moment when I crossed that threshold for the first time, when I signed the document to begin work. I was twenty-four at the time: a trajectory of thirty-six years, now reduced to a few papers in a file, transferred to the archives, the dust accumulating on top of lines written at different times, on top of signatures and reports to which I didn't have access and decisions that once meant something.

The end overtakes me abruptly. When I started out, I thought I had infinite time—looking forward took precedence over looking back. At thirty, I paused. My writing was an expression of my surprise at the completion of three decades. When you reach such a juncture, it's as if a door closes firmly behind you, making it impossible to go back. After thirty, time is compressed. Reaching forty is faster. Fifty arrives in no time, and now here I am, "with a distance of two bow lengths to go, or less" (Qur'an 53:9). Finishing out the term of service—retirement. Pension? How can the word for "ceasing to work" share the same root in Arabic as the word for "living?" How is it that I haven't considered this expression before? In calling the end an exit, are there echoes of a hidden code from the time of our distant ancestors? They thought of eternal silence as a mere phase, a transition from state to state.

Departing into daylight. Retirement—perhaps. Regardless of the terms, the phrase is nothing but an expression of the expiration of a life and the beginning of a different time—more reminiscence and less expectation. I recall the phrase as it appeared in the ancient, sacred book:[1]

Yesterday I completed my life

And today I go out into the day.

I repeat it when I'm on my own, solitary, a situation that's familiar to me. My acute awareness of the passage of time spurs me to write in these notebooks. Yet beginning the practical steps of what had been merely an expectation takes things to a different domain. My colleague's smiling voice, glowing with friendship, calls my attention to what I've understood, in its entirety, for a while.

---

1   Widely known as *The Book of the Dead*, the original title in ancient Egyptian ("Birt emhaaro") is "The Departure into Daylight" (author's translation).

Those tiny specks remain after the extinction of time—mere traces that remain after the erasure of the moments I've passed through or that have passed through me, some which exhausted me and caused me pain, others which delighted me and transported me to rare heights.

As the end draws near, everything is compressed, time is condensed into particles that shoot past me without lingering. If I were to describe it in this way to those who have put up with me and endured my company, they would be taken aback. Traces, what are left of me, that matter to no one but me. All that I've accomplished is nothing but a shadow of erased shadows, wisps of dispersed clouds. A presence unnoticed by those who pass by, some of whom I knew, others who came from nowhere, from gates hidden from me, and then disappeared. Moments which have now passed—mere signals of what used to be, suggesting or signifying the hidden cycles of the universe, that enfold me completely.

My traces are echoes of desire. Fear, longing, sadness, yearning—shadows of the dew formed in the recesses of the soul. My inner world is crowded with unheard cries, unuttered laments, whispers of planets and the glimmer of stars that I once sought with my limited vision. For a fleeting moment, I wondered about their locations and their moons and about what remained of their life spans. After I'm gone, some will live on for millions of years. Others are already long extinct, even though I can still see their light shining from the past. I no longer take any notice of my own continuing disappearance. Now, I observe what remains of me just as I observe those fading stars—as we all disappear. It's not me who beholds them. It's someone else, someone parallel to me and now departing. I try to gather what's left of his traces—my traces—as the end of my allotted time draws near, when my life will be plucked from me.

In hope, I cling to fragments . . . setting out to record whatever remains, whatever I can capture, whatever flashes through my mind, free from time and space, questions that I won't be able to answer before I go, that I can merely say out loud, with no intention of putting them in order or arranging them. Maybe what occurs to me will reveal something about me. Maybe what I capture will show something of what I was, of the yearnings I felt and the sighs I emitted as I prepared myself to go there. That will be enough for me . . .

—⚬—

Yesterday—where did it go?

—oo—

Are we born just to die? Or . . . do we die just to be born?

—oo—

Ten years from now, from this very moment, ten months, ten days, ten hours, ten minutes, ten seconds—where will I be, and where will my loved ones be, those who are close to me?

—oo—

White, black. Black, white. Which comes first?

—oo—

When we look in a particular direction, does our vision travel from within us, or do images reach us from outside?

—oo—

Why is a baby born upside down? It emerges from the mother's womb into the womb of life with its head toward the ground. Why should it be upside down? Would emerging feet first mean its demise?

—oo—

That gentle little breeze.

At the beginning of spring, the breeze caresses the surface of my body as it passes. Is it a descendant of the age-old breezes that passed over the ancestors, arousing their melancholy, their whispers, and their nascent hopes? Or was it born in my own time, this very minute, from a place and a moment I will never know?

Is it old or new?

Is it eternal, coursing through the universe, through time?

Or does it begin and then vanish completely?

Does it create its own law? Or is it subject to the same law that impels me to track the ashes of those faded stars?

Fear

It presses from within until I'm on the verge of fainting. It happens so often that I thought at first it had to do with when I looked out at the wide horizon from my office window, on my own. But it happens when I'm among people, in the warmth of companionship, the height of gaiety. I wonder if it has snuck into me by way of my aversion to reality, my seeing the opposite wherever I look. But when have I ever been in harmony with my surroundings? Haven't I always been averse to things that define and confine me? All there is to it is that my ambitions have turned from the impossible to the less impossible.

Nothing of what I suggest explains the fleeting, startling moment that crushes me when I'm caught unaware, when I'm not expecting it.

Rain

Rain . . . rain . . . rain.

I wake to the fall of the drops, to their crashing against what sounds like a metal roof. I listen attentively to the rain outside, with the covers wrapped around me. A comfortable bed. I take in the blessing of the warmth, of lying down. How wonderful to hear the storm from a secure shelter! A changing rhythm: rapid, then slowing down, then the intensity of a downpour followed by an intermittent slowness, until the end comes. The rain resembles the sequence of heartbeats, indicating the continuity of life and its renewal.

Rain . . . rain . . . rain.

A night in which it falls more intensely, a long time ago. I can almost distinguish the sound from other cloudbursts to which I've listened, or under which I've walked, or which I've observed from behind a window pane. But I'm unable to place that cozy bed in which I luxuriated or the night that reminded me of the rainfall.

Rain . . . rain . . . rain.

A dove

My father tells me about a toy. A dove that flies. He promises he will buy it. He points to the ceiling to show how high it can go. He used to buy a toy for each of us for Eid. A train, a fire engine, a toy car. But the dove, which I never saw, always preoccupied me. I didn't know whether he'd actually seen it or if he'd imagined it.

I saw it at a different time, when it caught my attention only because it matched my father's description. It was in the Place Trocadero in Paris, between the Musée National de la Marine and the Musée de l'Homme. Among the African street vendors standing there, one had a cord around his neck from which doves were hanging. They were white, brown, and gray. He had one in his hand and with the turn of a small key he would release it into the air. It would ascend upward—the exact height of a room in the old style of buildings. It would go right, then left, then stay still for a little while, before descending slowly to the ground, just as my father had described it with the movements of his hands some fifty years earlier.

The one I used to be

He who I used to be and am no longer. Several times I was he and we grew apart. We were separated from each other. What connects them all to who I am now? And now, what connects me to who I will be? What hidden bonds?

The one I used to be stands in the yard of Muhammad Ali Preparatory School. He tends to be on his own. He doesn't play with his peers, just reads and reads. His classmate is called Is'haq and lives in Qait Bey, that is, among the dead: he looks like a different creature from a distant reality, strange and fearsome. In front of him—the one I used to be—stands Is'haq, who's first playful, then teasing. Is'haq puts his hand in front of the pages of *Scaramouche the Noble*, snatching him out of a moment in which he's totally oblivious to everything around him.

"Come on—play with us, pal. All day long you just read and read."

The one I used to be gets up angrily and shouts, "You scoundrel, you have insulted me! I cast the glove in your face!"

Is'haq's face registers surprise, while angry sweat drips from his forehead. His face changes from sarcastic to serious. The one I used to be shouts again, "I challenge you to a duel! Choose your witnesses!"

After a moment of surprise, Is'haq makes a sound closer to a snort. A glove? What glove? What does that mean? And what witnesses? Are we in a film? Meanwhile, his face—the face of the one I used to be—grows pale.

The one I used to be leaves a small hotel that looks out over the ancient waterfront of Copenhagen, where timber yards, warehouses, and shipyards have been transformed into hotels and galleries, already the most expensive parts of the city. He goes out of the door and then continues to the corner. When he reaches it, the modern port appears on the other side. A huge and towering ship is entering slowly, coming from Oslo. It spends the entire night in the North Sea, bearing hundreds of containers, connecting the two Scandinavian capitals. So . . . this is the North Sea, associated in his mind with the painting *The Scream* by Edvard Munch. A terrified face emitting a terrified scream—or a cry for help—in a cold vacuum and a lingering night. Just one step from the corner, he's struck by a piercing, roaring gale. Thin and sharp, it attacks one's bare face directly. Where did he read about that thing called frostbite? It seems as if he should have taken other precautions. What made him think of going for a walk so early in the morning? With hurried steps, he goes back to shelter in the warmth of the hotel, making fun of himself. How painful, that arctic wind!

As a child, the one I used to be went down to the irrigation canal called Tirat al-Bir accompanied by his parents, his uncle, and others he didn't know. Almost middle-aged, the one I used to be goes down to the canal alone, slowly heading west. No one knows him, and none of the villagers stop him. He doesn't yet notice the elderly. He goes to the house of his uncle, whose wife, wearing black, and their only son receive him. He insists on going directly to the cemetery to recite al-Fatiha, the opening surah of the Qur'an, for his uncle's soul to rest in peace. He stares at the headstone above the grave, which looks like an abstract rendition of a stray camel or one about to kneel down. He spreads his palms while reciting al-Fatiha and thinks the headstone looks like modern art!

On an autumn afternoon, the one I used to be boards a military aircraft by the rear door, from which a short ladder extends to the ground. He takes his place at the end of the bench, facing his colleague the photographer. As the aircraft takes off, the paratroopers start reciting their enthusiastic slogans. He looks at the small, yellow lamp: when it turns red, the door opens and the jump begins, right over the Dahshour desert. The space seems bottomless and gray. Everything to do with autumn is gray, mixed with the red of the approaching sunset. The men's jump proceeds. As they pass through the gaping door, they're quickly transformed into clumps that disappear immediately into the air. The air. He's fastened to the wall of the plane by his safety belt. The photographer is absorbed in capturing the moment in which the soldier is parted from the aircraft. There, down below, the parachute begins to open. The one I used to be begins to think: Next time, I'll be with them.

The one I used to be is riding in a car in a desert. All deserts look alike, yet knowing that it's the Gobi—the one the Mongols once crossed—gives it some significance. The one I used to be stands in front of a loom at which girls in brightly colored clothes are sitting. They work quickly, fitting the knots tightly together and cutting them. He smiles a quiet smile, the meaning of which his companions do not grasp. He says to himself: *So this is Kerman then, the style of Persian rugs I loved. I learned all about its design and execution. Here I am, at its birthplace, where the designs are the memory of the tribe.* The one I used to be stands obstinately facing the sun, clear and bright in its ascent. His lips are parted, and in his eyes there's a mysterious expression that can't be ascribed to joy or sadness.

The one I used to be, or the ones—what connects one to all the others? If I seek out one of them, will I find him in a time and place between the others? If I were to meet up with any of them and say hello, and if I spoke to him and he spoke to me, would he recognize me, the one he is now? And would I recognize him? Perhaps that's my quest. The one I am now is merely a memory of them—all the ones I used to be.

—m—

Where do breezes originate?

Where do winds begin?

What's the source of the first wave? Which drives the other, the winds or the waters?

How indebted I am to that breeze which gently caressed me as I crossed Hussein Square. How it inspired my love for the universe—what I know of it and what I don't know. So from where does it come, and where does it go?

The Biter

It was as if I could see Ahmad the Biter in front of me, right then. I don't know what had brought him back to me, so many years after I'd last thought about him. I was lying on my bed, enjoying a break between the afternoon shift and the one that started after sunset—a habit dating back to my student days and continuing when I first started working to earn my daily bread. Whatever job I did—from designing rugs to journalism—was only a way of making ends meet. For that reason, I considered daytime hours to be in vain, a waste, doing work I neither loved nor hated. I would do it well because I'd been entrusted to do it: out of loyalty, not love or solidarity with the work. That I could achieve only through writing. I focused my efforts only in the few, brief hours I would spend alone at night, dividing them between reading and writing.

Over the past few years, I haven't been able to sleep, neither at night nor during the day, but I still must lie down. I listen to the BBC news report or summon my thoughts. In other words, I surrender, perhaps, to thoughts and images of mysterious origin.

Suddenly, I saw Ahmad the Biter. He appeared before me, out of the blue, coming from nowhere.

To this day, I don't understand how memory works, what drives it. Why does one image take me by surprise while another does not? People who have disappeared entirely look out at me. I see the moment frozen in time, without movement. This is how Ahmad the Biter appeared before me.

I saw him approaching me, looking as if he were dancing, his arms stretched out, his mouth open as wide as possible, baring his teeth, spinning around, and circling us, letting out screams that filled me with terror. This was the image of him that came to me. For fifty years I hadn't thought about him: I hadn't wondered what had happened to him, nor had I asked my father, who used to protect me from him. Many figures came and went: a few lingered for a moment or two, others vanished completely, while all that remained of some of them was a gesture, a bow, their way of walking, or the way they talked.

Why did Ahmad the Biter come to mind?

I stayed where I was, lying down. I wasn't trying to recall my childhood years or my youth. On the contrary, despite his sudden appearance, the thoughts I was preoccupied with were as far as possible from him. Nevertheless, I shut my eyes, recalling the times I'd seen him. The vividness of what I saw startled me, as did the details of what I remembered of Ahmad the Biter.

He appeared suddenly in the middle of the street.

Not emerging from around a corner, or from the door of a building, but surprising us without warning. At that moment, I was gripped by fear. I hid behind my father, clinging to the hem of his *gallabiya*. My father had to move in order to prevent Ahmad the Biter from grabbing my hand. He shouted a warning at him, but if his voice was really as it seemed to me at the time, it didn't have the anger that accompanies a stern warning. He seemed to be joking with him or teasing him in some way. He didn't take him very seriously, as if he didn't realize how terrified I was when I caught sight of him, a terror that grew the closer he got to me or when he was about to touch me. Was he threatening me or teasing me? I didn't know.

He was short, with a yellow *gallabiya* with black stripes. Even if he sometimes wore different colors, that afternoon I only saw him in yellow, with a brown felt hat and shabby slippers. His bushy chest hair peeked out from the opening of his *gallabiya*. His nails were long, and his face was broad and flat—as broad as it was long. He had a snub nose and wide eyes, but the source of my inexplicable fear of Ahmad the Biter was his teeth: specifically, that wide gap between his front teeth that made his mouth seem huge and coarse, as if ready to gobble me up. It was my father who nicknamed him Ahmad the Biter, because he would stay silent for a long time or sit for a whole day beside Hussein Mosque, without moving, and then suddenly stare at someone and run after him, grabbing hold of his *gallabiya* or shirt and opening his mouth as wide as possible, aiming for a specific place that never changed—right near the wrist. If he succeeded in sinking his teeth in, it would be difficult to shake him off or push him away, no matter how many blows or kicks rained down. However, as it happened so often, the patrons of the Burhan Coffee Shop—to the east of Hussein Mosque—discovered that he would let go and run away at the merest touch on the tip of one of his ears. This was what my father told my mother one night as they whispered to each other, exchanging information about the neighbors, the town and my father's work, the news of deaths and marriages, births, and divorces. Conversations that filled me with satisfaction and serenity, that made me grow drowsy, comfortably satisfied, looking ahead with hope.

I knew Ahmad the Biter through my father's stories: I can even say I knew him before I saw him. At that early age, I wouldn't go on my own to the area where he used to hang around. The furthest I went would be the entrance to the alley, to Sidi Marzouq Mosque; I wasn't allowed to play beyond that point. The entrance led directly to Qasr al-Shawq Street. Going there meant getting lost, the threat of going missing or being kidnapped. There were those who preyed on children, who carried them away to the mountains to torture and abuse them, then teach them to be pickpockets and to steal. I heard some say that they burned children with irons and submerged them in water. At best, they beat them with sticks. They didn't send a child out pickpocketing until he was so adroit that he could split a cigarette paper in half as it floated on the surface of the water in a copper bowl.

I was wary of going beyond the only entrance to the alley, as it led nowhere—a dead end. I would look at the people entering Qasr al-Shawq Street, which led to Habs al-Rahba Street, asking myself what lay beyond Ali the coppersmith's shop, beyond *Amm* Shams's place. *Amm* Shams would sleep all day and come out to his little shop at night, selling cigarettes by the pack or individually as "singles," as well as beer by the glass.

I might see someone who frightened me for some reason—an obscure, indeterminate reason—and I would turn back immediately. Sometimes, I would run all the way home and leap up the stairs. I wouldn't calm down until I'd entered the room and was sitting by my mother, without telling her why I was afraid, fearing I would be forbidden from going out to the alley to play.

What prompted this fear? Why did the image of a particular person instill such panic and terror in me? I still shiver every time I remember the fair-skinned mother of Nabil, the roundness of her face. The mere sight of her looking out of her window would make me tremble. As for Ahmad the Biter, nothing separated me from him except my father's body, who stood between us. I would fear that at any moment he would get hold of my hand and sink his teeth into it, even though it never happened. My father always prevented it. It seemed the whole thing was really a joke, but how did my father accept that, knowing my fear of him?

I don't know.

Why did it seem that it was some kind of joke? Perhaps because I'd caught a glimpse of laughter on my father's face when he should have been angry at the Biter for trying to grab my hand. Instead, I was surprised to find out in later years that my father used to give him something for Ramadan. At Eid, he would give him a portion of the *kahk* cookies, those cookies my mother so expertly made, which she would prepare long before Ramadan began. I asked my father why he'd taken pity on him if he was attacking people and biting them. He said that Ahmad was alone in the world—he had no family, no father, mother, or children. This was the state of many who wandered aimlessly before taking shelter in Hussein, where they sought protection, sprawling on the sidewalk outside the mosque and receiving alms from the visitors and faithful.

When I learned of this, I felt pity for Ahmad the Biter. I was on the verge of tears, unable to imagine anyone without a family—no home to go to at the end of the day. But my fear of him didn't go away, especially the fear of his teeth sinking in, which could be prevented only by touching his ear. Once I heard my father talking about someone from our village who'd been bitten by a rabid dog. They hadn't given him the rabies shot in time, so his voice had changed into a bark and he'd begun to crawl around on all fours. If he saw water, he would become agitated and flail about in all directions. His family had been forced to tie him to the trunk of a palm tree until he bit himself and died.

After I heard that story, I asked if Ahmad the Biter was ill with rabies. But the answer was definitely no, as he was a feature of the Hussein Mosque neighborhood for over twenty years. He only ever got hold of a few passersby: it seems that only the particular smell of a very few would set him off and make him bite.

When I got older and began to walk that street on my own, I used to see him either sleeping, stretched out on the sidewalk by the green door, or walking slowly with precisely the same features that I remembered, except that he was now shorter and thinner. His head was smaller, but the way he opened his mouth was still the same. His eyes would meet mine. I wouldn't turn away, and he didn't come toward me. There was no sign that he remembered me. This is the question that troubles me: Did he attack just for fun? Why didn't my father explain this? Couldn't he see my panic and my fear? The whole thing is confusing and hard to understand.

Telegraph poles

Telegraph poles follow me. No one takes notice of them in cities, but when the train sets off they appear alongside. You don't see them until they pass by. If the train is moving at top speed, they appear in a flash and quickly disappear. If it slows down, they slow down, and if it speeds up, they do too, even though they're fixed in place.

In my childhood, when I used to travel with my family, I would wish I could count the poles from the moment we set off until we arrived. Sometimes I would try to spot the unusual ones or the ones that branched off along another line, growing smaller in size, leading to a town or some village—there, in that direction following the horizon.

I imagined them with human features: this one was female, while another looked male. This one was middle aged and that one was a young man. This one was happy, that one was sad—or smiling, scowling, willing, annoyed, content, curious. I would try to get to know one of them, choosing one pole I thought I would recognize when I was coming back in the other direction or during my departure in the same direction. But it was impossible; I could never do it.

However close or far away they are, however firm or obscured, however silent or still, their regularity carries news of birth and death, sadness and joy, through those connected wires. In Juhayna, the arrival of a telegram meant a disaster. When Abd al-Maqsoud the telegraph operator appeared in the courtyard, everyone would hold their breath. If he said, "Telegram for the Basha family," the sound of screaming and wailing would ring out before it had even been delivered, until old Ahmad Ismail, who wove wool from the moment he woke up until he went to sleep, would scold the women, shouting that wailing was a needless harbinger of disaster. Still, some of them went on, entreating God: *Protect us, O Lord. Protect us, O Lord.* Husbands and sons who lived abroad were forced to send a telegram only when it was very serious; to indicate a funeral, they would use the expression "send off." My name was transmitted along those poles. For about a week, I remained without a name. They'd informed my father in Cairo of my arrival. He sent a reply, asking that I be named Gamal.

When the train comes to a stop, I leave the platform. I look at the poles that carry on beyond the station, parallel to the track, extending to a point further than I have been. Night and day, hot and cold. For this reason, they say the wood of telegraph poles and railroad ties is worth its weight in gold, since it resists rot and corrosion and is capable of withstanding all storms and weather conditions. The wood comes from far away, from the north. Now, I always look at the poles when I travel, at what's before me, and ask myself: Are these the same poles or have they changed? Who passes whom, me or them, in their completeness?

—⁓—

She points to the photo, asking her father, "Who's that lady?"
    "That's Grandma, sweetie . . ."
    "And who's he?"
    "That's Grandpa . . ."
    "Your mom and dad . . . ?"
    "Yes . . ."
    "They're with God . . ."
    "Yes . . ."
    "So Dad, you and Mom will also be with God, like your mom and dad?"

14

"Yes, my love."

"So you'll see them again?"

North

The train comes to a stop just past a station called Daraw. After a long while, one of my scout friends says the driver got off and is sucking on some sugarcane. From the window, I see passengers below, and people from the village selling sugarcane or goods made from palm leaf, others looking at the carriages and chatting. After I realize how long we'll be here, the presence of the driver outside restores my peace of mind. I get off. Now I can see three narrow steps. The carriage is gray, with beautiful calligraphy that says "Egyptian Railways."

A man of about thirty approaches me. He's wearing a turban wrapped with a brown woolen scarf.

"Where're you from?"

I reply, stressing every syllable, intending to show my pride that I'm from Upper Egypt: "I'm from Juhayna . . . "

He gestures backward with his head. "Ah, from the north."

I glare at him, furious. "Juhayna, in Sohag Governorate . . . "

"So, north of us . . . "

I stare at him, for the first time discovering how relative things are. What I consider to be southern is northern for others. This was at the beginning of my journey.

—ɯ—

Why do I not remember the first moments following my birth?

Why, despite the fact that emerging from a mother's womb into the womb of life is such a shock?

Do images remain in our subconscious, in our inner mind? Of all beings, is man not the most ignorant of himself, of what happens inside him? Of what motives, what hidden powers drive him? How is it that we're able to remember fleeting features, yet we're unable to recall who phoned us, or lived near us, or with whom we shared our sustenance? Do I not sometimes look at a faded old photo of me with friends on a trip and recognize some of them but fail to recall the others? Not knowing the beginnings confuses me, likewise the endings. What images will appear before I close my eyes forever? Will it be an image from among those traces? Will it be an idea that

15

I will never be able to express? How limited I am. I long to know an end whose time has not yet come, despite my ignorance of a beginning I truly experienced but about which I know nothing at all. How to explain this?

A dream

I wake up intending to go to the bathroom. I know it's my house, but it's not the place I know. Some unknown place is overlapping with the place that's familiar. I'm torn between the two. I don't know in which one I'm setting foot.

The domes of the monastery

I know where the building is located. Definitely between Assiut and Tanta. I'm pretty sure it's Abu Tig.

What I can't pin down are the circumstance in which I spent a night there. Was I alone or with my father? Do I think it might have been with my father, because on more than one occasion he mentioned his connection to the Bishop of Abu Tig in front of me?

Sometimes, what we hear is transformed into images and scenes, so that we think that we've experienced them and seen them for ourselves, even though we haven't. We know them only through others' experiences, whether spoken or written. I wish I could remember the circumstances and the reason why I went as easily as I can recall the color of the paint, the moment, and the details of the monastery. A dark yellow, imbued with a touch of red—not orange, definitely a dark yellow, and it's the paint on the wall, specifically on the second floor. The rooms are beyond; in front of them is a wooden passage, supported by green columns, forming a square balcony overlooking the courtyard. What I can see now are the wooden balcony, the columns that support it, the doors to the rooms on the second floor. This means I'm looking from below. I also see domes with yellow paint—three, possibly four—with a cross on top of one of them. An oval dome. Palm trees growing in the courtyard whose fronds don't extend above the building. The blue of the sky is clear—the building is open from the inside. It's the afternoon, the light is faint, either because it's winter or the sun is in the west. What I'm sure of is that the building adds a certain something to the light— it receives it and transforms it. The light is altered as it passes through.

The moment appears just as I envision it now. In my mind, it's steady: it condenses what came before it and what comes after. This is quite normal. But the moment is framed by confusion. I'm unsure whether I really experienced it or it experienced me. What I'm certain of is the specific location—its Copticness. Perhaps because of the cross on top of the dome. Perhaps because of the nature of the colors, the dominance of that particular yellow. I saw the same shade later in Muharraq Monastery, which I visited a few years ago. I stayed in the town of Qusiya, where I'd been invited to give a lecture at its church. It was a sensitive time, when the Copts were experiencing difficulties as a result of extremist Islamist groups. I asked to visit Muharraq Monastery. I passed through the small villages and farmlands. I still recall their colors and the impact they'd made on my thoughts and on my visual memory since the earliest days of my southern upbringing: the clover, the corn, the wheat. At the end of the fields stood the monastery— just like the ancient Egyptian temples, on the border between green fields and desert, between green and yellow, between life and death. The wall was high, the door open. Only a few months had passed since an attack near the entrance during which a number of the monks had fallen victim. I was startled by the clarity of the light and the unlimited space, as if one could rise up into the core of the universe from within. Just as I was passing through the entrance, that uncertain place in Abu Tig came back to me. Through the yellow that surfaced in my memory, I recalled surroundings lined with wood and the difference in age between the buildings. In the reception area of Muharraq, the heads of the monastery and some former bishops came to see me. One of them was dark skinned, apparently of Ethiopian origin. The archbishop welcomed me. Several of his questions seemed direct and pointed, including one that surprised me:

"Why are you interested in the problems of the Copts?"

By the time he'd invited me for lunch, we'd got to know each other well enough for me to answer: "Because they're my problems as well. They concern me as a Muslim just as much as they concern you as a Copt."

We sat facing each other. Our food was different. In front of him they put a plate of fava bean *bisara* stew, fried eggplants, tomatoes, and lettuce, while in front of me were assorted plates of meat—duck, lamb, and chicken—as well as vegetables cooked in rich fat.

I excused myself from eating what was in front of me, smiling: "Not out of courtesy but of necessity . . . "

"But my food is for Lent . . . "

"It suits my diet . . . "

Throughout the conversation, I tried to remember any discussion that had taken place in that building of Abu Tig, which looked out at me from days past. The details wouldn't come to me, and I couldn't recall a single sentence or word, as if I were looking at a silent photo or standing in a place utterly empty of people.

I visited the oldest part of the monastery, the church, and the oldest place there, the altar. Each place had its own distinctive feature. Just as certain occasions—like holidays and anniversaries—are fixed in time, the sacred plays a part in determining them all. For this reason, we visit a specific place, no matter how hard it is to reach, to await a particular moment in order to perform a ritual that has been passed down or to accomplish something.

"The Holy Family came here on its journey to Egypt," my companion the priest said. "This was the last point reached by the Virgin Mary and her little child Jesus, peace be upon him, and with them, Joseph the Carpenter. They ended up here. And that was when the construction of the monastery began."

I recalled what I'd read about that journey, about the ancient Egyptian priests and their wariness when they met the Holy Family. It was as if their intuition was telling them what would happen and—with the appearance of the new religion from abroad—of their inevitable demise, despite the fact that any scrutiny of the religion's origins would have revealed that it started here. Perhaps aware of this, they greeted this family that had arrived in Egypt with reserve and a lack of civility. As I walked around, I hoped that my memory would latch on to some stimulus—the sight of something, anything, that would render clear a tiny part of the building in which I'd stood that day in Abu Tig. I hoped to see something else in it, an area still hidden, so that I would be sure that I'd been there, that I'd lived in it for a while—for how long, I'm still unsure. I'm fairly certain that I did spend a night there, yet perhaps this certainty is based on my father's account and the details that he told me several times, and perhaps that which relates to him is intertwined with what's related to me.

I strolled through the passages, gazing at the ancient trees, at the movements of the monks, their black garments, their head covers, the prominent crosses hanging fixed in place. It seemed to be a time for walking. Walking in closed spaces is always similar—going, coming, going. In prison, I would dream of walking in a straight line with no locked iron door or walls to block me, forcing me to turn back. The monks in their black clothes resembled the prisoners in Tora Farm, and they merge together. To me, they're all coming and going—not in a straight line, not in different colors. What we see is what's familiar to us, nothing more.

In the manuscript library, I listened to a young monk talk about its contents. The oldest volume belonged to the sixteenth century. I expected older manuscripts, but I didn't find them. I asked him about the particular smell of the place. He told me that it was a type of chemical used to prevent vermin from chewing the paper. Looking at him as I listened, I was surprised by the delicate, slender sadness revealed in his eyes. He was looking directly at me through moments of the present, yet his presence, his slight stoop, his unceasing stare brought back another look from long ago. I couldn't place whose it was, but another person looked at me through the monk's gaze. Was he linked to that building, of which I could only see a small part, as if it existed in a void? All I knew was that it was connected with the bishop of Abu Tig. A lodge or a church? Or part of a monastery?

Past and present intertwine. The distant becomes more prominent, the indeterminate becomes present: the tangible, that which we feel with our senses. Within the imagination, we roam between the two, attempting to find the barest link or to confirm a feeling that we've doubted. The act of looking merges faraway places with those nearby. Do they emanate from this person before me? I can make him out in his black, clerical garments, as well as the melancholy in his eyes. Or does it come to me from another absent person, one who is no longer present in this space that contains light and voices, concealed shadows, revealed places and locations fallen into the realm of illusion?

A "red night"

Fawzi, the electrician's window, one Friday night. Around nine in the evening, a night unlike any other, glimmers of red appear through slats in the wooden shutters. He brings a piece of transparent colored paper and covers the electric bulb installed by Abu Ghazala, the expert in stealing electricity from the government.

Beams of light emerge from upstairs. The room is on the top floor. Its door leads to the roof—anyone entering the *darb* can see it if he looks up. There's no streetlamp: the space is lit by whatever light filters from the windows and the balconies. *Hagg* Hamid's house, just before the corner, has a small lamp but its light isn't enough. In the dimness, the red looks distinct, clear. It's also the object of interest of a number of the neighbors who know its significance. Some, like Said the Communist, or Sheikh Faris, who hands out perfume to people praying at Hussein Mosque, come out onto their balconies. Sometimes, when things go right and the mood obliges and the light is still on at dawn, Sheikh Faris catches a glimpse. At that moment, he asks God for protection from accursed Satan and says out loud, "For shame. Has he not heard of the Prophet's saying: 'Seek help in fulfilling your needs discreetly'?"

Badges

Hussein Square. A bright day. A sky bound to be clear, not a hint of clouds. So . . . it's summer. What confuses me is my panoramic view of the square, as if I were seeing through the eyes of a soaring bird, although I know that I'm walking along the ground, coming from Azhar, heading to the street parallel to Mashhad, the route I usually take on my way back to the *darb*.

So . . . it's some point before 1971.

A pushcart, meaning the owner is pushing it or, if it's empty, pulling it behind him. Stacked on top are small goods: from combs and brushes to matchboxes and sometimes incense, chewing gum and gum Arabic, and perhaps treatments for sexual potency, like nutmeg and paper cones containing creams. The man walks silently, his head down, extremely sad, miserable, desperate, neither calling out nor advertising his wares. A quick glance at the goods arranged on top makes me lean over to have a closer look. I walk beside him, looking at him intently.

"Wait up, *Amm* . . . "

I got used to calling any streetseller "*Amm*," even if he was the same age as me, perhaps influenced by many years in the *darb*, where men and women would call out to the streetsellers: "*Amm* with the corn," or "*Amm* with the flour . . . ." If I were to call out to this thin one, with his gaunt neck, would I have shouted out: "*Amm* with the badges"?

Badges of different kinds, medals, round symbols, stars, small rectangles. A collar of thick fabric in green, red, and white, ending in a round medal, and within the medal an engraved cross with thick edges. Not hooked, but there's something in it that makes it seem to be: connected to it at the end of the fabric is a smaller, octagonal star with four ribs, neatly forming a silver-edged cross. The dominant color on the inside is a deep green. The edges cross at the connecting point, making what appears to be a small knot. On the front, a cross and a circle—from the circle, something that looks like a ship's anchor protrudes. On further examination, I see two expertly intertwined letters. The Latin letter *l* and another I can't make out, just as I'm unable to confirm the name of the country, which seems to have worn out, although I can read the word "republic" in Latin letters. An elegant medal, which could be hung from the chest with a pin. It's still intact, with no rust, the metal is solid, heavy. Is there a trace of red? Perhaps . . .

I pick up another larger medal. A five-pointed star painted with white enamel, with a golden circle above. I'm not sure . . . is it real gold, gold plating, or just painted? It surrounds a circle of deep blue, with Arabic script, but the two words are close together, not Arabic—perhaps Turkish, Persian, or Urdu, or a language I've never heard. The star lies on top of a circle, bordered by an engraved frame, decorated with a pattern of some kind of flower, like a lotus. The circle lies above another that is bigger, dome shaped, its edges indented like the decorations in mosques. But it's a miniature: a small, raised ring that connects to an oval ornament with a small, eagle-like bird inside it. It's not an eagle or a falcon. Above the decoration is a ring from which emerges a ribbon with blue edges, turquoise in color, and another bright red ribbon. The rectangular center is a deep, dignified ruby red.

"Hurry up, sir . . . "

I realize I'm slowing him down. Perhaps he's afraid of the police. He's in a bad mood, looking elsewhere, not letting go of the handles of the cart, holding on to them all the time. Many questions: Does he know the name of every badge? Will he tell me how he got them all? How much are they? I look again quickly. Some of them are military, stiff looking. Others are more delicate, more artistic and miniature. Some have a womanly touch. I become confused—which one should I choose? He turns to me expectantly. He looks without staring, as if blind. I point to a red medal the size of a pin, to be worn on the lapel of a suit.

"How much . . . ?"

Abruptly, he says, "Take it."

I repeat, "How much, *Amm*?"

He speaks as he pushes the cart forward. "I told you, just take it."

The Building of Silence

We could see Abdelrahman Katkhuda School from the roof of our house. The school lay parallel to our house, to the south, where Qasr al-Shawq Street opened onto our *darb* and wound around it from the top and toward the east. The school building turned its back to us, adjacent to a wide courtyard. *Amm* Radwan the plumber would appear in the courtyard from time to time in order to practice his trick of getting a male horse to breed with a female donkey. He had a special way of mating them to produce mules. He was completely bald. He walked among people silently. Yet he was totally different when carrying out this task.

The school building had only two floors, though it was the same height as the house where we used to live on the top floor, the fourth. It must have been older, perhaps dating to the end of the nineteenth century or the beginning of the twentieth. Its windows were rectangular, the outer shutters made of wood, the inner ones of glass. It had a covered courtyard, which the open passages leading to the rooms overlooked. It seemed to be covered with shadows, so right now it's difficult for me to remember its details, even the faces of classmates. Through the years I can see only the features of a fair-skinned face, flushed with red, plump. I don't know his name, but he's linked with an impression that has come back to me at times—that he's "kind." The courtyard is associated with food. Beginning at twelve o'clock, we would smell the frying of onions, the cooking, rich, red soup, with ghee from the countryside—we could see the empty cans. Hot bread, the best bite to be had was before you dipped it into anything. *Baladi* bread—soft, with a welcoming taste. I still consider it to be the best, after *shamsi* bread that rises in the sun. We would stand in line, waiting for our turn. At the head of the table, the hard-wearing enameled plates, with blue flowers on a white background. A heavy spoon made of copper. Aluminum wasn't yet widely used; every home was equipped with copper pots. They were an essential part of every bride's trousseau, the value of which was determined by the quality of the copper and the number of the pots. I would hold out my plate and keep it balanced as the cook ladled out the soup. I would get a loaf, then move on—to where?

Perhaps to a table where we would sit, or perhaps we would go back to the classroom or gobble down our food standing up. Radwan Effendi—Mr. Radwan—supervised lunch. I remember his voice commanding that we take our time eating, that we chew our food slowly, that it was healthier that way, that we keep the noise of cutting and chewing down, that if more than one person were eating from the same dish, each should stick to his own side. We were told to start by invoking God's name and to end by praising Him.

Lunch was served for only one more year after I enrolled at the school. In the second year, the hot meal was replaced by matured *roumi* cheese and boiled eggs. I've always liked the combination of these two flavors, especially when I needed to have sandwiches, since I worked all day. In the third year of school, lunch was discontinued altogether. Once or twice they gave us a tin of yellow margarine, a block of cheese and flour. The margarine tin was round, with English writing on it and two hands in a handshake. Later, I found out that it was painted with the colors of the American flag: red, white, and blue. I only saw those cans once. Were they part of something called "friendship" between Egypt and the US at that time?[2] Perhaps, I'm not sure. I won't attempt to confirm via any other source what my memory can't supply; rather, I will seek certitude from what remains, from the traces of what has passed, in the time that is left. I mean fated time, the time granted to me. The lunches came to an end in the primary schools but continued in the vocational schools. I was destined to enroll in one after preparatory school. That is another story.

The shadows of the building surround me. No detail of any lesson remains. The features of the teachers have become blurred and intertwined, except for two: Mr. Radwan and Sheikh Mustafa, the Arabic teacher, due to his dignity, the hugeness of his body, his Azhari garb, his elegant turban, and his slow gait. Whenever I saw him in the street, I would swerve away and hide until he'd passed. I wouldn't dare face him, even if I were to approach him meekly, seeking to kiss his hand as my father often advised me.

As for Mr. Radwan, little remains of him except how he sang Umm Kulthum, and his gleaming baldness. He used to live around Bayt al-Qadi Square. He would always come from that direction. The square is very close to Darb al-Tablawi, where we used to live, and Abdelrahman Katkhuda School, the first educational institution I attended. I can only recall him being dressed in a wool suit, whether in summer or wintertime. His face seems to match his total baldness. He stoops forward, as if on the verge of weeping all of a sudden. He was in a state of permanent nostalgia for the unknown. I never saw him laugh. He would suddenly shut the door and command that the windows be closed—especially the glass panels. Slowly, he would begin singing:

Egypt, the one on my mind and on my lips
I love her with my blood and soul

His voice was the twin of Umm Kulthum's. Whenever I remember him, he's like a shadow of her singing. He used to say that this song could teach us more history than the history books approved by the Ministry of

---

2   This is a reference to the United States Agency for International Development (USAID), which some Egyptians referred to locally as the "Friendship Project." American food aid to Egyptians included items like cheese and butter.

Education. He would sing not only with his voice but with his whole body. He would sway to the right and the left, his fingers expressing what he wanted to communicate to us. I would gaze at him silently, immersed in the melodies. His touching voice would seep through me. The strange thing is that everyone would listen, whatever their age and however peculiar his behavior: a history teacher bold enough to sing. Back then, a teacher had his prestige and his respect.

If I saw Mr. Radwan in the street, I would try to hide, dreading that he would catch sight of me. But from the moment he shut the door and the windows, the signal of his secret collusion, we would be seized with a comrade's solidarity, although we feared him and were wary of angering him. There was also pleasure in the departure from the familiar, the con-ventional—from sitting for hours, staring at the blackboard and the white or colored chalk.

In June 1967, I often remembered Mr. Radwan. I wondered where he'd ended up, where he'd settled. I no longer met him by chance, going to or coming from Bayt al-Qadi. When news of the defeat of 1967 broke and the rout was plain to see, the songs that were broadcasted changed from the triumphant to the mournful. We began to listen to what made us sorrow-ful, rather than what stirred our zeal. Each time I heard that song by Umm Kulthum, I would feel the burden of sorrow and Mr. Radwan would appear before me, standing in a void or in the position he used to take up before singing, or his hands would appear, brimming with vitality—just his hands, as if detached from everything else. Sometimes I try to recreate what he would have felt while singing those songs during those painful times.

Mr. Radwan, as he appears to me, is a part of the building, but not how it exists in reality. The school has been closed for about forty years, its windows unchanged, the brown door fastened by a chain with a dusty lock. I wonder where the key is? With whom? From whose hands did it pass to another's? Where is it kept? One day, my father stood behind the shutter on the right, facing the building. He made sure that I stood back. He was talking to Mr. Ibrahim, a man who wore a jacket and *gallabiya* and a dark red fez. I understood that my father wanted to submit a certificate or a request to be exempted from the school fee. It was no more than one Egyptian pound, but a pound was worth something back then. All night, he and my mother had talked. She refused to allow him to submit a poverty certificate, saying that its name was a bad omen and that we weren't so poor as to be destitute: it was true that times were hard, but not to the point that the child should start school with a poverty certificate. She'd said she would write to her brother to send her an advance from the annual land rents. Her voice seemed decisive and resolute. I hadn't heard my father's response, even though the conversation took place at night, in our room in Darb al-Tablawi. Yet seeing the school gate causes me to recall it, long after that meeting with Mr. Ibrahim, whose features are clear and vivid to me, perhaps because they're linked with the green, circular tattoo in the middle of his forehead. His face and his accent revealed his rural background. Perhaps he was a secretary or an administrator.

The building's interior is associated with the features of my classmates. I only remember one of them, although I'm not sure of his name: Idris, Bassem—it has the letter *s* in it, I'm sure of that. Despite my difficulty in trying to pin down his name, as his features become intertwined with others, what's certain is the way he sat, with his arms folded in front of his chest, looking upward, a little chubby, plenty of hair, his skin almost white. Inside the class—the location of which I no longer remember—stands Mr. Saadallah. His is a long story.

Although it's still standing, the building appears to have been forgotten. It wasn't demolished in order to build another in its place. It was left boarded up. There are many buildings like it in Old Cairo. I call them the Buildings of Silence or the Buildings of Oblivion. People pass by them all the time; they don't attract any attention, despite their existence. People don't reflect on the transformations that have happened to these buildings. I never go to that place without stopping, trying to savor the scent of the food that used to waft by, or the tune of a song, a look of praise or reproach, or the dignified entrance of a teacher we feared.

Bat Alley

Very short, taking the form of a right angle connecting Habs al-Rahba Street with Mashhad al-Husseini—an alley connecting two streets. During my childhood and youth, crossing it meant departing a secure, defined world, one with a known beginning and ending, for another, one open to every possibility. Bordering the alley were two old houses and Muhammad Ali School—the name of which was changed to Hussein Preparatory School—where I went for three years. A short alley of many tales. The older inhabitants say that it used to be covered with thick papyrus matting in which bats lived, which gave it its name. By day, they would hang from the old bamboo reeds, and at night they would hover around the buckthorn trees—most of which disappeared with the vast, old homes. None of the homes remain except the Suhaymi house in Darb al-Asfar. That's how the alley came to be associated with those flying creatures that make those who see them tremble.

For me, the alley is linked to the smell of fish and old paper. Before you enter, there's an old, three-story building with two shops on the ground floor. The first shop had a blue facade and sold fried fish. In charge of the place was a man with a bushy, white, and awesome beard: *Amm* Ali, the fishmonger. Behind him was the huge frying pan, in front of him the cooked tilapia, *makaroona* fish, and prawns. My father would ask me to go and buy a fish special for five piasters. "Special" meant that it was fried in front of the customer. I would stand there, steeped in the smell of oil and garlic and the catch of the day.

Once, as I was waiting, *Amm* Ali the fishmonger told one of his customers: "The kind of fish is not important. The important thing is that it's fresh . . . the catch of the day . . . "

How often I've said this precise phrase subsequently—perhaps with the same rhythm—in front of friends and in the hearing of fish experts. This part of the street is characterized by the smell of frying. I savor its smell as I wait. After it's done, *Amm* Ali spreads out some white paper, arranging the fish side by side on smooth, green parsley. He places them in rows with care, adding a small cone of yellow salt mixed with cumin and ground pepper. He reaches for the prawns, filling his palm, and places some on top of the rows of fish, free of charge. I carry the warm package, my mouth watering as I head back home with quick steps. It may have been the most delicious fish I've ever tasted, despite all I've eaten at restaurants and ports or on remote islands. I've eaten fish with different sauces, with fruit, with herbs that have traveled the Silk Road, yet I've never forgotten the taste of the fried fish in *Amm* Ali's shop at the entrance of Bat Alley.

Hagg Diab, a southerner from Girga, my family's area—fat and short. A paper specialist. Remnants from newspaper presses, old pamphlets, volumes, books: he buys and sells them by the kilo. The paper is a must for wrapping food and sweets, small items, fabric, and anything sold in shops. I spend time there after I discover the books, popping in frequently to look for old editions and periodicals.

In *Hagg* Diab's shop I acquired various treasures and oddities. If I start talking about them, I won't stop. Among them, I remember the dinner menus of King Farouk. Thick, blue sheets—azure—the name I learned later, when I worked in the Khan al-Khalili Association.[3] How did these menus reach *Hagg* Diab al-Girgawi's shop? I wish I knew the details of that journey. I see the moment when I found them—the royal seal, dark blue, raised letters. Some of them date back to 1944 as well as 1945, the year I came into this world. Menus printed daily. They would have been placed before the guests to inform his majesty of the order of the dishes, what they contained, and what music selections would accompany them. Each dish is paired with a special piece of music played by the Royal Orchestra, led by Lieutenant Mustafa Ouf. Who are you, Mustafa Ouf, whose name I said in a loud voice, one afternoon in Bat Alley? Who are you?

Carob

The thin-bodied man stands behind the counter inside the little shop. He wears a white hat and thick prescription glasses. Despite his height, he always seems to be looking up from below. With lips pursed, he rarely speaks. Only three sentences are ever repeated within his earshot:

"One carob juice . . . "

"One tamarind juice . . . "

"One *khushaf* . . . "

The jugs for the carob and tamarind juices are made of plated copper, narrow at the middle, with covers that open slightly. Each stands at some distance from the other. The *khushaf* is served on small metal plates: figs, raisins, and dates soaked in water, an apricot and sometimes a prune. The syrup has the smell of rosewater and the taste of pure honey.

What interests me most is the carob; I wish I understood its secret, its fragrance, the feel and smell of it, which lead me to the spirit and scent of a blissful paradise. Throughout my life, whenever I was near that shop, I would become susceptible to anything that touched my senses and framed my soul. I would watch as the amber liquid was poured, and the moment I picked up the small beaker, I wouldn't rush and slurp it down—rather, I would take my time to savor the pleasure. Later, this would also be my way with women. As I began to taste it, I would travel without leaving the spot; I would fly without taking off. With the taste of carob, various paths opened up for me. I wished the beaker would never be empty. Once it was finished, I looked at it with a sigh. I could drink another, but I tried that once and wasn't satisfied. I've come to realize that anticipation is one of

---

3   The full name of the association is the Egyptian Cooperative Association for Artisans and Manufacturers of Khan al-Khalili.

the conditions of pleasure—that not quenching one's thirst complements one's satisfaction. The taste of the carob gave me what I haven't understood from traveling long distances, from turning pages, or from deep thought. It was this drink, from precisely that location. I've tried carob juice in other places—from cafés that I frequented, from vendors recommended to me in Alexandria and Damascus—but I never experienced what I did at the hands of that eternally silent man, who prepared and served with so much care.

When the shop reopened after years of being closed, someone I knew to be his son appeared. I approached him, driven by a deep-rooted nostalgia, but I didn't finish the cup, so that I wouldn't lose the flavor of the olden days.

Appetite

I sit at the table, between my father and mother. A spacious hall. A house near the Citadel, perhaps belonging to Sheikh Muhammad Hassanein, the scholar at Azhar. His son Salah faces me. His mother enters the room, carrying a tray of *fatta* adorned with chunks of meat. She puts it in front of us. Hunger stirs me, and I reach out my hand, but there's a powerful kick under the table. My mother is looking straight ahead, as if she hadn't done anything. I realize that I've done something serious. I'm sad but not afraid. I don't like to anger her. When they begin to stretch out their hands, I don't dare. I remain with my head bowed, revulsion rendering my saliva bitter—putting me off the food and ruining my appetite. Salah notices.

"Why aren't you eating?"

I cast my eyes to the ground, and when my mother offers the spoon I'm slow to respond.

—⁂—

What hidden law governs memory? Puts it in order, organizes its contents, hides what it hides, shows what it shows, bringing features to the center of consciousness while concealing the name? Or allowing the name to emerge but blotting out the features? Disclosing what the errant moment contained and destroying intimate times that I thought would never be erased. What arrangement? Where? And who does the arranging?

Moments

I'm afraid of recalling them. When the association happens, when one occurs to me, I become anxious. I push other images to the forefront of my consciousness, I recall different situations by force until I eliminate what corresponds to them. There are many moments I don't wish to recall. But now, I focus on three, none of which are connected to any harm to my body or my mind, or to any confrontation with death, or to hearing painful news, but rather to difficult times that I experienced. One of the moments concerns me, and the other two relate to my son when he was a child.

Azhar Street, which begins in Ataba. The fifties, perhaps toward the middle or the end. Tram number nineteen: it sets out from in front of Azhar and ends at Ataba Square, specifically between the vegetable market and the flea market—the first is south of Muhammad Ali Street, and the second is in the direction of Muski Street. The two are parallel to each other. The tram has two carriages. When they reach the last stop, the driver steps out, gripping the brass lever, switching to the other side of the tram car. Meanwhile, the conductor steps down to shift the position of the pantograph connected to the electric cable hanging in the air over the road. The line is considered a connection between Azhar and the main lines, meaning you can use the same ticket for trams going to Giza, Shubra, or Abbasiya, and vice versa. As the tram returns from Ataba, it switches over to the line leading to Azhar, following the angle of the two rails. When I get off at Ataba, I usually walk by myself, mainly to stop at the stalls selling second-hand books stacked against the fence in Azbakiya. I don't know what made me take the tram home that afternoon, hanging from the left-hand side, which wasn't allowed, the side that faces the stops, where you get on and off. Anyone riding on that side would be dodging the fare—which at the time was nine milliemes. (Sometimes, there was no one-millieme piece available for change, so the conductor would give you a matchbox instead.) Hanging on the left side required being able to jump off whenever the inspector showed up, while the tram was still moving or when arriving at the stop. I must have been copying others who I'd seen doing this, especially my classmates. But I was never good at jumping on or off while the tram was moving. Or while any vehicle was moving. I didn't master many skills in my youth, like playing football, riding a bicycle, or swimming. The strange thing is that the only sport I ever loved was the one I never played: boxing. It remained wishful thinking. And until this day, the only two things that can wrest me away when I'm absorbed in something are a boxing match or a Leila Murad film on TV.

That afternoon, I see two tram carriages, one of which starts to move. It moves along with its two short connecting wires. I don't see what comes before or after, yet I see myself quite clearly. I'm hanging on to the door handle with one hand, trying to let go of it, my body bent forward. If I take too long, the carriage behind will overtake me and run me over—over my body or my knees. For a moment, my steps are falling behind the increasing speed of the tram. Did one of them hit me? Did I manage the maneuver? Was I able to get into a position that allowed me to escape? Until this day, I don't know what happened, but I shut my eyes every time that moment recurs to me.

In 1978, I arrive in Istanbul with my wife and son from Varna, Bulgaria. We'd spent a night on the sea and the Dardanelle Strait. Now we plunge into the city, where we've decided to spend an entire day and then sail back at nine in the evening. In Sultan Ahmad Square, I gaze at the mosque, trying to absorb the gray color that dominates the city. I'm about to ask the guide where I might buy some Turkish music. My wife is looking at the entrance of the mosque. Suddenly, suddenly, my heart sinks. I realize our son is no longer there. He's not between us. To this day, the moment in which I lose him still terrifies me. Lose sight of him. It wasn't even half a second, perhaps less. Yet it was enough to shake me. He was standing between two European tourists, staring at something he was holding in his hand. At this point, the "what ifs" start one after another: What if he'd wandered too far away from us, away from the mosque? What if a traveling gypsy had taken him by the hand? What if he'd walked in one direction and we in another? How would he have found his way, and how would we have found him? He, the two-year-old. Our time was limited: just a few short hours in a vast city where we knew no one, where we didn't know the language. What if? The money we had with us was only enough for a day and a night. How could we have gone back to Varna without him? Or to Egypt? Would we have gone back at all, crossing the wooden bridge connecting the jetty and the ship, with him somewhere far away? What if? At that point, I close my mind in order not to imagine what could have happened.

In Alexandria, we walk on the sidewalk by the sea. We've come with a friend of mine who is a photographer. We have work here. My son is seven; it's later in his life. He's happy that we're on a trip. Earlier, he'd gone with us to Sinai. When my friend begins to change the film or adjust the camera, using his good hand and as much as possible his artificial hand, my son avoids looking at him. Whispering, he tells me that he doesn't look at him, and he doesn't ask anything in order not to embarrass my friend. I tell him that my friend is used to it, but what he's saying is good and shows that he's sensitive. The three of us walk on the sidewalk. I'm holding his hand. A lamp post blocks our way. I free my fingers from his but too late. He'd been looking at something behind.

A forceful blow. I bend over him. My friend comes to look and says, smiling, "May you live on to survive another one like that."

He follows up with a look at me, meaning that the blow was in fact quite strong. I grind my teeth. The little one says, "Don't worry, Daddy." He assures me: "I'm OK." He speaks softly, through his pain, so as not to upset me. But he stops again after two steps, bent over, letting out a groan. I can't recall it without anguish tearing me apart. I make an effort to push it far away from me, as if what occurred then has just happened now.

Slaps
A small white car moves in front of us. It swerves all of a sudden, moving right, then left. A man's head. A woman is driving. They're looking at each other, furious. The car moves toward the sidewalk. The door opens, the man steps out, wearing a yellow shirt and a gold strap around his wrist. He leans forward a little, then begins striking his face as women do—the powerful slaps of someone in mourning, one after another. The beautiful young woman looks at him quietly. One hand on the steering wheel, one on the seat.

—w—

Through how many doors have I passed, entering and exiting, from my birth until now? If I were able to remember them, and what was associated with each, I would be able to recall the smallest detail of what I've experienced . . .

A dream
I'm traveling. The plane takes me upward. I don't know where it's going. A feeling that I'm heading east. To where exactly, I don't know. I don't know the passengers' faces. The captain announces that the plane will land in Tripoli, Libya, from where we will continue our journey—he doesn't say to where. We have to leave the plane during the stopover.

I haven't encountered an airport like this before. A high building with thick walls, all of them dark. It branches off from an old building stained with red and yellow. I take a look through an opening in the wall and discover that we're on a roof. A solid wall, leading to what looks like an uneven valley. The building looks like the paintings of Pieter Brueghel the Younger. Buildings like no other in reality, their purpose unclear. The exterior doesn't reveal the building's functions. The waiting room has no windows—they're blocked up. Intersecting, crowded passageways. I'm holding books wrapped in paper. I put them down by the door that I must bend down in order to pass through. Somehow, I realize from the movement of the people that the exit to the plane is in that direction. The movement of the passengers increases. I don't know the source of the instructions I'm getting, but I'm aware that it's time.

Where are the books?

I go out to where I've left the package. There are soldiers from some army, their bags strewn about. Some of them are stretched out, sleeping, their fatigue evident. The final call is announced. I realize that I've lost sight of the passage leading to the airplane. I speed up to a trot; I'm trotting but not going forward, I'm not moving. I accept the loss of the books. The source of my panic is missing the plane. I try to walk, but I'm running on the spot while the corners of the building close in on me . . .

It is what it is

For me, this recording in particular means more than my admiration for the melody, the meanings, the excellence of the voice. One night in 1945, Umm Kulthum stood on the stage in Azbakiya Gardens to sing "The Moonlit Nights."

A tender melody. Flowing, with no sharp rises or falls. What's certain is that the day was Thursday, her monthly rendezvous with her fans over the airwaves since the thirties. Two things I never stop thinking about: First, how that particular Thursday related to me. Was it before or after I came into this world? That is to say, I took my first breath on a Wednesday at dawn, the ninth of May.

Did her singing precede my arrival? Or did it come after? Was she on the stage, holding her famous handkerchief, before the ninth of May or after?

When I later asked a friend who was a young man at the time, of course I didn't put it that way; rather, I asked him to recall whether Umm Kulthum had continued to hold concerts during World War II or she stopped. If he answered that she'd stopped, the matter would be settled and clear—that voice would be from the following period—because I was born a few hours after the end of the war. He didn't frown or look off into the unknown. Immediately, he said that there had been no break in her performances during the war. I didn't reveal the motive for my question to him, but my confusion remained. Naturally, I didn't declare what I wanted to find out, what I wanted to grasp. The voice—not Umm Kulthum's voice, but that of someone in the audience. I can place him in the front rows—reserved mostly for certain people, known for their passion for the Lady, her voice, and the beauty of her singing. It was he who shouted that phrase. No, not the one who uttered it, but the phrase itself:

"Like that, again, like that."

All of a sudden, I hear the phrase anew. I recall the rhythm, its expressiveness, the moment it took place—the night, the month, the year. It indicates a time that has faded away, as well as other matters I can't pin down. Some are brimming with mysterious contents—inscrutable to me but opening a way to things I can absorb, from which I can depart or to which I can return.

Between two periods, interludes of singing framed by tender music. During a brief moment, the instruments stop, apart from the murmur coming from a band that had been assembled for a day. Suddenly: "Like that, again, like that."

Within it, a reproach for the abundance of pleasure, a complaint against the profusion of beauty, joy seeking out closeness, a proclamation of exceeding admiration, expressing hidden implications, yearnings that have only to do with the one who possesses them. It's not possible to perceive the details; it's only possible to absorb them in their entirety.

"Like that, again, like that . . . "

Melodious and distinct, to the point, without restraint. Perhaps it's the only thing left of the one who pronounced it. I don't know a thing about him. Yet through this phrase I know everything about him—a shout like nothing I've heard before. It is what it is . . .

The *dawsa*

Early morning.

The shops facing Hussein Mosque are not yet open: those selling rosaries and carob juice and walking sticks and offal meat. *Hagg* Zakariya's real estate brokerage. The shop that sells shaving instruments and sharpens blades, the furniture showroom. All the shopkeepers are gone except for Mahmoud al-Labban, the milkman, who never closes, night or day. I'm coming from Bat Alley, passing Muhammad Ali Preparatory School—which in the sixties changed its name to Hussein, following the belated recognition of the founder of the Muhammad Ali dynasty—and the modern Khawanki Building, whose owner had been brave enough to build higher than the mosque and the venerated shrine, which initially had made renting the top-floor apartments difficult, even without key money. Later, attitudes changed, and people talked of the legendary difficulty of finding an apartment in Khawanki.

From the point at which the street forks, one direction leading to the Egyptian Club Hotel and the other heading west, where the Café Magazeeb is, I can see Hussein Square and some of the domes of Muhammad Bek Abu al-Dahab Mosque. The street is usually empty at this hour of the morning, except for the milkman, a few pedestrians, and some people lying on the sidewalks facing the shrine of our saint, Hussein, appealing for his help throughout a long absence from home or for lack of shelter.

On this morning, I'm surprised by something I've never seen before or since: men stretched out on the ground, the face of one alongside the feet of another, the head of a third beside the feet of a fourth. They're wearing short, bright, white clothes, their legs exposed below the knees. Each holds a sword with a sharp, unsheathed blade, its edge against his chest, gripping the outer edges to hold it in place. They stare upward, none of them looking at the one beside him. Wide belts gird their waists.

From the square comes a sheikh on a black horse with a graceful stride. He approaches as if not moving, swaying right and left. He grips the reins. He's wearing white, a tassel hanging from his grand turban. It's as if he were doing a dance with the horse. They move from one man to the next, the horse's hooves touching the polished sword edge planted firmly on the chest of the reclining bearer.

I come to a complete stop. I'm trying to figure out what's happening; I don't know how long it takes for the sheikh to reach the end, at which point he turns around nimbly to retrace his steps, he and the horse in harmony, their limbs as one. As he returns, everyone fortunate enough to have been trodden upon jumps up. Some spin on the spot, as if doing a dance, brandishing their swords. Soon, the sheikh disappears. I follow him with my eyes until he reaches the square. Then he seems to vanish behind a curtain. Two days later, when I tell my father what happened, he says, astonished, "It's the *dawsa*! We've heard about it, but we've never seen it. They stopped doing it a long time ago."

Gypsies

At the door of the restaurant in a small, old theater famous for its flamenco dancing, stand two people. I'm watching with fascination—dances that come from the core of existence, from a point impossible to distinguish from another, impossible to specify. The dancers' steps on the small, wooden stage reverberate within me.

One of the two men is stocky and tall, with a large head and coarse hair. On his right cheek are the scars of some old wounds. He's wearing a brown coat and a woolen sweater with a high collar visible underneath. He has a thick silver chain around his wrist.

The other is thin, shorter, bushy haired, always looking at his friend.

For reasons difficult to pin down, I'm scared of gypsies—wary of them, despite sympathizing with them on a human level, after reading about their nomadism, their exile, and their oppression. Perhaps this goes back to my childhood in Upper Egypt, when the gypsies would arrive at the bridge outside of town, beginning their stay out in the open, east of the bridge. We knew them as *halab*. And because their stay was only for a short time—we knew neither their destination nor their origin—and their presence was temporary, people would worry and be wary, especially given what was known about them.

When the gypsies appeared, small children were guarded more closely. Men too. The fear was that the children would be kidnapped, especially if they were babies or one-year-olds, or toddlers. Gypsy women needed a child to elicit pity when they begged in the markets or knocked on doors offering their services. The motherly appearance reassured people.

As for the men, wives feared that their husbands would be enticed away for brief periods. Although it was said that the gypsies never allowed things to get serious and contented themselves with flirting—with rare exceptions—the risk lay in their expertise in the arts of flirtation and flattery, which so attracted men's attention and created a distance between the men and their wives by way of glimpses of ideas and techniques that stirred what had lain buried.

Despite the caution and fear toward those migrants, doors were not shut to them: they were open to the women, who were experts in the divination of sands and telling fortunes. They understood what the shell whispered; they had precise prescriptions to bring back someone who'd strayed and to drive away what brought misfortune.

I'm looking at the two men in the doorway when my friend who had invited me stops talking. He has been living here in Madrid for about twenty years. I don't know who stops whom or who had started the conversation. The bigger man—the one wearing the coat—points to the camera I'm holding. My friend says he wants to take a picture with us. I remove the cap and take a picture of him and his friend. My friend joins the two of them, the flash goes off again. The thin one asks me to join them. My friend takes the camera. The big one takes his place beside me on the left, with the thin one on my right. He moves back a little to create an eye-catching pose. He starts talking to my friend again. I don't know Spanish; my friend tells me that he's talking about the skillfulness of the dancers and that they are—like him—gypsies from the countryside. He shakes my hand as he's preparing to leave with this friend, when I realize that he hasn't given me his address so that I can send him the pictures.

"Why are you so concerned about a picture that you won't see?" I ask.

After listening to the translation of my question, the big one looks at his thin friend, who is looking at nothing in particular.

"We live nowhere, and we want to be in a photo that captures a passing moment. It's not important that it reaches us or that you send it to us. The important thing is that we exist in a photo, somewhere."

Red and black

A manuscript in my maternal grandfather's house. My uncle's wife takes it out of the large, wooden chest that is sometimes covered with a cushion and used as a seat. The chest is filled with books, some of them printed, some handwritten. This one is handwritten.

Lines that are totally alike—their beginnings and ends don't diverge from the line. The titles are written in ruby red, in the middle of the pages; the lines are pitch black except for the space at the beginning of paragraphs. This is the manuscript's general form, but its contents have utterly vanished from my memory. I remember one name—perhaps it's the author's—written with a different kind of calligraphy: *Qadi Ayyad*.

I'm dazzled as I gaze at the skill of the rhythm of the lines, the letters, the dots, the yellowing of the thick paper compared to the paper of newspapers, magazines, and novels that I've begun to read. My uncle's wife approaches me, smiling; at the time, she was in the prime of her youth. She tells me I will damage my eyesight by looking for so long. "That's enough," she says as she takes away the manuscript. She turns to the oven. The circles of dough puffed up after absorbing the rays of the sun. Two by two, she tosses the paper in. I stare at the raging fire. In its depths, the letters perish: the black and the red and the yellowed spaces.

Killed

"It's all over!"

Dense, concentrated, out of the blue. Nothing before or after. The scream ripped apart the silence of the morning in our neighborhood. Then there was a before and an after. A specter that loomed large. The scream's significance was clear to everyone in earshot. My mother and my uncle's wife went to the door. My uncle had left early, before sunrise, heading to the Nazzat al-Hagir market. The two women looked out of the half-open door, from where they could see out without being seen by a passing stranger or neighbor. I snuck between them and looked out, curious: Dayfallah, dangling from the back of his donkey, without a turban, bare-headed, his arms pointing to the ground, his feet pointing in the other direction, his eyes closed, his features blending into each other. A bloodstain on his back. The donkey motionless, its head and ears bowed. It had come on its own from the open fields—the open, cultivated area outside the town where Dayfallah had spent his last night. There they had gunned him down, they had got him.

For the first time, I was faced with a killing—a startling, shocking murder. Over the span of years and decades, the moment comes and goes. My mother didn't let me stare for long; she took my hand and brought me inside, yet she and I would recall what had happened a number of times later on. Neither she nor my uncle's wife screamed. They withdrew to the courtyard of the house after the dead man's brother appeared to carry the corpse inside, his mother watching silently, suppressing her piercing grief. The shedding of tears and the slapping of cheeks in grief deferred for now. Until blood canceled out blood. It could be a week, months, years later—no matter how long, the moment would come, at which point Dayfallah's soul would be at peace in its place of rest. The family would be able to show its delayed grief and accept condolences for the precious one, the one who'd been so treacherously murdered. That moment on a hot, southern, summer morning, the sun scorching and its light piercing. The sudden quiet that followed the scream of a mourning mother. One fate determined and a life brought to an end, while another walked in some other place, nearby or far away—perhaps not yet born, unknown, not yet materialized. But from that moment he was marked.

Someone had placed the body on Dayfallah's donkey, which at that moment had looked sad, its eyes troubled as if shedding a tear. As soon as the body was loaded on, the donkey's slow steps began to take it past the open field, the bridge, and the dust track that rose to the nearby houses, where the relatives resided. It didn't need a map or a nudge to guide it. It knew its way, just as it was aware of the significance of the load it carried. After they'd removed the body, the donkey got down on all fours and stretched its neck forward. No one approached it.

A cart

The wooden wheels clad in aluminum make a loud noise, a rattling, on the road paved with polished stones with gaps in between. The sound means that it's now six o'clock. When Mokhtar al-Nubi returns, that means it's twelve, give or take a minute at most. Mokhtar's departure and his return are more precise than a timepiece—whether it's hung on the wall or worn around the wrist.

The cart is raised on large wheels, pulled by a sturdy mule that receives exceeding care from Mokhtar. He rubs its skin with soap and massages it with water two or three times a week; he disposes of the mule's droppings in a special bag so that no one complains about its odor. As for its braying—no one ever hears it.

The cart is raised unlike any other—except carts used for carrying sand. But Mokhtar's cart is completely enclosed. It's lined with zinc to maintain the temperature, so that the ice does not melt in the summer. The slabs of ice keep the slaughtered animals chilled. In the early morning, he gets the meat from the official slaughterhouse. After he's finished distributing it, he returns at midday, not leaving again until the following morning.

Olive-skinned, dark, with a white *gallabiya* and a silk turban, full-bodied, Mokhtar climbs gracefully into the rectangular seat. It's as if he were sitting cross-legged, firmly planted, solid, although his legs hang down. I never see him speak to anyone at all, I never hear his voice. He never looks down from his bedroom window on the third floor of the Foss house. The Foss family was well established, specializing in lamb and mutton. Many

38

claim to be descended from this family, like the Dahhan family, the famous kebab makers. More than one *kababgi* sneakily added the name Dahhan—the same for the Foss name. Yet Mokhtar al-Nubi has no connection to them: he works for butchers in Souq al-Laymun and Husseiniya who supply meat to several hospitals.

His eyes are wide, cold; they glitter from no particular direction. A mysterious trembling passes through me still, despite the fact that it has been more than fifty years since I last heard or saw the cart.

A dance

The women's hands lifted into the air, above their heads, one after the other, streaming away as far as the eye can see. I can almost hear the wails, the anguish that overpowers the features of the women. The movement of their hands shakes the sadness off into an unknown space. Within it too are gestures of farewell to Ramose, whose mummy is preserved for eternity. It's enough to see it once to be able to recall it forever, as if it were in front of me, there in my field of vision, wherever I turn. Every time an overwhelming sadness strikes me for an unknown reason, especially at times of transition—from day to night, from spring into summer, or when I set out from one place to another—I wish for that tearful release, when the women might appear before me and I could raise my hands like them, waving, wailing over my life. I spent much time in front of the southern wall of the tomb of Ramose, Akhenaton's minister, in the Tombs of the Nobles, in Thebes, the Western Desert, Gurna. Yet I always say that even if I'd seen that mural just once, I would have absorbed its colors and details. With time, the features of the women in those paintings become intertwined with those I've known in life, until one morning I actually see them.

I'm sitting in the car that is taking me to work: 26 July Street—formerly Fuad Street. Some of the entrances to the alleys of Bulaq are visible. The women emerge from one of them. First I see their unified movement, harmonious, undulating, connected, despite their distance from each other. It emanates from them at the same time. Not only is their movement as one but the differences between their bodies disappear. The color of their clothes is mournful—black *gallabiya*s. Since every movement has a source and a center, my vision is drawn toward the tall one in the middle. The tallest of all, she's wearing a dark *gallabiya* and a veil, her face spattered with blue indigo. I know indigo as a dye, its blueness tending to black—angry women use it to curse when they scream, "Indigo in your face!" Indigo covers her cheeks and forehead. Her body moves likes a dancer's—its undulations suggest a dance, but different from anything I've ever seen: a dance that attempts to escape, to cast something off, invisible, trying to hurl it into the void. The other women support her when she occasionally leans to the left or right, at which point she springs up, trying to exceed her physical presence. The movement embodies the torment of loss, where the body's movements are intertwined—standing doesn't work, sitting provides no comfort, reclining gives no peace, neither does bowing nor looking up. The hands are pointed upward, seeking refuge, protection, in a desperate attempt to find a protector.

I recall a friend's comments about the loss of a breadwinner and what it means in terms of deprivation or collapse, what the inevitable departure implies. In front of me, the women's hands in Ramose's tomb merge with those of the women I see at the start of a new day. The bereaved woman, swaying left and right, appears in front of me often, when I least expect it.

Lines

Many dots, joined together, next to each other, connecting two points: the simplest definition of a line. The line, I mean, connects two places. I recall lines associated with other meanings that didn't occur to me when I initially experienced them.

The oldest is a line with no number and no name. A green carriage pulled by two mules; the driver wears a yellow outfit and a head covering that hangs down on both sides of his face. The line has no name, but the company does: Suares. Later, I found out Suares was a Greek who'd established a transport network across Old Cairo, with carriages pulled by mules. I would take a carriage—along with my father and mother—from Hussein Square to Sayyida Fatima al-Nabawiya in Darb al-Ahmar. Suares: the name meant this particular kind of transport, the name of the Greek owner of the company. He had green carriages, donkeys, a standing driver, and passengers sitting facing and next to each other on two rectangular seats. The Englishman Thorncroft was the owner of a bus company, the main departure point being Ataba Square, in front of Ahmad Halawa's clothing and textile shop. Two colors: white and green. I would ride from the square to Dokki, where my father's office was in the Ministry of Agriculture. He would take us to the Agricultural Museum, leaving us to roam around its opulent buildings and gardens, returning to us after signing off at the end of a working day. It seems that Thorncroft was the first to establish a transport company because the name survived in all the companies that followed, like Tarabolsi, Darwish, Abu Ragila, and the Public Transportation Company. All of these became Thorncroft. The first one bestows his name on all who follow his line of business. That's what I noticed.

Line number twenty begins from Bayt al-Qadi. The Tarabolsi Company. The last stop is Kobri al-Qobba, but it goes via Bab al-Hadid Square, which was the first stage of the journey to Juhayna with my family.

Number seventeen links Sayyida Aisha and Abbasiya. It goes via Azhar; its buses are red and white. It represents my time at Abbasiya Technical Secondary School. I never took it south from Sayyida Aisha. Always north. It meant the time of ebullience, anticipating Suad's appearance, then reaching the wide-open expanse of Abbasiya's desert—which was unpopulated at the time—approaching the quarantine station near the school, and the hospital for mental illnesses, surrounded by trees. The whole area was associated with mental illness, and anyone suffering from such illness, or exhibiting a defect, would be referred to as "Abbasiya" or "Khanka," the latter referring to a place further away, a larger hospital for more severe illnesses. The crowded bus number seventeen approaches on Darrasa Street, which was dusty at the time. There would be many people hanging out of the two doors, so the bus seemed to be leaning to one side, and one would imagine that it would tip over. But it kept going.

Number sixty-six begins at Darrasa and ends at Bulaq al-Dakrur. This one represents my first job, the beginning of the sixties, Dokki's streets, Vanilla Road, which reaches the core of the senses, the beautiful trees.

Other than that, bus numbers run together—nothing remains except the way they look, their colors. Features that I can't pin down: of drivers, collectors, girls I used to look at, whose bodies touched mine.

The trams are more distinct for me. Number nineteen. Discovering places on my own, confronting danger when I was about to get caught under its wheels. The first wallet snatched from me, Sheikh Salih al-Jafari sitting solemnly, his eyes wide open, saying something about men covering up and women going bare.

Twenty-two. It begins from the slaughterhouse and ends at Abbasiya. The carriages are old-style, without walls. The benches run crosswise. Only a women's section and a first class. More like two compartments, front and rear. It passes through Khalig Street—which later became Port Said Street—and from there my relationship with it begins, the route to the school in Abbasiya. Soheir, a student in the Sarayat School—a brunette, plump, radiating the beauty of yesteryear, the first girl I approached and to whom I offered my friendship, speaking to her in the language of the heroes of classic novels. The conversation lasted only a minute, perhaps less. She listened to me, then said, "Sorry, I don't have time." Many evenings I would pronounce the sentence with different intonations, trying to approximate the exact manner in which it was said. I would look at the ceiling and say to myself, "What nobility? What purity?" Then I would say, "She could have brushed me off, but she didn't." I would recall her glances. I would stand, bowing down, saying, "My noble lady, please accept my respect and my sacrifice."

Number twenty-one: from Ataba to Shubra. I get off at a stop, the name of which I can't remember right now. I head to a quiet street where my classmate Abdelmonim lives. We review our lessons, then his brother's wife cooks dishes we've only heard of: stuffed artichokes, steak, stuffed pasta. He would invite me to lunch, but I would excuse myself, shy about eating at other people's homes. Abdelmonim is the only person from my class with whom I'm still in touch. I see him once every year or two. His son is now a police officer.

Number thirty-three: a tram whose destination is Imbaba. At the beginning of the sixties, it became a trolley bus—line number fifteen, destination Giza. It was said to be the best and cheapest method, environmentally friendly, with carriages that caused no pollution. Number thirty-three: its destination the working-class housing area where Ahmad Omar moved. He lived on the ground floor of the *darb* and was on the heavy side, and he used to wear a white, country-style *gallabiya* and a red fez. His wife's name was Wagida and she looked like Mimi Shakib. What interested me was his brother's daughter, Sorayya, with her arrogant way of standing, her looks and glances—always upward. I loved being close to her and breathing in her intense perfume. I never formed an attachment to her, perhaps because she had nothing to do with al-Hamra.[4]

Bus lines. Tram lines. I see the signs of some of them clearly, plainly, even though they're no more. While for others, only their outlines appear and perhaps a tram line gets mixed up with a bus. Yet all of them begin and end with me.

---

4   Al-Hamra ("The Red") refers to a figure to whom the author repeatedly refers in the third volume ("Streaks of Red") of the present series, "Composition Books." She serves as both his first love and the ideal of womanhood.

Abu Hagar

Once a week.

My father would come back from dawn prayers on a Friday morning, carrying a plate of fava beans from Abu Hagar and a jug of milk from Mahmoud al-Labban, the milkman, or from al-Maliki. The names of the latter two remain in my mind to this day. Abu Hagar disappeared without a trace; no one knew what happened to him.

Abu Hagar would stand with his cart to the east of Hussein Mosque. The cart held the fava bean pot, bottles of oil and all the other requirements, including salt, cumin, chilies, black pepper, and bread—some of it chewy and soft, freshly baked. As for the oil, there was flaxseed, olive, and French, each with a particular flavor, sharp or mild.

I've eaten all kinds of foods, tasting the best whenever it was available, but only a few have shaped my memory. Among them, fried eggplant dipped in garlic and potatoes, molasses and tahini, *shamsi* bread, and *molokhiya* with *taqliya*—garlic, cilantro, and ghee—and mint tea. These are the foods I yearn for and seek out, regardless of changing circumstances or the disappearance of their source. But what I hope to recapture most of all is the taste of Abu Hagar's fava beans.

He would start selling after the dawn prayers, not before. After prayers in the Hussein Mosque, he would head to his spot, where he was a fixture for over fifty years. He came to be associated with the place, and people would use him as a landmark, saying "right of Abu Hagar," "left of Abu Hagar." He'd always find a pot of fava beans on top of the cart, in its usual position. The workers from the furnace that heated the Sultan Turkish Baths would bring it for him at the regular time. They never missed it or arrived late, out of respect for their venerable old colleague. They would place the pot in its place and leave it there, closed. When Abu Hagar arrived, he would take a piece of cloth and wipe it carefully, fastidiously. He would uncover the containers of crushed garlic, parsley, cilantro, cumin, ground pepper, and both types of salt—coarse and fine. He would shake the three oil bottles. Then, in an audible voice, he would invoke the name of God and gesture to the first of the customers. He would work through the line, repeating "now your turn" again and again until the sun rose, when he would stop. At the same time, the last of the fava beans would be served. If anyone approached then, he'd say, "We're done." It would be a customer who didn't know Abu Hagar; he had to be a stranger. Anyone who knew him would seek him out during his regular times. The chief of police in Giza, who was sure to perform dawn prayers in the Hussein Mosque every day, would some-times come by or send his driver. If he came himself, he'd stand obediently, waiting his turn, as would others of authority and high social standing. Whatever applied to others also applied to them—no one was exempt. While Abu Hagar was serving, he was completely devoted to preparing the fava beans. He would take the dish from the customer and pour in a drop of oil. Then, he would turn the dish right and left and scoop up the fava beans slowly. Light brown fava beans, a special crop from a small farm located to the west of Esna. After maturing the fava beans underground, the farmer would send half his crop to Abu Hagar and the other half to three specialty shops in Alexandria. After scooping up the cooked beans— mixed with the water from yellow lentils—Abu Hagar would slowly gather some crushed garlic with the tip of the spoon and place it in the middle, at the very center of the dish. Then, even more slowly, he would surround it with parsley. Then, he would lightly sprinkle on the salt. He would look at the customer as if making sure of something. He knew each one of them. Each had a different character and a different palate: this one liked chilies, that one couldn't stand them. Ahmad liked flaxseed oil, while Ali preferred French oil. If he saw a face he didn't recognize, or one he hadn't encoun-tered before, he asked for his order in a quiet voice, then filled the dish.

For his careful preparation, al-Khodari, the pastry maker, also stood out. He would bend over the tray of *kunafa* to cut a piece as if he were kissing the little shreds that had been soaked in butter and sugar. He was like al-Bagirmi, who sold offal. I never encountered anyone with a cleaner *gallabiya* except the man who sold *ishtingil* sandwiches and Osman al-Nubi, who sold *harissa* sweets, hidden by the entrance of Souq al-Hamzawi. The existence of each of these men centered on what he did—not as a product of his work, whoever he might be—but as a blanket, an abode for his soul and his inner being.

Fear

A real Cairene sky. I stare at the incongruity of the building styles, the juxtaposition of contradictions—the modern towers, the poor buildings, the piles on the roofs. In the vast horizon, the peaceful clouds seem eternal, settled, but I know they will quickly disappear. I wonder, Where do clouds come from? When do they form? And where do they disappear to? I smile at someone I can't see. All alone in a dialogue with the unknown, I get angry, I laugh, without any expression.

A weak light, with a firm, comprehensive goal, but suddenly I'm struck by a fear that affects the regularity of my heartbeat. Unknown, for no reason, no direct source, unable to determine its direction. Not from within, nor from outside—a fear of fear.

—⁓—

Does light flow, or is it solid? Does it arrive from its distant source in one stream, or is it composed of adjacent atoms? Does it travel in straight lines, emanating from sources difficult to determine, to destinations too difficult to pinpoint? Does it really bend when it passes an ultra-high-density magnetic field? Does this bending mean that it's a material? And if so, why can't we catch hold of it?

A dream

Fish of various kinds swimming in the open sea. Colors I can't identify. Funeral processions suddenly pour forth. Coffins, one after the other, but I don't know whose. When I ask, I'm told that they're for some official in charge of youth. I wonder, All these funerals for one person? "The coffins are all empty except one," I'm told. I turn around and see my friend Magdi standing there, silent. I ask him, and he answers me with that distinguished tone he uses when he speaks standard Arabic: "They're afraid he will be assassinated . . . "

Kunafa

My mother stands in front of the portable kerosene stove—Primus brand, lit with a low flame. She's holding a brass tray, spreading it with a fine layer of ghee. She puts it on the stove. As the ghee melts, she starts arranging the fine threads of *kunafa* pastry in lines, then sprinkles raisins on top. She begins arranging a second layer, the raisins, then a third layer, turning the tray slowly over the flame. She holds it by its edges with two pieces of wet cloth, sometimes humming songs of longing for the countryside, for the south.

At times she might go quiet, showing her steadfastness and patience. She doesn't stop turning the tray until the bottom half is done, turning a color between yellow and red. She holds it away from the stove, moving it right and left. She flips the *kunafa* over onto a round pot lid and then slides it back onto the tray. The bottom, completely browned, is now on top, and the fine threads that are still white have become the bottom, nearer to the flame. She tilts the edges—so that it cooks through and the mixture shrinks, forming a gap between it and the edge of the tray. In the sixties, a great advance took place in the house. We bought a propane stove with a built-in oven—locally made, produced by the army factories. It had two powerful flames and a smaller one for making tea and coffee or boiling milk. The oven helped my mother to make *kunafa* more quickly. She would put the tray in the oven and only have to flip it over once. She mastered the oven.

Before that, I'd known of a different oven in Juhayna. It sat in the corner of the courtyard, made of clay, and had two halves. In the bottom half, you would put the fuel to make the fire—discs of dried dung and small pieces of wood. In the top half, you would place the circles of dough, bread, *fatayir* crepes, *fayish* bread for breakfast, *bittaw* cornbread, clay pots. I didn't know of *kunafa* in Juhayna, but I did know *makhrouta*, those steamed threads of dough eaten with milk and butter. Only older people remember this now. Last year, when I went to Gurna, I asked my friend to make me *makhrouta* for breakfast. I yearned to taste it. He looked confused. He said he hadn't eaten it in many years; he asked his wife, but she politely declined. He spoke to some of his relatives, and one of the elderly ladies voiced her readiness. She came to his house to make *makhrouta* for this guest who was clinging to the distant past.

My mother didn't tell me where she'd mastered her method of making *kunafa*; she must have learned it from one of her neighbors, either in Khosh Qadam Alley or Darb al-Tablawi. I didn't ask. I deferred questions for a long time—either out of laziness or thinking that there was plenty of time, until her time was up before I understood things thoroughly.

What ingredients produced that taste—and that tenderness?

After the *kunafa* was cooked, it was time to sweeten it: a syrup made of sugar and lemon boiled over a flame, then chilled and poured over, slowly, mixing with the fine threads that had stuck together. Bit by bit, it softened: the surface was firm, while the middle was softest, the part I loved most. Mother's *kunafa* was for Ramadan, just like al-Bulaqi's eggplants. If I saw him looking the same way, in his white *gallabiya*, with that precise way of bowing his head, in the same place but in a month other than Ramadan, then he wouldn't be al-Bulaqi with his pickled eggplants. It was the same with my mother's *kunafa*. If she made it any other month, it wouldn't be the same.

After the evening call to prayer, we would start by eating *khushaf*—soaked dates, figs, and raisins—and then we'd have the meal, followed by a dessert of *kunafa* or *qatayif* sweets. My mother would cut the *kunafa*, the yellow threads moist with syrup, looking like chains of pleasure. Her *kunafa* was halfway between firm and soft—the way I prefer it and what I seek out even today. As time went on, buying it ready made became easier and faster. I discovered various types, including round *mabrouma*, *osmanliya*, Nablus-style, and "hair *kunafa*." I've eaten it stuffed with cream, walnuts, almonds, hazelnuts, pistachios, or cheese, dipped in syrups of different colors. But I've never rediscovered that original taste.

I went to Syria. In Homs, at dawn, I stood in front of a shop called Natour, with various gourmet varieties. In Latakia, I went to a famous pastry maker whose specialty was *kunafa* with cheese. The shop was on a hill overlooking the sea. Short, plump, solid—he cut the *kunafa* with care, as if he were a surgeon. In Damietta, on Egypt's northern coast, there was an old pastry maker named Abu Sitta who specialized in *harissa*, a sweet I've only known from his place. What he had in common with the one from Latakia was that both of them opened for just one hour a day: the supply was exhausted in the final seconds, so he locked his doors. I ate at a place in Amman whose owner originated from Nablus; the shop was called Habiba. *Kunafa* with cheese is a Nablus specialty—its scent signals its presence from far away. Mouthwatering, tasty, yet lacking that particular aroma of my mother's *kunafa*. In Paris, I saw finger-shaped *kunafa* in the window of a Greek restaurant, the fine threads looking like those my mother prepared. I entered and ordered moussaka and *kunafa*. The waiter looked as if he was hearing it for the first time. He asked me to wait, returning with a young Egyptian man who worked in the kitchen. He smiled, saying that they called it *kataifi* there. It tasted similar, but not the same—I might even have imagined that closeness out of my intense desire to find it.

Abu Ghazala

He's always staring downward. Toward his lips. The top lip is turned up, thicker than the bottom one. Something connects his two bulging eyes; his nose is long too. He's always silent—I never heard his voice, as if he spoke in signs, although I never saw him use his fingers or facial expressions.

He seems to have something to do with electricity. I can only see him wearing a khaki suit with shiny brass buttons. He works in some department or company—perhaps the electric company in Sabtiya or one of its branches. In the alley, he's known to be an expert in supplying electricity—in other words, stealing it. There are lines leading to the lampposts that provide light for the streets and paths; they were lit by gas until the end of the forties. The gas company workers would appear before dusk, carrying long ladders. They would climb up in order to light the lamp posts, and in the morning they would come back once again to put them out. They were among the indicators of the city's activity. I knew them, especially those lamps that lit the front of Azhar Mosque, the main entrance of which faced Muhammad Bek Abu al-Dahab Mosque and the stop for tram number nineteen. After the revolution, perhaps in 1953 or 1954, the situation changed: electricity was supplied, and although the lampposts were now lit by electricity they kept their external appearance. Abu Ghazala was known for his skill at breaching the government's electrical lines and splicing wires in different locations, hiding their paths carefully, each of them ending in a sixty- or one-hundred-watt bulb, in a room or hall, inside a home. For doing this, he received thirty piasters, nothing else. At the time, it wasn't a small amount for the residents of the alley, but it saved them the trouble of using kerosene lamps, of which I knew two kinds: lamp number five and lamp number ten. In addition to their dim light, which could not be compared to electric lamps, there was no end to the chores they required to maintain them. They needed continuous care to clean the soot from the glass cover and to be filled with kerosene.

Abu Ghazala stands on a stool in the middle of the room. My father observes him carefully. He moves silently. For me, the bulb is of little interest, although it's a big change for us. What I'm staring at, what I look at for a long time, are those features that, if I'd seen them three or four years before, would have made me shudder at their strangeness, their oddness. I'd never seen anyone who looked like this. He would be looking down all the time, even if he was staring upward, at the sky, his torso half-leaning back. A prominent chest. Disproportionately tall. Even though I'd seen him many times before he appeared in our room, I didn't see him in the years that followed until 1969, about sixteen years later. It was in Maspero, the TV building, while I was visiting a friend I'd met that year, a talented director. In the studio, I saw men and women waiting—extras. The director or his assistant was examining their faces in order to choose pedestrians, or people sitting in cafés, or passersby, for some scenes. I was surprised to see those bulging eyes, looking down at that thick upper lip that was turned upward as if looking back at the eyes. I passed in front of him twice—of course he didn't recognize me. My friend the director said Abu Ghazala's face was strange: if he could have acted, he would have become something. But he spoke only with difficulty and was content to walk slowly through the scene of a horror film: his silent appearance would terrify the star. When I sat in the observation room, I saw the scenes via the control screens. His eyes looked at me. I didn't ask my friend how he'd found him, and I didn't ask Abu Ghazala to explain how he'd found his way into television. I only saw him once in a short episode, about two years later. I never noticed him on the street, despite visiting the alley and the neighborhood several times. But I would sometimes see him as I slept, close to the point of waking up: I would see only his eyes and the thick, turned-up lip. His features would linger after I woke, and from time to time, they seemed suspended in a location I didn't recognize.

Before and after

Most of the traces that come back to me are from the first, brief moments. That confused me for a while, especially since it's all the same, whether I intentionally recall them or surrender to the onrush of fragments from a distant past. A long time had to pass before I realized that the one who lived those distant, isolated stages of my life isn't the one who hurries toward the vanishing point. I bear his name and his characteristics, but he's not me. He's someone else, and when we recall what relates to another person, we see what we don't see in ourselves. He represents what does not seem to be us. We're not embarrassed to mention him, or to tell others about him, since he's related to someone else. At one time he belonged to me, and I was in contact with him, but he has gone. The rift kept us apart, and because I know a lot about him, I record him, proclaim him without hesitation, without embarrassment. It's strange: What we've experienced in the past and have cut our ties with, we can recall clearly, distinctly. As for what's closer to us, what's dear, it's as if it had no connection. I will only venture to mention him if he gets closer to my past, but I don't have a single past, and so I'll never be granted the time to examine what I am from the same distance that I'm examining the one I was. Time is so short. Will the one I don't know recall me after I'm gone? Will the traces of what I experience now migrate to someone I've never known, whom I will never meet, who is unknown to me—just like the one who lived before me?

Four by six

All that's left.

A truly tiny piece of photographic paper that was once glossy. Exactly four by six—that's what I knew photos to be. Either four by six or six by nine. The size, in centimeters, that was used in official documents: a photo of certain dimensions would be required to be affixed to a border—printed or drawn—either the smaller or the larger size.

Its colors have changed, taking on this faded, in-between color—neither yellow nor brown, red nor blue—a color that can't be categorized or traced back to any particular color. Just like time, we see its signs, the effect of it passing us by, or we experience passing by it, not understanding its essence. It's in front of me now, this photo, its edges eaten away. As I put it under the glass on my desk so that I can see it when I'm sitting there, I wonder—between a moment gone by and one that follows—whether it's a photo of me or someone else who once existed. Is this really my brother Ismail, or is he someone else, someone somehow connected to him, who looks vaguely like him?

The oldest photograph that remains of me. Rather, the only one. There are none left from before then, since the officer who came to arrest me at dawn confiscated the envelope containing my graduation pictures and the rare photos of my family. At the end of each year, the entire class would line up in equal rows. In the front row would be seated all the teachers. Three rows for the students, standing on the wide steps so that all would appear clearly. I kept the photos from primary, preparatory, and secondary school until I graduated with my diploma. Though they showed no other phases of my life, they were all seized. I used to look at them from time to time, saying the names of the ones I remembered in a loud voice, making an effort to recall the other names, starting with their expressions, expectant and intent. I wonder about the places they've settled in, now unknown to me. I recall the features of those standing near me.

Another photo, as if I were seeing it before me right now—one among the things that got lost. My father took us on a trip to the gardens in the Agricultural Museum, next to his work. He told us one day about a new fountain that sprayed water into the air, accompanied by colored lights. Days of expectation and flowing optimism after the revolution. Between afternoon and evening we headed to the huge square. We were dazzled by the fountain of colored lights. We sat on the marble benches around the square. The droplets of water touched my face. A man wearing a yellow suit came over, carrying a camera with three wooden legs. My father agreed, and the photographer slid his head into a long piece of fabric that looked like a huge, wrinkled arm. My mother sat, her features expectant, my father beside her. Ismail to their right and me to the left. Nawal was leaning on my mother's knee, holding Ali, the youngest.

Other photos from my first trip to the south, by myself. Others that do not remain in my consciousness. Nothing remains from that early period except that photo. Maybe because of its small size and its delicateness, the officer didn't notice it—the one who went on to stack the confiscated items in front of him and around him: envelopes, letters, papers with writing on them and others that were blank. He was boorish, a brute, though I'm not malicious, nor do I hold a grudge, even against those who have wronged me. Yet this one, whose name I don't know, I recall him sitting in the hall and going through my belongings. I send out loathing toward him, though I know nothing of him except the image that appears before me. I don't know if he still exists in this world or has departed it. Nothing escaped him apart from that photo. Four by six.

A Photomaton. I believe instant photography started in the fifties. Before, you had to wait a day or two to pick up your photos. The Photomaton was a large machine. The curtain would be lowered on the person while the technician would stand on the other side. After a minute or two, the photos would appear. For a while, this method wasn't approved for use in official documents—I don't know why. On Umm al-Ghulam Street, under a modern building, which its owners painted bright red, a photo shop opened, its large banner proclaiming the modern method of photography—immediate delivery for a very low price.

Inside the shop hung an *iqaal* and *ghutra*, a cowboy hat, a fake beard, Zorro's black mask, a pistol and dagger, and a pirate's leather eye patch. I picked a red and yellow Arab *iqaal*—the original colors were still distinct—and a pistol. Who was I aiming at? I must have been posing like some movie star or as a stand-in for Arsène Lupin. I used to reenact how he walked, his sneering and sidelong glance, how he would brandish his pistol while lighting his cigarette, defying the rich, whose property he would seize to give to the needy. Why do I seem serious, even angry? My brother is next to me—shorter in height, smiling, a child's features. He's speaking into the receiver of an imaginary phone, holding an open book—some novel, the cover doesn't show. I would have been afraid of leaving the book outside. I look like someone who kidnaps young children. But my brother's not worried, just smiling. I wonder, What occurred to the man when he pressed the shutter button? Did he make fun of us, or did he think of mundane matters that had nothing to do with us? What did he look like? Yet . . . why am I thinking about him, while I don't know how many of my own features remain with me? I've come to know my brother better than I know myself. If, one day, they acquire the ability to get old photos to speak, what will someone who sees me say? What will that person tell me? And how should I answer? Will he ask me what I've done for him? What I took from him and what I gave him? Will he recognize me?

Eclipse

The sun rises and sets and none of the city dwellers notice, especially in such a cramped, crowded place as my Cairo. The stars appear in the sky, then disappear, the meteors and shooting stars pour forth, filling the sky; no one notices them. In large cities, the planets are lost, lights obscure the distant stars. People pay no attention to the movement of the stars except when the extraordinary happens, a breach of the regular by something that occurs only at long intervals. That day I looked up: it's rare for me to observe the sky during the day. Perhaps during the winter, to try to classify the colors of the clouds and explain their path, or to stare at the sun as it appears silver, shining, with a clear roundness. It's possible to look at the sun when it disappears behind clouds. I don't go outside specifically to look at the sun but do it when I'm in a car on the highway leading out of the city or when I'm in the countryside.

That day I wasn't alone. Thousands, if not millions, of my neighbors were looking up that day, at the time that it was fated for me to follow it above the earth. All of us looked up at the massive celestial mass to which our planet is bound. Some got ready and went out under the open sky, and some travelled to particular places, to that island in the vastness of the Atlantic Ocean, where the eclipse was most visible. I had special black glasses that I'd bought in Paris with a book about the sun, printed in the shape of its orb. Its publication was part of the event; I happened to purchase a copy during a quick trip. I went up to the balcony on the top floor of the building where I worked.

As I put on the dark glasses, I grew closer to the sun, in spite of the distance separating us. Eight minutes at the speed of light—that is to say, twenty years of continuous flight on board the fastest aircraft in the world. Just by looking, I'd taken a place on a balcony that overlooked the universe.

What for me appeared to be a glance upward was perhaps a straight line—from the broadest perspective—a position from which I wasn't looking out at a street, or a favorite corner, or a pretty little tree, but at the movement of the stars. I saw the circular shadow of the moon—this cold mass devoid of any atmosphere, orbiting the earth—start to crawl toward the center of the sun, eating away at it. Here it was, covering the origin of the origin, obstructing the center and the periphery, between the line and the point. Only its cold shadow, lifeless, advanced on the scorching furnace, the explosive body whose surface temperature is 5,600 degrees Celsius, melting all kinds of metal—both known and not yet known. The solid substance, down to its smallest particles, is liquefied beyond the reach of our senses, which operate in accordance with the conditions of the possible. The branch of the branch began to cover the origin, covering its cosmic flame little by little, gnawing at it, sawing away with its bent, circular edge, until the orb—which under normal circumstances can't be looked at with the human eye—became merely a thin crescent that withered, little by little, captured by the spectators, the observers, those searching out the mystery, those engrossed by the matter, and the curious. The beginning and end of a body to which we've got used to seeing as a thin crescent transformed, through its shadow, its source of light and its radiance, into a crescent—the beginning and its opposite resembled each other, the origin and the branch of the branch. Yet what we conceive of as the origin is nothing but a branch of another origin, around which billions of similar stars are organized. Perhaps this was all merely a dense shadow of a hidden origin that was truly remote, impossible to grasp, even with the imagination of the heart. An original origin measured them out in harmony with those spheres in their orbits, organizing their movements so that anyone with a little knowledge could predict solar and lunar eclipses—not just the immediate occurrences but their cycles for the next three centuries by our measurements of time.

As the shadow advanced, the light changed, fading little by little. Gusts of unusual winds were blowing that summer, an unfamiliar chill. Neither autumnal nor hibernal—a chill from afar, an inestimable distance, that penetrated the most minute of cells despite the delicateness of its touch. The light faded with the dimming of its source. An unusual cosmic event was made visible, suggesting an even more unusual event in which those suspended masses collide, at which point the matter ends for those who care, who attempt to understand.

The shadow over the origin was complete. An unprecedented darkness, incomparable to any other. On the horizons of the city, collective supplications rose up from the mosques—the eclipse prayer. Collective voices, muffled, from no specific person, with no suggestion of an individual: the supplication of a group, all facing an indeterminate point. I was looking from my own position, indifferent to the discomfort. Everyone was watching, even those who offered prayers within closed places. No matter how high the voices rose, there was a silence. The most we can understand is what we see. The only sound that can be heard in the universe is of that distant origin which vision can't grasp but which I almost glimpsed a trace of.

Al-Bulaqi's eggplants

Nothing compared with the way he bowed his head, as if he'd been born that way, looking at the plates and their contents. He wouldn't show up except during the month of Ramadan—after the sighting of the moon had been confirmed, to be precise. He would take out the rectangular table and arrange the pickle utensils on top. He would be at his place facing Banan Café until the night of Eid. Al-Bulaqi—was that his real name, or a nickname given to him by the people of the neighborhood? I don't know, just as I'm unaware of his real profession, though I'd see him wearing a shirt and pants throughout the year, heading to work or coming back. Yet for me, he's simply what he was during the month of Ramadan, nothing else. Beginning in the afternoon, he would come out in front of his house, wearing his pure white *gallabiya*. His hair bushy, pitch black. It was impossible to make out his eyes, as he was always looking at the pickles, his eyelids drooping as if closed. He would speak so rarely that I can swear I never heard his voice. He would stand in front of the door of the house in which he lived, but I didn't know on which floor. I never saw him looking out of any window; I never saw him sitting in Banan Café, opposite, or speaking to anyone. Only that Ramadan stance of his, taking a piaster from me, not asking what I wanted or what my father ordered. He knew his customers' desires—he could even guess them. He would move nimbly between the ceramic pots, the glass jars, and the large, deep dishes. In the tightly closed containers lay the green olives, dark yellow lemons, onions big and small, red and white turnips. Dishes covered with light fabric, gauze: inside lay the black eggplants, the tomatoes, the slices of cucumber and various kinds of chilies.

He would appear before the afternoon call to prayer rang out from Sidi Marzouq al-Ahmadi Mosque: was the time linked to his return from work, or would he receive a leave of absence the duration of Ramadan? He would roll up his sleeves, holding the pickle not with his fingers but with metal tongs or a ladle. If a customer pointed with a finger, he would warn him not to touch. He seemed more dedicated than a surgeon whose instruments had been sterilized in preparation for surgery. He would arrange the eggplants and tomatoes in straight lines patiently, carefully. I remember the powerful breaths he took while he was absorbed in his work, like someone who took pleasure in a job.

Just as Artin the Armenian was known for his *roumi* cheese, despite the many varieties in his grocery, and al-Khodari for his *basbousa* pastry, despite his expertise at making other desserts, al-Bulaqi was known for his eggplants—the distinctiveness of their flavor and the uniqueness of the mixture he used to stuff them. It was difficult to separate the mixture's individual ingredients, to trace them back to their origins. No one laid eyes on his secret. The eggplant's flavor shot to fame, and so the demand for it rose. Celebrities and people of high social standing who prayed at Hussein sought him out, as did the major merchants of Khan al-Khalili, Sagha, Nahhasin, and Khurunfish. It was said that he supplied the royal palace in Abdeen. Each day, at a fixed time, a solemn man would arrive in a cart pulled by a horse. He would enter the house before al-Bulaqi came outside and would come back carrying a large, wrapped dish of the pickles of the day, especially eggplants. Due to the high demand, it became the only item that you had to order in advance. He paid no heed to some people's advice that he should make more, instead giving priority to his longtime customers, whoever they were—dervishes, traveling salesmen, merchants, or prominent pashas accustomed to visiting the neighborhood. The only word I ever heard him say was when someone tried to push in front of someone else:

"Wait your turn . . . "

No one was an exception, ever.

Amm Shams

He peers at me through incalculable distances—his hair is white, as are his eyebrows. His eyes are narrow and pinched. He has on a striped *gallabiya*, with a collar I only ever saw on him, tight around his neck. He moves through his little shop carefully, precisely, only opening the door after the evening prayer, after the doors of the mosque located near the entrance to the alley are closed.

A rectangular shop, its interior camouflaged by the cartons of Cottarelli and Matossian cigarettes, both empty and full. Each carton held a hundred cigarettes, sold individually. I used to collect them and use them to play "Boys and Girls," where I would arrange them on the landing with Camellia and Azza and Mahasin: that carton would be a closet, this one a bed, another would be a dining room table, and the fourth the kitchen. I would eat breakfast before going to work, and when I returned from the ground floor, Camellia—my wife—would greet me with kisses and start to prepare lunch. The empty cartons were from *Amm* Shams's shop: he would throw the extras outside.

I only saw him at night, after the lighting company workers had lit the gas lamps, and most of the shops on Qasr al-Shawq and Habs al-Rahba were closed, except Banan Café and Abdelhadi the grocer. It was difficult to see the door during the daytime, as if it were a part of the mosque's wall; it didn't show until after he opened it and stood behind the shop window, which had nothing inside it except cigarette cartons and the smell of tobacco. As for the beer bottles, long necked and green—I don't know where he kept them.

In Azhar and Gamaliya, there were no shops that served alcohol except *Amm* Shams's place. There was no written law forbidding it, but it was customary that in places with shrines, and the resting places of saints and deceased sheikhs, no alcohol of any kind was served. Hashish was permissible—indeed, its powerful odor hung in the air throughout *moulid* celebrations. "There's nothing in the Qur'an that forbids it," teased one veteran smoker. "Even if it were forbidden, we're only burning it!"

Amm Shams lived in a room on the roof of house number three. He would go to bed before sunrise, sleep all day, and wake up before the evening call to prayer. No one knew how he managed his affairs: no one saw him coming home with loaves or meat wrapped in paper, or a bag of fruit, nor did the neighbors detect the aroma of frying coming from his home. Throughout the day, whether winter or summer, he made no sound, and no one heard any noise coming from his room. He would be standing in his shop throughout the night. At exactly ten o'clock, he would start serving beer, pulling out a green bottle with a square yellow label in Arabic and English—Stella Premium. He would open it slowly, place a rectangular glass beside it and ask the customer:

"With foam or without?"

If the request was with foam, he would pour it straight in; if without, he would tilt the glass at a certain angle, pouring it painstakingly from the mouth of the bottle, which would touch the rim of the glass. With a delicate sensitivity and rare dexterity, he was utterly engrossed, whether the police officers of the *thomn* were calling out to him or Sheikh Ali al-Girgawi came for a visit. The sheikh was fond of *Amm* Shams, was close to him, occasionally prayed for him, and gave no indication of his disapproval of *Amm* Shams selling beer to God's creatures. *Amm* Shams remained focused even when the woman with upright posture came by, whose features no one ever succeeded in seeing. No one knew her age—how young or old. She would appear once a week, minutes after he'd opened the shop, whisper good evening and wish him well. She would pass him a package and he would put out his hand for her to take something from it, which no one, however near or far, could make out. But what was certain was that his features would change only when she came near. His features were connected by an invisible thread: anyone who saw her approach would confirm that other features on his face emerged in her presence, only to disappear again with her departure. Despite all of this, even if she appeared while he was painstakingly pouring a glass, he wouldn't turn his face or pay her any attention. During such moments, he would be utterly remote. In fact, *Hagg* Nassif, the baker (who was familiar with the taste of beer and its calming effect, who found it helped him to sleep after insomnia had exhausted him, and who, once he'd gulped down his first glass, couldn't get enough), confirmed that *Amm* Shams wouldn't open his shop or come out of his isolated top-floor room except to pour the beer. What was sure was his pleasure in pouring it with such care—skillfully and warily. His eyes wouldn't stray from the chain of golden liquid coursing from the depth of the bottle into the domain of the small, compact glass, which he would hand to the customer. He would never sell a whole bottle—it was by the glass, and only by the glass. No one saw him taste it or let it touch the tip of his tongue. As soon as the beer glass had passed from his hand to the customer's, he would retreat inside the shop. Everyone would step back beside the door, sipping slowly, silently, taking care that no one made any noise or went too far. Only someone inexperienced would dare do this, someone ignorant of the essential rules of drinking at *Amm* Shams's place. Whoever knew him was in awe of him—of his silent, unmoving features that showed neither pleasure nor anger, that provoked only fear. Despite a hint of melancholy when he looked at people, whoever knew him was familiar with the significance of the way he looked at anyone who upset him. He would stand still in the confined space, looking straight ahead, unwavering, and wouldn't resume serving. At that point, anyone standing and waiting their turn to get a drink would start to drive out the one who'd caused the problem, urging him to leave, to go away, while Shams remained unmoved, unmoving.

Al-Banan, the owner of the nearby café, claimed that *Amm* Shams had influence with the officers and the soldiers of the *thomn* area. How and why? There was no stated explanation. The incident concerning Sergeant Hagras was widely known. Familiar to all, he would patrol the alleys and lanes, inspecting the soldiers, making sure they were awake and signing off for each one in a small notebook. At that time, officers of his rank didn't carry firearms or knives—just a short, thick stick strapped to a wide, leather belt. But he only had to appear in order to cause fierce hearts to quake—except for Shams. No one knows what night or moment in his life—or what motive—made Sergeant Hagras taste his first sip of Stella. He'd only become acquainted with it late in life, but this wasn't a passing sip. He started to frequent the place, his posture and body tilting backward. He would order the Stella in his Upper Egyptian accent, gulping, not drinking, wetting his twisted mustache, before paying. What annoyed Shams was the noise he made: he looked at him with disgust, angrily. In a rare moment, he let his feelings show. One of the veteran customers understood and tried to explain to the imposing sergeant the difference between this golden drink and sugarcane juice. As the days went by, Hagras increased the amount he drank until he exceeded a bottle and a half. He would quaff glass after glass. One night, he suddenly disappeared from the shop, taking the empty glass with him. He ran off as far as Darb al-Masmat where he stood in front of the last entrance to Musafir Khana Palace, looked up at the darkened central window, and started to scream in a powerful voice. At this point, the people in the building opposite hurried to shut their windows to prevent the women and children from seeing him, now totally naked. *Maallim* Landi, Abdelhadi the grocer, Abdo the vegetable seller—all were in a state of shock. There were no repercussions against Shams from the policemen. Hagras was punished and lodged safely in Abbasiya Hospital for the mentally ill. Yet *Hagg* Nassif, the baker, called them all idiots: Was there nothing else to talk about apart from what happened to Hagras? What about the shop carved into the wall of the mosque that housed Sidi Marzouq al-Ahmadi? And what about al-Sunni, the pious dervish who handed out perfume to the devotees of Hussein? He would emerge before dawn, stand in front of his shop, and take out a flask containing a special blend, which he would open slowly. Shams would reach out, palm facing upward, to get a drop of the perfume. The air was redolent with the scent of ambergris as al-Sunni would ask him for his forgiveness and supplication.

The procession of *ajam*

Sikkat al-Tumbakshiya—the street of the tobacconists.

A street connecting Gamaliya Street and al-Muizz Lidinallah Street. I only knew of two streets in Old Cairo called "Sikka." The first of them was Sikka al-Gadida, which ran from Hussein Square to Muski. This was built at the time of the French occupation in order to facilitate the movement of troops—including foot soldiers and cavalry—to Azhar Mosque, the seat of the revolution and the call for jihad against the foreign invasion. A century later, after the events of the 1919 Revolution against the British occupation, the wider Azhar Street was built, perhaps for the same reason, when military equipment had become bigger and more sophisticated. The opening up of this street split the city into two parts that have not been reconnected at the time of writing, the beginning of the twenty-first century.

There are so many names that I know and repeat without understanding their meanings or what they signify. Tumbakshiya is the place where all kinds of *tumbak*, or tobacco, is sold: from Iran, Aden, Latakia, and Turkey. There's also *noql*, a word whose origin I don't know but which refers to *mukassarat*, the mixture of Ramadan nuts that includes walnuts, hazelnuts, and almonds—both shelled and unshelled—as well as dried figs, raisins, prunes, and dried apricots.

Most of the traders were *ajam*, meaning they had Persian roots. The newcomers among them didn't speak Arabic clearly, and I still recall their accent: the way they emphasized certain letters and jumbled others. The ones who'd been here for years, or those of the second generation, who were born in Egypt, spoke Arabic perfectly.

My father knew some of them, the *ajam* on Tumbakshiya Street and in the shops of Khan al-Khalili, especially the ones who sold carpets, woodwork, ceramics, and silver candlesticks. In the afternoon, my father would accompany me to a gallery. It had a narrow facade, but its interior was deep. Inside was every curiosity: from China, Singapore, India, Malaysia, Yemen, the lands of Persia, Anatolia. The owner would be constantly smoking a shisha, sitting with his face toward the shrine of Our Master Hussein.

The detail that stands out in my memory is the green tea with mint, fresh mint—a penetrating, fertile green with a distinct aroma. I never came across another like it, except in Morocco.

On Tumbakshiya Street, one of the men wore a dark yellow *abaya*, in summer and winter. I only ever saw him bending forward. I can't make out his features. My father knew all of them from the dawn prayer at Hussein Mosque. I passed many of them, yet Tumbakshiya Street has a different significance for me.

Early morning. The street was empty. I was headed to Khurunfish from Bayt al-Qadi. I was surprised to find them coming toward me: the *noql* sellers, others from Khan al-Khalili, and strangers I didn't know, swaying right and left in an orderly movement. Fists clenched, they beat their chests rhythmically and cried out, closer to a scream: "O Hussein! O Hussein!"

Turbans, *gallabiyas* lifted, bare feet, faces full of longing, their fists striking their chests, shaking them to the core. I stopped, struck by sadness; I wanted to cry but held back my tears. Later on, I shed many on my own in front of the enclosure of the holy shrine. It's one of the places that draw out my buried sorrows and brings tears streaming from my eyes.

I told my father that I'd seen some of his friends in the morning, describing what I observed. He said, "It's the procession of the *ajam*, Ashura."

I thought that this description was his own, but later on I heard it again from Muhammad, the perfumer, and Abdo, the waiter in Fishawi Café.

Umm Saad

Midday, on a day I can't recall now—between twelve and two o'clock. The timing is associated with a degree of natural light that floods the alley, when there's less activity, when the women are busy preparing food for lunch and the children are called back after playing outside all morning.

An unusual knock at the door. My mother touches her hand to her chest: "Shield us, O God . . . "

She hesitates. Nothing is more frightening than sudden knocks. I stand behind her, at a distance.

"Help me, Umm Gamal . . . "

She recognizes the woman's voice and hurries to open the door.

"Umm Saad, what's the matter, sister?"

In later years, whenever anyone mentioned "panic," I recall the way Umm Saad looked. Especially since, at that age, I couldn't take my eyes off her from the moment she would enter and sit cross-legged in the narrow room. I would sit behind my mother, staring at Umm Saad: comfortable, secure, believing, submissive, under the spell of her composure, the mysterious stimuli that she radiated, that drew me to her. It was the same as when I saw al-Hamra in town—I saw her in Umm Saad, grown up. I might have been around nine or ten, maybe eleven, I don't know. As for al-Hamra, what I know for sure is that I wasn't yet five years old when I became fixated on her image, which I can still see to this day.

Umm Saad would come once or twice a month, carrying a large bundle of fabric or headscarves. Sometimes she would bring bars of olive oil soap for preventing hair loss, or a fine powder to treat rash, or *mifatta'a*, a preserve that gave off a pungent aroma: a blend of seven ingredients, the ones with the most powerful effect, the most penetrating, were molasses and fenugreek. It warms the body in winter and gives off heat, and it's fattening. At that time, plumpness was a sign of beauty. Umm Saad wasn't plump, not even on the plump side.

Her face was oval, her eyes an alluring point of focus—exciting, vast, deep, lined with deep black, her eyebrows prominent, commanding. Her nose and mouth forming a mysterious composition, which I can see but not hear. Despite the absence of sound, I can only listen and obey. Her physique was delicate, gracious, neither tall nor short, close to statuesque, almost perfect. I don't know which aspect gave her that special quality. Not because it was difficult for me at that early age—I believe that if she were to appear before me right now, that same confusion would overcome me, and I wouldn't be able to identify the source of her beauty and attractiveness! Everything about her was calm, delicate, the very source of excitement and contentment. As I recall her presence across different times and distant places, she arouses only tranquility and surrender. For that reason, I recall her alarm as something unique, an alarm that became for me a characteristic and a mark.

She rests her forehead against her palm. Under her shawl, her *gallabiya* is pulled back to reveal a glowing loveliness that still, despite the passage of time, fulfils my needs. The roundness of her shoulders, their incline, leading the way to her arms, her hands that dazzle with their proportion and their poise. I recall her from all angles, from in front and from behind, from above and from below—as if she flowed through me.

That day at noon, she does not spread out her wares. Instead, she seems horrified, in panic. I can't think of the definition of fear without her face appearing before me. Her turmoil, her restless eyes, staring at an indeterminate point, saying from time to time that she only wants to mind her own business. She struggles to make a living. She doesn't sway or twist when she walks, and she doesn't look anyone in the eye. Isn't her toil enough? Isn't her misery enough, her constant scurrying around to look after the three souls, the orphans whose father left them so early? Aren't her efforts enough, running between the districts Otouf, Kafr, and Darrasa just to sell an item of clothing, a bar of soap, or a bag of tea to earn an honest piaster?

The rhythm of her voice is like mourning. In the middle of her delivery she suddenly becomes animated: what amazes her, she says, is his boldness, his audacity. When she'd reached the entrance, she thought that he wouldn't do it—the alley was a dead-end, leading nowhere. Only someone who lived there, or someone visiting, would enter. But she was shocked when, in front of the bakery, she'd turned around to find him close behind, about to reach his hand out to touch her, his eyes plunging into her back like a knife. She was terrified—she hadn't known what to do!

My mother stands up: "Wait . . . "

She opens the door. I follow her, torn between the desire to look at Umm Saad and the fear of something unknown that I've never encountered or heard of before. This wasn't Umm Saad. I longed for and looked forward to her visits, to watching how she sat, her features, discreetly, calming my breathing. It was as if terror had transformed her into someone else.

My mother knocks on the door opposite. *Sitt* Atiya, the wife of Abdo, who was the distributor of cigarettes to grocers, small shops, and kiosks in the squares. My mother refers to her quietness and gentleness and always calls her "the bride," even though it has been a year since she arrived, still waiting for her first child. Her brother would come over during the day to rest. He worked as a conductor on the tramway—quiet like his sister, shy, not raising his eyes lest they fall on a woman, a neighbor, or a passerby.

My mother asks if Abdo is home. As Atiya asks why, she realizes that something is up, especially as my mother's features show that something has just happened. Briefly, she says that someone was harassing Umm Saad.

"Imagine, he came up behind her . . . "

Atiya beats her chest with her hand. "Oh, how horrid . . . " Screaming, she asks who this criminal was, this son of a criminal. The matter doesn't require her husband to be home—she will call the neighbors to get rid of him. She goes back into the room in order to cross over to the window overlooking the neighborhood. My mother tries to stop her, not knowing what might happen. I run to the window in the inner room, climb the sofa, and look outside, through the two slightly parted shutters. In front of Umm Eid's house, there he stands, looking at our house, his pupils wide—ready to fight. He's dark, with bushy hair and thick lips. He's staring—ready to fight. When Atiya's voice rises up, screaming, provoking, he shows no sign of having heard or noticing anything. It's impossible to make him leave.

In a later moment—one linked to another, distant day—I ask my mother where Umm Saad disappeared to. Why had she not come over after that day? With a gesture of her hand, she declares her silence, at the same time telling me to be quiet.

Firyal

Due to the unusualness of her name, she appears clear and distinct: going down the stairs, going up, from top to bottom, from below to above. Her breasts drew the eye in no uncertain terms, her cleavage was plain to see. Her *gallabiya* was too tight for her body, which seemed about to break free of the fabric into some indeterminate place.

The names of the girls in the alley were few and well known: Zaynab, Aisha, Khadiga, Hind, Rohiya, Suad, and perhaps Layla, as well as Safiya. Firyal was an unusual name at the time, belonging to what people called "high society"—the likes of the artists Sirag Munir or Mimi Shakib. Perhaps some didn't dare to give their daughters such a name because it was associated with the ruling family: King Farouk's sister, Princess Firyal. On the other hand, the king had another, incredibly beautiful sister: Princess Fawziya. The shah of Iran, Reza Pahlavi, married her, but they divorced because she couldn't have children and he wanted an heir to the throne. And Fawziya is a common enough name in Gamaliya, Bataniya, and Otouf districts, as well as in the countryside. Yet Firyal still has a uniqueness, a special quality.

Firyal was married to Atiya's brother. There was nothing about her that would suggest a royal name. Her skin was dark olive. Her hair hung down. She had wide eyes and full lips which were always parted, revealing the gap between her teeth. The expression of her face wouldn't be complete without her ripe body, her full breasts, her arms that were ready to embrace, her elegance—from her legs up to the point where they parted—especially her stomach, the slenderness of her waist, the curve of her thighs, and the inability of her dress to hide her curves. She was "all woman." The women neighbors would look at her, discreetly or directly, especially when she appeared on the roof to hang out the washing, in sight of the neighboring buildings, one or two stories high, or when she looked out from her bedroom window in the afternoon. Her proud breasts held sway over the whole neighborhood. Samir the Communist would stand there for ages, as did *Hagg* Ahmad, who sold perfumes in Hamzawi, and Gharib, the train driver's assistant. The times of her appearances became well known, predestined: whoever lived below would look up, while those who were at the same level would glance around casually, looking beyond and then letting their gaze pass over her slowly, as if by chance. Some of them wouldn't look away, like Fikri, the bachelor electrician, and Abdel-hadi, the conductor, who promised his neighbors that he would soon be traveling to bring his wife home from Fakous and that only hard times prevented her from joining him. As the afternoon approached, Firyal's appearance meant that both men and women would come out onto their balconies and windows to look at her. Through a variety of reactions, she controlled them all. People said that after a short while her particular, provocative scent would begin to spread through the air to all the senses. The neighborhood had never known anyone like her, with her indirect provocation, hidden incitement, and lethal attractiveness. She became a source of worry for everyone: the fathers feared for their adult sons, while for the mothers it was twice as bad. They worried about their husbands as well as their children, specifically the girls—the way she stood, the bareness of her body, even the way she wore the light *gallabiya* of *rimsh al-ayn* fabric. All was a source of temptation to adolescent girls, who secretly yearned to break the rules.

Yet what made everyone even more anxious was her disappointing husband. It was obvious that he didn't fulfil her needs, that he couldn't quench her thirst or stoke the fire under that female cauldron. To this day, I have no idea how the tiniest details of the most intimate moments managed to leak out, so that the women began trading stories about her when they chatted in the mornings, on the staircases inside their homes, as did the men in the cafés—even the children as they played.

How did everyone know that he would be finished even before he started, that she no longer took him seriously? Or that no sooner would he get close to her than her mocking gestures would compound his apathy for his task? Or that once, in defiance, as she kicked up both legs while he was on top of her, he looked at her with tears in his eyes and said, "You're a brute, you are."

She would give him her back as she slept. At night, she smoldered with a flame her husband could not smother or put out. Umm Soheir, the midwife who lived directly below, confirmed that all the bed's creaking from Firyal's tossing and turning would wake her up at night and didn't allow her daughter—who was in secondary school and preparing to go to university to get a degree—to get enough sleep. Yet she didn't confront her neighbor about what was going on upstairs. This was for many reasons. First, how would she react? What excuse would she offer? What objection? Second, there seemed to be a hidden desire to observe what was happening, a conspiracy to watch, especially since her husband grew even thinner and more bent, keeping his hand on the wall as he went down the stairs. He would cross the street hunched over, his eyes on the ground, not looking at anyone or responding to the jibes he heard—sometimes so obvious, it was as if someone were talking directly to him.

Once, Firyal poured water into the alley and soaked him. Umm Soheir said it wasn't unexpected and that the frustrated girl couldn't find anyone to satisfy her. His sister Atiya was the only one who didn't seem to pay any attention, as if it was someone else's business—nothing of concern to her. When Firyal would come down, strutting around in the *gallabiya* that revealed what it should have covered, she would open the door and hug her, asking her what she needed.

Atiya

Morning. Perhaps ten or eleven o'clock—definitely before noon. Some afternoon on some day, some week, some year, perhaps fifteen or sixteen years old, perhaps younger, but definitely older than thirteen, and after the signs of adolescence and discovering an unusual source of a mysterious pleasure that was followed by that demeaning, paltry fluid. I was fully aware of the transformation and kept the matter from all those close to me. For certain, that morning came after, not before.

I'm standing in the narrow living room by myself. Where had my mother gone? She must have left to take care of something. It was after we'd come back to the area, after moving to Darb al-Asfar for two years. We hadn't been able to stay there because the rent increase had been too high for my father's salary. Things were difficult for us, so we went back to Umm Kawthar's house—a smaller apartment, but cheaper, with Atiya's apartment facing ours. She was an ambulance nurse, but after her marriage to Ahmad, she'd retired. She stayed at home but kept a syringe and needles.

She was quick to put it on the flame if she received a call from any house in the neighborhood. She had a deft touch.

Morning, almost noon. I'm standing looking at the door as if I'm expecting her. Perhaps I'm thinking about me being alone here and her alone there. I can't be sure, especially since my heartbeats quicken when there's a knock at the door. I'm certainly surprised to find her standing in front of me in her *gallabiya*, which hangs from her shoulders by two straps.

It reveals the pleasurable sight of her shoulders and her cleavage. The *gallabiya* is short, just a little below her knees—more like a nightshirt. It was normal to see some women unveiled—at windows or on balconies, as they hung out the washing. It was also normal for one to breastfeed her baby within sight of passersby. It isn't her uncoveredness that stirs the unknown inside me but her expectant features, bold and defiant. This is how the moment of that morning appears to me. She asks for some salt, then says that she's going to check the flame on her stove. She asks me to bring her the salt. I don't go to the kitchen—I remain standing, as if her leaving for a moment was a chance for me to get ready. I don't know what I'm supposed to do, exactly—how I should act. I don't know a thing. I think about my friend Hassan and how he would act. He told me that he'd slept with a divorced woman who lived around Muski; he said she was alone. She started kissing him and the fire spread through his body and soul, so that he didn't know what happened. She took his virginity, and he got used to stopping by her place at prearranged times. I go back and forth in my mind—should I go to her? Why did she go back? Was it really to check on the flame? Did she give me any hint? Why was she delaying? Did she really need salt?

The door opens. It isn't her but rather my father. Contrary to habit, he has come home early. I wasn't expecting him at all—he usually comes between three and four. He asks about my mother. I say a few words in return. Then he asks why I'd left the door open—was I waiting for someone? It seems that something about my appearance made him suspicious, but he has no idea about what might've happened just a few moments earlier that morning or what would happen on many subsequent mornings. In fact, it was about ten years before I would know what I should've known that morning.

Saadiya

She's a sculpture—her features well defined, even when seen from far away. The junction of her sturdy eyes with her nose, chin, and cheeks—and that which can't be identified or pinned down. She suggests an ancient Egyptian statue, not yet discovered, still hidden somewhere.

I have two images of Saadiya, the sister of *Amm* Muhammad, the newspaper vendor. This one, the first, is framed by the emptiness of the small shop, located under the mosque after which the Gamaliya neighborhood was named. There were three shops below; I don't know if they'd been there ever since the building was constructed or whether they were built later, after the death of the founder, Gamal al-Din al-Istidar. The shop belonged to *Amm* Muhammad. Strongly built, with a squat neck and a circular tattoo on his chin, he would wear a short *gallabiya* with a country vest over it, as if he were a peasant going to work in the field and not to the alleys and lanes, shouting out the names of the newspapers—specifically *al-Ahram* and *al-Masry*. I would see his feet before his face, flat with long toes. He always went barefoot—was it because it was difficult to find his shoe size or because going barefoot was common at the time? I would always see him from behind, with his head tilted upward, calling out of course. On Friday mornings, my father would go down to the alley to buy *al-Masry* from him, which he would read at leisure.

At first, I didn't know where *Amm* Muhammad would come from. I would wait for him to appear or to hear his voice calling out. When I began to go beyond the alley, out to Gamaliya Street by myself, I would turn left and see him in the store that was below street level, facing the fava bean and *taamiya* vendor, as well as Atrees, the charcoal vendor, and Abbas, the laundryman who pressed clothes with a pedal-operated iron. At first, I saw a young woman with narrow eyes, wearing black and mostly silent, *Amm* Muhammad's wife, standing behind the small, narrow shop window. Above her were round, glass jars filled with different kinds of cheap sweets, and packs of cigarettes, mostly unopened. She would sell the cigarettes as singles or by the pack. The shop was small and compact and dark inside. I couldn't tell what was inside, even when I was standing in front of the door and talking to *Amm* Muhammad or his wife. He must have come by himself initially, then taken various jobs until settling down to distribute newspapers in Gamaliya. The truth is, he didn't continue doing it: I don't know what happened to him later on, during the sixties—fifteen years after I'd met him for the first time and got used to his calling out the newspapers. I was surprised when he started working in *Hagg* Nassif's bakery, in the middle of the alley. He would carry trays arranged with circles of dough or bread after it had been baked. He would deliver it to houses here and there. In my mind, *Amm* Muhammad is always going here or there—either distributing newspapers, bringing dough to the bakery, or delivering loaves to houses. Why did he leave the newspapers and the shop, which a watchmaker took over, replacing the shop window for another, rectangular one? I had nothing to do with his shop, since I had no watch to repair at the time. My eyes would settle on the watchmaker whenever I went to Cinema Fath on Khayamiya Street, or when I came back from Bab al-Nasr. He would always be bent over, fixing a watch. What amazed me was how he did such precise work in the midst of the store's darkness, where it was impossible to see anything except someone standing at the entrance—and even then only the face, neck, and chest. As for the rest of his body, it would merge with the darkness of the narrow place, which appeared to exist independently, unaffected by daylight or the lamplight after sunset. From this frame, Saadiya's face looks out as I see it the first time, looking left toward Gamaliya Street or right to Habs al-Rahba Street—in both cases, in profile. That's why it's the side of her face I always see, the same pose that the ancient Egyptian artist was in the habit of drawing as he painted the faces of gods, kings, and nobles. Even the position of her eye has that slight tilt, as if she were the sole center of attention.

Saadiya . . .

In my mind, *Amm* Muhammad is associated with her—as is the shop, her silent sister, Gamal al-Din al-Istidar Mosque, the shops opposite, the smell of *taamiya* frying, the black of the charcoal sticking out from sacks of various sizes—as I approach the corner from which one can see Bazaraa Market, and the *sabil* fountain of Odah Pasha, by the entrance of Mayda Alley—and the variations in light during the day. All those items—some of which have anchored themselves within me without my realizing until later on, especially the ancient buildings—revolve around her, fall within her orbit. The way she would stand, making me slow down as I passed in front of her, the mysterious bonds that connected me to her, the desire to stare at her for a long time, to be with her, which was never satisfied. I would try, whenever I encountered anything that reminded me of her or brought her back to me: whenever I passed by the shop that made my heart flutter each time I saw it had changed, whether from a watchmaker's to a baker's, or to a pickle shop, until it closed years ago and I had no idea what it would become. Or whenever I saw a face in profile, like hers. I never found myself in front of a painting that showed a face in profile, whether in a museum, a gallery, or a book, without recalling her, despite the passage of time. The jolt that really shook me, and which reverberated within me for a long while, took place as I entered the Osiris suite, in the Temple of Seti I in Abydos, as I stepped inside it for the first time and walked slowly through its space, which was once sacred.

What's the link between the carved relief of Isis, the mother goddess—the ancient, the departed—and Saadiya, sister to the always roving newspaper vendor?

I'm uncertain, yet it's related to that profile, those repeated echoes of human inheritance. I could only see Saadiya, looking into the distance, touching her chin—her hand supporting it—transported in thought to somewhere I couldn't know. As I would get closer to the shop, I would slow my step. Once or twice I bought something from her. Her voice was sweet—broad and husky. She knew my father:

"Hello to the good man's son . . . "

I didn't say a word. I was at an age of timidity and shyness. I would struggle to put words together as I stood before her on the pretext of buying something. After I'd moved out of Gamaliya, no matter how long I roamed the world, and throughout all my wanderings, I would remember her, seeing in her what I hadn't seen when my eyes first fell on her. It was as if my connection to her developed and grew by way of my imagination, despite her remoteness and my absence from her—even as she stood silently, in profile, staring into the unknown, she was nothing but an image. For me, there's no difference between what I'm looking at, in the moment, and what I recall in my imagination. But many years later—maybe ten or fifteen—I did see her on two occasions.

She was crossing Tahrir Square with quick footsteps, even hurried, as if wanting to catch up with something or running away from something unknown. She wasn't wearing the black headscarf; she was in her black country *gallabiya*, but without a scarf—her hair was disheveled and her face was tired. Her posture was proud, statuesque, just as I remembered it, but with her face turned in some unknown direction. She passed swiftly by. She was crossing at the traffic lights, while I was in a friend's car. If I hadn't caught her profile, I would have been overcome by doubt and not believed it was her.

The second and last occasion, I stood face to face with her. We spoke. I recognized her although she didn't recognize me. I was with Hassan, my oldest friend from primary school until now—an expert with women, with many adventures and exploits. We were on our way to a solid old building with an imposing entrance, which overlooked the Egyptian Museum. It was some apartment or other, on some floor, I don't remember which one. It had been rented furnished by some foreign friends of his whom he wanted me to get to know. When the door opened, I took care that my expression didn't change, that the shock I experienced didn't show.

It was her . . . Saadiya, as if she hadn't changed her black, country dress, as if she was unconcerned by the people arriving. She wasn't the least bit curious. Someone came from inside the apartment, happy to see Hassan. He gave me a friendly handshake. She stood with the left side of her face toward us. He addressed her:

"Mushira . . . ask the gentlemen what they want to drink."

I spoke to her silently, starting with her first name, wondering what on earth, what by God Almighty, had brought her to this moment, to this situation?

Escape

During their quiet evening conversations, my mother would tell my father the news from the alley. Who'd left, who'd come, who'd scuffled with whom, who'd sold, who'd bought. One evening, her voice suddenly dropped to something resembling a whisper:

"Atiya ran off."

"Ran off? Who with?"

"With the man who took over from Umm Saad, the vendor."

Atiya, tall and tender, whom I'd only seen wearing a *gallabiya* directly over her bare flesh, revealing her curves. I recalled her standing on the balcony, looking at the man in defiance, angrily. I won't forget how he stood there, fearless and aggressive, exploding with desire. How did these two come together—how did she leave her home?

"It looks like her husband didn't satisfy her. Just like her brother, who failed his wife."

Atiya was somewhere now, with that bold, anonymous man who'd taken over from Umm Saad.

"God most high, the Lofty, the Glorious."

Umm Khayriya

The distance between Darb al-Tablawi and Salihiya: today it seems so short, yet it used to feel so long. When my mother asked me to go to the apartment building where Umm Khayriya lived, the way was full of perils. Her building

70

was at the corner of the alley. I went to ask her to come and see my mother, who wanted her to sew some clothes out of two pieces of *kastour* fabric. Winter was coming and the cold would descend suddenly. I knew where the fabric was kept, in the small cupboard that my father had bought secondhand from *Hagg* Fuad, the furniture dealer on Amir al-Goyoush Street, which people pronounce "margoush." *Kastour* is a special cotton. To this day, I don't know what the name means, but it's thicker, with a light nap resembling down. At that time, crossing this distance meant leaving our alley, with its dead end. In the corner of the alley was Sidi Marzouq al-Ahmadi Mosque, with its door leading to the dome overlooking the beginning of Qasr al-Shawq Street. Going there meant the beginning of the unknown, a brush with danger. The street led to another and then to Hussein Square and to Azhar, where the tram was and the big stores, including Dawoud Ads—from which my father would buy his winter and summer suits—and Benzion. The owner of the former instituted a system known as the "form," meaning selling via installments to employees whose salaries provided a guarantee. My father would fill out one form for the summer and another for the winter. Dawoud Ads remained the name of a chain of department stores. Furthermore, when I later met the owner's son in Paris, he owned the hotel where I stayed.

Dawoud Ads, *kastour*, what lay between home and the alley and the street—leading to Umm Khayriya, to a certain place, a room in an apartment building occupying a square plot, with several entrances. My mother had described it as the one facing the side door of the Egyptian Club Hotel, which was always shut. On the second floor, I would have to ask. Umm Khayriya was well known and had many customers.

The entrance to her building was narrow, a stairway without a banister which curved sharply after about ten steps. Several turns led to the first occupied room, which you had to pass through to get into the building and its internal divisions. No one knew if it had been arranged this way for that elderly blind lady who sat cross-legged by her doorway, receiving the charity of the people entering. She never left her post, making people wonder when she went to the bathroom or changed her clothes, if she changed them at all. The contents of the room were visible from any distance. It led to a long corridor, lined on both sides with rooms of different sizes, both vast and tiny. It was even discovered later that one of them consisted of two rooms, one on top of the other, a sort of duplex: the family that lived there belonged to a classmate of mine from the Abdelrahman Katkhuda School. I heard about doors leading to vast residences, with countless rooms and corridors and stairways. Various types of trees grew in spaces that formed kinds of gardens. There were flowers and little henna trees, tamarind and basil. I've heard people say that no one in all of Gamaliya—or the governorate—knows exactly what lies within the Salihiya building. It's said that famous scholars from Azhar lived there, preferring its nearby location and cheap rent. They would live there when they came from their distant villages and countries to study at Azhar, some from Egypt and others from various Arab countries. They would choose to live there at first, and when they completed their studies and became professors at Azhar, or taught in other mosques, they would move to spacious, independent accommodations, where residents lived their own lives separated by high walls. Unlike the building, where rich and poor lived side by side—the merchant, the scholar, and the simple citizen. It didn't matter whether people knew each other: everyone had to go through that first room, the door of which was never shut and led to another door or passage. The complex also contained small handicraft workshops, producing leather bags or *bulagh*, leather slippers decorated with gold engravings, as well as boxes with pearl inlay and plates of various sizes, engraved with Arabic or pharaonic designs. There were also some famous goldsmiths and silversmiths. On my way to Umm Khayriya, I used to pass by one of them: a short old man, always bending over small, handheld tools with a black loupe stuck to one of his eyes. I often asked myself what he was able to see through it. His room had no door—that's why I saw him. But I never paused to satisfy my curiosity; I would carry on to Umm Khayriya's room, asking for directions as little as possible. I was guided by her name, as if it contained something significant. It attracted those who were heading to her, guiding them. I wouldn't ask, in spite of the cramped corridors leading to her and the interconnected rooms—despite my conviction that those alleys would change each time I came to the building, carrying my mother's messages. I only asked for directions the first time; the following times, I would almost close my eyes, not looking at anyone, walking in the direction of Umm Khayriya. And I would get there. I never got lost. I heard that some people got lost in the building. After entering, they'd lose their way and no one could trace them. Some took refuge in the place and didn't leave. I was afraid to look at them, to look at strangers, especially after I'd left the alley. In my memory—which no longer retains all the details or views—there are stories of children who strayed far away from home and didn't return to their families.

"Beware of anyone who tells you, 'Come here and I'll take you to your daddy.'"

The thing I feared most was being kidnapped, being forcefully separated from my family. Numerous warnings sank in, took root, with frightening details about kidnappings. Torturing victims, breaking them in, subjugating them to the point that they forgot their families and neighbors. They'd be sent onto buses and trams to pickpocket or to sell packs of cigarettes or small items like combs, clothes pegs, or cheap sweets. The fear of being forcefully separated from my family remained an anxiety of mine until it happened, at dawn, years later, but in totally different circumstances. For this reason, it belongs to the traces to come.

When I would reach Umm Khayriya's room, tranquility would descend on me—not because I'd arrived safely and informed her of what my mother wanted but because of the serenity of the place, the beauty of her greeting, and reasons that connected me to her, which were difficult for me to comprehend. As soon as she opened the door, I would look at her and her lofty body, her full hair—without headscarf or headband—hanging down her back, with a few braids in front. Her house *gallabiya* was short, sleeveless, generously enveloping the slope of her shoulders.

She would look at me from above—with her deep black eyes, round and full of something I could not explain, although I did so later—as I looked at her. Umm Khayriya means those two piercing eyes, lined with kohl, which reveal her inner depths to those who look at her.

I never saw Khayriya, her supposed daughter, and I don't even know if she existed or was merely a name that people had added to the mother's. In the neighborhood, a woman was known by her son or daughter's name, while her own name remained hidden, especially after marriage or having a child. Few women were known by their first names.

I never saw Khayriya, but I did see the son. He was like her—in liveliness, in height, in the fullness of his body, his fair skin. I saw him in a full suit, looking elegant, passing through the door of her room. Even though I have no name for him in the depths of my memory, I've bestowed a name on him—I often name those with whom I'm not familiar or whom I don't know.

"Talaat, my son . . . "

Did she say his name to let me know who he was?

I only saw him at her place once. Where did he live? Why didn't I ever see him again? Was it because I went there so little or because he rarely came in? Was Talaat really her son?

Sometimes I imagine him going up the stairs in the apartment building, or some other place, all neat and tidy—apart from that, he doesn't cross

73

my mind or enter my thoughts. As for her, she looks out over everything, standing at the door for a while or bending over in front of me, exposing all of her curves—the visible and the hidden—the cleavage of her breasts and her buttocks, everything. Those moments that aroused my curiosity, that provoked my looks—my excuse was my youth. Her indifference as she moved throughout the confined space, in which there was only a wide bed and a black sewing machine with a logo on it, which I later realized was in English, when I saw it written over a shop on Azhar Street by the corner leading to Souq al-Hamzawi. I would watch that Singer sewing machine for as long as Umm Khayriya sat at it, bending over it so entrancingly, frequently surprising me with a glance, a smile, her eyes twinkling with hidden meaning that flowed through me like warm milk. Umm Khayriya inundated the place and me—touching all of my senses, accustoming them to the world, to things that need to be known.

After a certain point, she no longer appears. That time she was in our house. A sharp conversation with my mother, some dispute. Umm Khayriya was wrapped in a black scarf, a yashmak on her face, with a golden disc parallel to the nose. Her senses were represented by her uncovered eyes, which for me became the point of reference for all women with penetrating eyes. I summon her to my memory as she looks at me from an inaccessible place. But what puzzles me is her visible anger and the harsh way that she left, while my mother stood there silently, saying goodbye—with no regrets—to that festival of femininity.

A bride and groom

Imbaba, Kit Kat, some street, some road. A house, the floors of which are unknown to me, a room inside, an Ideal refrigerator sitting on a wooden base facing the entrance, a wide couch. I'm with my friend Nabil Mahrous Hussein; we're visiting a teacher friend of his, for some reason. He comes out after inviting us in and leaves us alone for a couple of minutes.

He returns, smiling. Before we go upstairs, Nabil says that the teacher got married two weeks before.

Lips move, eyes meet, there's some talk—I put in a few words. The teacher's eyes are wide—there's ease and satisfaction within them. His bride appears and my heart throbs as I make an effort to conceal my shock at seeing her. It's as if Layla Murad has emerged from a film to parade in front of me with her radiant smile, the twinkle in her eyes and the grandeur of her presence.

She places a tray on top of a table in the middle of the room. Something to drink—tea, coffee, hibiscus, fenugreek, rose syrup drink, I don't know, although I sip it and it settles inside me. But what matters is her presence. She sits next to him as he looks at us with his wide eyes, conscious of her beauty. He's proud of her, full of himself. I struggle to hide, even from my friend Nabil, the way I tremble before her beauty, to display good manners in front of the bride and groom . . .

Confidential talk

My father and mother are preparing to host my uncle, Muhammad, who will arrive from the village in a few days. My father does as my mother asks, saying that he will not make her angry again, that she should forgive him. Hardship and limited means are what pushed him to those moments he doesn't want to mention again.

My mother reminds him of his threats to send her to live with her brother.

He says that he didn't mean it, that a moment of anger can drive a person to say what he might not want to.

What she wants, she says, is mutual understanding between them.

He assures her that what's done is done—the important thing is for Muhammad to spend his time in peace and quiet. He then says that during dawn prayers at Hussein Mosque the previous day he spoke to the mufti, who is also a doctor, and that the two of them will go to his clinic on Fuad Street to examine his nose and prescribe the necessary remedy.

I'm listening to their conversation, which becomes a soft whisper. My uncle's scent overpowers me: wool, wheat, corn, *shamsi* bread, dry *molokhiya* leaves, wheat-stuffed pigeons placed on top of dates, and everything that the woven palm-leaf basket contains, all covered with the fabric of an old dress. I fall asleep.

My uncle is generally quiet. His turban is made of brown felt. And around his neck he wears a scarf woven and spun in Juhayna. He wraps his neck in it both in summer and winter. I've heard the saying that "what shields from swelter protects in the winter."

Sunrise

I don't know what time it is. The thick curtains block out the light completely and I haven't brought my little radio. I usually tune to the BBC to find out the time, to hear the pips of Greenwich Mean Time with their universal echo. I reached the rest house at night, just a few hours earlier. I go to the living room, seeking the postponed moment. I should have done what I usually do as soon as I enter a room: open the balcony shutters and look out for the first time at what I can see, at what I might return to or what I may not reach. But I was tired, so I went to sleep.

I now go outside to a totality of light, shocked and almost melting. I'm faced with a brilliant light—concentrated, radiating in all directions, canceling out everything else, dissolving it, merging it with its opposite. In this way, it engulfs the mountain boulders, the palms, the trees, the plants, the banks of the river. The building overlooks the river; its course is wide at this point, ancient and deeply rooted. On the eastern bank are rocky heights with palms below. If the sun's disc is only just appearing, where is this brilliant southern light coming from?

How long did it last? How long did this sunrise continue?

I can't be sure. Yet its brilliance still radiates within me, and perhaps it will exceed me.

A victim

Ghouriya Street, the afternoon. Coming from the direction of Bab Zoweila to Azhar Street. The fabrics on display are a festival of colors— taffeta, organza, batiste, *rimsh al-ayn*, *dammour*, *dabalan*, calico, wool, the fez shop and its brass ironing equipment, with Roqayya the chemist next door. It was there that my father used to buy medication for my brother before he passed away. I can't walk past it without remembering him. The Migharbalin Entrance, Khoshkadam, the juice seller, the passages leading to the cheaper shoe shops in Fahhamin, piles of goods. My mother would say you could find everything a bride would need in Ghouriya. Near Azhar Street, between Ghouri Mosque and its dome, between youthful and aged bodies all closely wrapped in black cloth, between *gallabiya*s, shirts and pants flapping around their owners, a boy rushes past, maybe eight or nine years old. He runs . . . as if he were in a wide-open playground—in spite of the congestion, coming out of nowhere, from somewhere, underneath the tires of an enormous bus, falling between them as the back wheel of the bus runs straight over his head. I stop suddenly, as if I'm listening to a description, as if I'm watching a scene that is being filmed, standing so close to the small body that is no longer whole, and wondering how the wheel had been so accurate.

The princess

Samia the White. Samia's children, Samia's husband. The snowiest white of all the women of the alley. Although the corpulent Umm Soheir sees in her only a chalkiness, a coldness, and doesn't know why she should look down on everyone, showing no interest. Samia never pays her respects, whether at birth or death. Her husband is a butcher from the Foss family or from one of its branches. Her husband is fair skinned as well, with sleek, pitch-black hair, a well-made *gallabiya*, pride in his walk. He enters the area as if walking on tiptoes. However, he's the opposite of his wife—friendly, with a nod here and a greeting there. No one knows of anything bad about him.

Samia the White appears to me in the afternoon, visible at the window as she looks out—occasionally noticing something and craning forward to make it out, then going back inside. I know her by what has been said about her. She knows the smallest items of news about Princess Firyal. She cuts out any piece of news about the princess and mounts it. She frames the large ones and puts the small ones in a scrapbook. She asks her husband to inquire about the princess's circumstances. He's diligent about listening to the foreign broadcasts, especially the BBC Arabic service, with its nasal newscaster. He reassures her and swears, each night, that he hasn't heard anything about the princess, at which point she screams in alarm: "*Her Highness*, the princess . . . ." Neither he nor any of her three children may say the princess's name without the title, nor her title without the word "highness." When she hears that Her Highness will be traveling abroad, she asks her son Mosaad to write her a letter wishing her a safe return home, and when God delivers her safely, she dictates another letter for him, congratulating her on the safe return. She cries in rage, expressing her great heartbreak because she hasn't learned to read or write. As for her husband, God granted him the ability only to sign his name. He forms his signature with large letters, deliberately, carefully, since an incorrect signature can cause him trouble, and he's honest—never summoned to the police station or late paying his taxes. If she'd learned to write, she would have written to Her Highness directly; she would have initiated a direct link to her, she would have visited her in Abdeen Palace and the princess would have returned her visit and come to the alley, on one occasion in her Girl Scout uniform, on another dressed as a nurse—"angels of mercy," as they were called by the weekly magazine and the daily papers—or as a sailor. Samia retreats to a corner of her home after using the bathroom and finishes sweeping, cleaning, and preparing the food, so that when her man returns he'll find something to eat. She sees the princess coming, the convoy entering the road as the neighboring women look out and the men discreetly steal a glance. It won't do for Samia to greet the princess from the second floor where she lives. She'll wear a special dress for the occasion, going down to the entrance of the building. No . . . to the beginning of the alley: this way, all the neighbors will be able to see the two of them together. They'll know her worth, and she'll see their reactions, and what will come over them: silence, amazement. Of course, Her Highness will not come alone—rather, someone will come first to clean the alley and cover up its flaws, to confirm that it's free of criminals and beggars. Perhaps banners and decorations will be put out. She will walk on her left, smiling at what she will say, nodding slowly when she gets close to the house:

"Welcome, Your Highness, you have honored us."

Samia knows how the upper class behave from watching films with her husband at the open-air Cinema Fath and Cinema Masr, some distance away. She will imitate the walk of Sirag Munir and the look of Mimi Shakib. The history of the alley will be defined by what came before and what comes after this event.

How many times does Samia repeat her preparations? How many times does she change things around? When she reads that Her Highness is unwell, afflicted with some ailment, she interrogates her husband about the exact nature of the illness, while he swears that he doesn't know. It's not customary to announce the details of the royal family's illnesses. She isn't convinced. She puts her hand in her bosom and pulls out two pounds she has saved from the household expenses. She asks him to go to Abdeen Palace and press them into the hands of some officer or soldier from the palace guard to find out what kind of disease and how far it has progressed, so that she may do her duty.

Her husband looks at her silently—she looks preoccupied, sad, as if one of her beloved relatives was on the verge of death. She follows him as he leaves. She stays at the window, watching out until he returns. She doesn't make supper for the children. When she sees him return, she rushes to the door, wanting to know.

"Put your mind at ease . . . it's just a little fever!"

Her white complexion becomes flushed and when he touches her forehead, panic overtakes him. It's if she were sitting on burning coals. He runs to the tap, wets a piece of cloth and rushes to put it on her forehead, muttering the name of Almighty God to ease her feverish tremors.

A victim

My mother asks, "What's the matter, Ahmad?"

When she says my father's name that way, this is compassion itself and the ultimate expression of worry, at which point he must speak, however difficult it might be.

"Sheikh Muhammad . . . may you live a long life."

"Muhammad Hassanein?"

"Yes . . . killed by a truck."

He was crushed between the truck and the wall of the mosque to which he was heading to perform the dawn prayer—meaning that he died a martyr. From my bed I hear the sadness of my mother and father, their elegy for the righteous man. I see the slightly plump man, wearing a jibba and a caftan with a wide silk belt around his waist and a red turban with a white scarf wrapped around. The way Azhar scholars dress, as well as people of education and knowledge. I see the old house, the courtyard, at the center of which lies an old fountain, bathed in a quiet, damp light. Dense shade—it must be winter. The windows, covered with engraved wood, the walls of the vast living room and the inner room are all lined with books, so many books. After lunch, I retreat to look at them. Under the name of the sheikh, near the middle of the cover, the titles are written in gold lettering: *The Treatise on Clarity and Clarification*, *The Raging Torrent*, *Commencement of the Mission*, *The Qur'anic Exegesis of al-Maraghi*. Books standing upright, with others lying flat on top of them. I feel as if someone is watching over me. I turn around and bow my head shyly. I don't know when he entered the room and sat cross-legged on the sofa, looking at me quietly—kindly, encouraging. When he notices my fear, he asks me, "Do you like the books?"

His appearance, his way of sitting in front of me. I can't recall his features. But the time and the location of the house transport me from what I don't know back to Citadel Square, to a group of old mosques, my knowledge of which accumulated bit by bit: first, Muhammad Ali Mosque in Mahmoudiya Square, then Qani Bey al-Rammah, and—facing Sultan Hassan Mosque—Rifaei. My reference for all of this is a moment I can't pin down. I see myself crossing the square to Sheikh Muhammad Hassanein's house with my father, my mother, and my brothers. I cross it with my friends, I cross alone, I plunge into it, I return to it—I carry on beyond it and don't stop. But on each occasion I turn around and all of sudden his look and that lost compassion are there before me.

Houses

Some houses on the road were known by the names of their owners or their wives, like Umm Kawthar's house, or Umm Sabri's, or Umm Nabil's. Others were linked to the most famous people who'd lived—or were living—there. Among them was the house of *Hagg* Nassif, the baker—whose owner was known to be Yahya Ibn al-Barrayn, the Nubian flour seller—near Umm Ghulam. Maybe the name was related to someone who once lived there and had passed away. Like Sheikh Ali al-Girgawi, who was burned to death when his gas stove exploded while he was bathing. He used to live alone. He was a bachelor—he didn't marry and didn't mix with anyone. They found large cans of al-Mizan brand ghee at his place near Bayn al-Sourayn. They'd originally been filled with ghee and were now filled with silver coins: hexagonal two-piaster pieces, with the image of the young King Farouk at the time of his coronation. These were known to people as "sixty silvers," and were worth a standard two-piaster coin at the time they were struck. Now, at the time of writing, they're worth 2,600 piasters. Each piece of pure silver was eighty grams. The cans were moved to some unknown place, and the news of them stayed on the people's lips. The house was known as the sheikh's house before the fire. The sheikh was an Islamic law attorney, renting the apartment that occupied a whole floor, but the owner of the building was unknown—completely anonymous—and it didn't cross any of the residents' minds to ask about him. The residents would give the rent to a lady of advanced years who came every three months—silent, speaking to no one, standing and watching with her hand tucked into her chest, pulling out a receipt after obtaining the money.

Other homes without names. Perhaps the residents feared mentioning their owners, like Umm Aliya's house. Rumor had it that she conspired with her husband to kill their daughter after she was raped and the signs of pregnancy had appeared, when her situation was about to come to light. The neighbors would refer to it with vague words like "that house" or "the house over here." If the person asking the question insisted, he would be told "the house of someone best left nameless."

Facades

The facades—those we've passed by or lived in—look out through memory like the features of people we once knew. We were familiar with some of them and steered clear of others, or we had a strange fear of them. Some of the facades have eyes—windows or balconies, or openings for light or air—while others are obscure and have nothing to justify their survival in the memory. Facades with a feminine look, perhaps due to their association with women for whom I harbored a desire and a passion, the ones I always yearned to see.

Among them was the house of *Hagg* Hamid, the Arabic language teacher and uncle to Soheir, who set my heart racing for so long even though we never exchanged a word. At the time of writing, some half a century has elapsed since she had that effect. I don't know where she settled, where she now lives. But the rectangular facade is there before me, the shutters on the windows move up and down, the transparent whiteness of the curtains is vivid. Three floors up, six windows—she lived behind the first, moving around and looking out before sunset. The whole facade is associated with her: with her presence, her movements, with my looking forward to seeing her, even a glimpse. It was as if the song of her voice emanated from the whole building. After her family moved to a bigger home in the Khurunfish neighborhood, I always felt she was still there inside, despite my knowledge that she'd left. With the passage of time, her features became confused with the lines of the facade; the walls and the windows became humanized and her face became part of it. She appears to me now only with her eyes gazing in my direction, from the windows that are now shut.

The facade of Umm Sayyid's house is mysterious, despite its six rectangular balconies with railings made of iron in the shape of leaves and its wooden floors supported by protruding beams. On the second floor, on the balcony on the right, stands al-Sunni, in his white *gallabiya* and Moroccan-style burnoose or a turban wrapped with a green scarf. With him are boxes containing little bottles, all of similar size and none larger than a finger. I used to see him while I was accompanying my father to dawn prayers at the tomb of Hussein, where he would be dabbing the backs of the hands of the people coming to pray: a powerful, penetrating smell that I later associated with the street corner, combining musk, ambergris, and basil. The musk meant transcendence, the ambergris meant the living presence, and the basil signified eternity that defies sensory comprehension. Each of the three evokes the enigmatic, the hidden. This is the essence of scent, implicit rather than explicit, a hint rather than a statement. In this way, the facade of Umm Sayyid's house and its balconies became associated with concealment, appearing to me only through questions for which it was impossible to find immediate answers. Just as al-Sunni, with his distracted look and his clothing, stirred fantasies of departure.

The facade of the Foss house—the famous butcher's family, who were related to Fadia and Mahasin's family despite the fact that they rented only two adjacent rooms on the ground floor. Fadia had an upright posture and the features of a Sixth Dynasty Egyptian statue—the princess of Giza alongside her husband, the ruler of the region. Every time I thought about this expressive sculpture, Fadia's posture and the details of her proud, supple, lithe, and bejeweled body would surprise me by way of that ancient time. But what preoccupies me is her scent, her aroma, her fragrance: the first female odor, musky and powerful, that penetrated my sense of smell and became a reference point, an essential understanding of an all-encompassing truth. "Essential," because even today I measure by it and refer back to it. "Understanding," because I gained knowledge at an early age through my experiences and the knowledge that every woman has her own fragrance: I don't mean perfumes applied externally but rather the scent which emanates from within, from an unfathomable depth. None resembles another, whether before or since. A lot could be said about this, but what concerns me is that, for me, the facade was associated with the scent of Fadia. The whole building became connected with it: the door, with its arch, meant the arrival or departure of her father, who was a salesman at a famous coffee roaster's in the Bab al-Louq neighborhood. I never saw him wearing a *gallabiya*, always a full suit with jacket and pants, a European-style waistcoat, and a fez, perhaps with a handkerchief beneath it in the summer to prevent, and absorb, the sweat. The windows are openings that lead to her. The building frames her—Fadia, she who fertilized my imagination, who watered my meadows and inflamed my passion, even though I never exchanged a word with her.

And then the facade that warns, that sends signals, that belongs to the other side of the alley. I call it the other side because I live on the right-hand side whereas the left-hand side is bordered by this mysterious palace, which our families warned us never to enter or try to explore—not to follow our curiosity, no matter the circumstances. A thick, solid wall, with a latticework-covered window protruding from on high, suspended, with an intricate and varied design of different lines and patterns.

What lies inside the Musafir Khana Palace, or beneath it?

At first, I only knew of the stories that increased the mystery and deterred any attempt to go near it. Some people used to say that what was hidden under the palace was more than what showed: underground vaults leading to each other, still occupied by the pasha's men, marrying, having children, generation after generation, waiting for the great cry, to rise up and fight for the pasha.

Rise up against whom?

Fight for whom? For which pasha?

However, what I read and understood later is that it was Muhammad Ali who chose this palace to host guests of the state (thus the name Musafir Khana, or Travelers' Lodge), and that he himself stayed there in the eastern, winter room where Khedive Ismail was born. I would always look at its grandly proportioned facade—the latticework-covered window made it no less imposing—and in 1969 I had the opportunity to see inside it, when I was twenty-four. In that year, a great celebration commemorated one thousand years since the founding of the city of Cairo. The palace underwent improvement and renovation and was also designated to accommodate some artists, among whom was a dear friend who allowed me to go in and have a look around. After that time, my connection with it grew stronger—I breathed the place, lived it in its shadows, sounds, and curves, its inscriptions and calligraphy and poetry written on the walls, until a fire destroyed it toward the end of the century. In my mind, I started to rebuild it by way of a long elegy that I've not yet published. In the elegy, I mention everything great and small, down to the tiniest detail, without relying on any references or resorting to photographs or drawings: I rebuilt it from memory, except for the facade, which I still look at, wondering what it hides.

Whenever I stay in a city for the first time, I look at all its facades as if they were echoes of those that I knew in my old neighborhood. On arrival at a destination, the first thing I do is to recall those enigmatic facades via the new ones I see. They've become the focus of my expectations and the heart of my quest. Even now that many have disappeared, they linger in my imagination as uncertain, elusive, trembling visions. From them, all facades burst forth and to them all return . . .

Osta Sayyid

Mashhad Husseini Street.

I've always said that if a rock were to be moved anywhere on this street, I would know. I don't think I've ever looked at any walls, windows, doors, or corners in the same way as I did on this street. I define my street as the part parallel to the mosque that contains the shrine in which the Noble Head of Hussein is entombed. It's my route to the city, to the four corners of the country, to other countries, to the universe. Throughout the first three decades of my life, not a day went by without my entering it: first coming out of Gamaliya, to Hussein Square, to Azhar. Getting there by myself was a rite of passage, a step toward discovering the world and traveling its alleys on my own. Being independent.

On my travels, I always think about leaving the street at the beginning of the day or arriving at it before sunset, crossing it from the square, coming home. My back turned to the square—this means I'm heading home. In my childhood and until the age of six, I never left my father's side; he would always take me with him, hand in hand. For this reason, all the great buildings are associated with him: the Egyptian Club Hotel; *Hagg* al-Sawi, the traditional tailor; Bayoumi, the owner of the furniture shop; al-Asfahani, the rug seller in Khan al-Khalili; and *Osta* Sayyid, the barber.

Each time I crossed Mashhad Husseini Street as a child, the first thing my eye would seek out was the barbershop. If I recall the street in my distant memory, the first thing that comes to me is *Osta* Sayyid.

When I used to accompany my father, I would look at the *osta* with fear and curiosity. His shop was narrow, with a large barber's chair that was raised and lowered according to the position and height of the customer. The chair also had a moveable headrest, a small pillow covered in green leather. It slid up and down until a comfortable position was reached, when it was fixed in place with a small key.

Once a month my father would go there to have his hair cut, and three or four times a week he would have his beard shaved. He had to book an appointment in advance. *Osta* Sayyid was very organized and was assiduous about the cleanliness of the shop, to the point of paranoia. Three or four flyswatters of different sizes had a special shelf of their own. The mirror had an intense shine and he would sweep the floor continuously, sometimes while he was giving a haircut. The white towels that he used for clients would be put in a covered basket, not to be reused. But the oddest thing in the shop was a tin can. He would remove its cover to spit inside: he chewed tobacco incessantly, dried tobacco leaves. Sometimes he would take out a small, round, silver can, open it carefully, take out a pinch of brown-colored snuff, bring it close to his nostrils with a deep breath through the nose, and close his eyes. After a few moments, he would sneeze successively. As soon as the sneezes started, he would take a white handkerchief from his pocket in order to stop them from spraying, as the blood rushed to his face. He would go back to holding the scissors or the razor and resume shaving. On the three walls were three large mirrors; perhaps they were what lay behind the feeling that the place had a special quality of light. On a shelf facing the seat were cans of powder and bottles of cologne, ointments, and balms. An arm's reach away were cubes of alum used for smoothing and moisturizing the skin after the threading process: he would start pulling out by the roots the small hairs that remained after the razor had done its work. I had to restrain myself from laughing at the way his head moved and the expressions on his face. He would tie the ends of the thread around his fingers so that they would cross in the middle. With a particular movement, beginning when he touched the thread to the skin, he would rock forward, then backward, then forward. My father would look somewhat pained, pursing his lips. But, as I heard him say once—I wonder where?—it was the perfect way to give the skin an incomparable smoothness, especially after rubbing it with alum. When *Osta* Sayyid used the thread, his features were completely transformed. He who was always scowling, whom I never saw smiling—who moved between the clients in his shop with precision and deliberation, as if measuring his steps, counting them, or treading in particular places—as soon as he leaned over and approached the client's face, at the moment he began threading, his features would be transformed. His eyes would grow wider, his lips would part, his eyebrows would arch and the thing that made it even more comical was his repeated movements, his advance and retreat, and as each movement was repeated his features would change even more, and I would suppress my desire to laugh. This must have taken place all throughout my life. I can only remember with amazement the way his face and his expression would change—but not in a mocking way. It's as if he's watching me and about to scold me. For some reason, I used to fear him and be annoyed at all the time I spent at his shop, waiting for my father to finish, whether it was his hair or his beard.

Perhaps it was because of his constant scowl, or the way he would order me to sit on a small, round stool without a cushion, for children, fearing I would move around and smash something or cause trouble. Once when I picked up the newspaper that used to hang from a bamboo stick to keep it flat while turning the pages, he snatched it away from me.

"He reads the paper every day . . . " my father said.

"He might tear it," *Osta* Sayyid answered, aggressively.

I stayed where I was, in silence, suppressing my anger and irritation. True, I was a child, but I wasn't like he imagined. Even before I went to school, I learned to read from my father, who was in the habit of buying *al-Ahram* every Friday, and on some days *al-Masry* too. *Al-Ahram*'s font and logo will always remain among the landmarks of my memory, just like the green Egyptian flag, with its white crescent and three stars, that flew on the front page. I remember the names of other papers I used to see with other customers in the Egyptian Club Hotel, such as *al-Zaman*, *al-Balagh*, and *al-Gomhour al-Masry*. They didn't last after the revolution, nor did *al-Masry*, but its logo remained with me. As for *al-Ahram*, it's still going. My father used to read slowly. I learned the shapes of the letters from him before I went to school. Sheikh Mustafa and Mr. Nasr, the teacher who loved Umm Kulthum, were pleased by this. Sheikh Mustafa took an interest in me and cared about me. He was distinguished; he had presence and an aura. He used to live in Darb al-Masmat. One day we bumped into each other on the street. He was affectionate, the opposite of his scowl in class. He patted my head, saying, "*Bismillah, maa shaa' Allah, bismillah, maa shaa' Allah . . . .*"

How could Sheikh Mustafa be so pleased with me in this way, praying that God would keep me safe for my father, while *Osta* Sayyid wouldn't let me read the newspaper for fear I would tear it? I would be restrained, holding back my anger, and when the moment was over, I would blame myself: How did I not answer? How did I not respond immediately? The further away it gets, in time and distance, the stronger this feeling grows. This is still my nature—how it has cost me!

Perhaps it was because of *Osta* Sayyid's constant silence and his calculated movements. Or perhaps it was because he circumcised my youngest brother. I still remember my brother coming back, his legs spread, the bandages wet with blood and antiseptics—some yellow and some dark red. I'm not certain that it was the same man who'd circumcised me; I'm still not able to say for certain at the time that I write this, but there are signs that confirm it as far as I'm concerned. He only carried out circumcisions during the *moulid* of Hussein. It didn't take place in the shop but rather in a small kiosk of green fabric—covered, with men and women standing in front of it. After the operation was over, they would carry the boy while the trilling cries of joy rang out. Sometimes the father would carry his son, riding a horse that trotted down the street. For my brother, nothing of the sort took place. There was only my mother: all the relatives were far away, and my grandmother and maternal uncle were in the distant village. If a problem ever occurred, she would go to one of the experienced women neighbors.

To this day, I can't pin down a precise reason to explain my fear of *Osta* Sayyid. Despite how formidable he was, he took exceeding care of his shop, as well as his tools and his clients. As for the entrance, it's one of those curiosities that I can still picture: curtains of colored beads hanging in narrow threads, concealing the interior and revealing it a little too. It kept the flies out, especially during the summer.

I'm trying to forget the way *Osta* Sayyid looked the last times I saw him. It was when I reached secondary school. I used to leave every morning for the tram stop in front of Azhar Mosque, then change at Ataba Square for another tram to Abbasiya. On the way there and back, I would see *Osta* Sayyid. He'd become thin, shorter than when I'd seen him in days gone by, unshaven, always resting his cheek on his palm, a fly swatter in his other hand, never moving. The beaded curtains had holes in them, the mirror was stained as if it was rusty. I didn't stop to talk to him. We never exchanged a word. He always used to talk to my father. For many months, I would see him on his own, always bowing his head, looking at the ground. I didn't see him standing in front of any customers, or bent over, with his thread. Later, after the shop had been closed for a long time, I wanted to ask my father about him, but I couldn't find the words.

Rumi

Rumi the Disciplined. Rumi the Body. Rumi the Direct.

He was known for his intense seriousness, his strictness, his aloofness with others. He worked downtown at the European tailor's on Qasr al-Nil Street. In those bygone fifties, just saying someone worked in that area—with its European character—meant a degree of distinction.

Excellent at reading and writing, he was one of the few on the street to whom Muhammad the newspaper vendor would deliver *al-Ahram* whether he'd paid for it or not, whether he found him or not. He would leave the newspaper on the doorstep of the apartment on the right, across from al-Sunni's house. *Al-Ahram*, for Rumi, was the most respectable, the closest to the official view. He remained convinced of this even after the entire industry was nationalized and all newspapers developed similar voices. He inherited this from his father and passed it on to his seven children—four boys and three girls. He taught all of them to start by reading the *al-Ahram* editorial, the official view of the newspaper, and to stick to what it said if they ever discussed politics with anyone. The same went for the commentary on the radio, which followed the news bulletin at two thirty in the afternoon. The fact is that in this respect he was a model to be emulated: if any conversation about politics or current events took place in front of him, he would respond only with what he'd found from these two sources, whether it was about the Taiwan Straits crisis, the consequences of the Korean War, or the Berlin Crisis.

Among the distinctive early morning sounds of the alley—which remained in the memory of many who'd heard it with surprise as children or with confusion as adults—was the cry, in unison:

"Long live Egypt!"

"Long live Egypt!"

It wouldn't come from a school or institute, or military barracks, but from Rumi's apartment on the first floor. He would wake his wife and children at precisely six o'clock. After they'd all got washed and dressed—whether they were going out or staying at home, like his stoutly built wife with her voluminous bust and rear—they would all stand to salute the flag, its pole erected in the middle of the room. After fixing the flag in place at the top, he would raise his hand in salute, repeating the cry to prolong Egypt's life three times, at which point he would dismiss his family; they could then start their day. When he left the house, he would shake his wife's hand, extending his hand in greeting just as presidents and kings shake each others' hands when they meet.

Rumi would often watch the newsreel shown before a feature film. In the summer he frequented the Cinema Fath in Dabiba diligently, and in the winter Cinema Kawakib, as well as the Cinema Olympia on Abd al-Aziz Street and the Ideal and Royale cinemas near Abdeen. His passion for the cinema was well known, especially for the newsreel. Once a month, his entire family would accompany him to Cinema Kawakib in Darrasa. On Saturday evening or Sunday afternoon, he would go to the other cinemas by himself. As he was on his way out of the alley, some would come out to watch him, especially the women, even though they were used to seeing his military stride and his upright posture, with his right arm forward, his left arm back. At the corner, he would stop for a moment before turning on one foot and continuing. During one evening conversation, I heard my father tell my mother that the happiest moments for Rumi the tailor were when he spoke to his family about an important matter. He would start by saying:

"Ladies . . . gentlemen."

—⁓—

Are places truly stable? Do we really wake up in the same place in which we went to sleep?

How, while the earth is rotating?

How, while the earth orbits around the sun, propelled through space at the speed of sixty kilometers per second, according to astronomers? Can stability be achieved while its rotation on its own axis, and around the sun, is continuous? The revolution of the sun and the stars around the galaxy, the revolution of the galaxy around other galaxies.

How are the south, east, west, and north that we know in the evening the same that we face in the morning? Or what's above us and what's below? How can one define anything, when everything is rotating?

Sympathy

Afternoon, winter, the gray of the clouds dominates. They're low, almost touching the course of people's lives. They foretell heavy rain, a hidden sun. How am I so confident that these are the beginnings of winter, since the ends resemble the beginnings? A vast horizon hidden by the accumulation of the clouds. A low sky, close above the roof of our house in the alley. My *gallabiya* is striped—narrow and white, broad and brown. I'm standing, looking down silently, sadly.

Why?

I'm uncertain . . .

I feel sympathy for myself, through the time in which I would look at that wintry moment that explained who I was. The details of a time that lies between us are difficult to explain. It's possible to understand it in its totality. Tenderness flows from me toward myself; within me, it connects two separate moments that relate to me. They grow distant and grow near what is between me and myself.

The man who is now so old feels for the boy he used to be and who has now gone. Thus I look at me from myself. I speak and I listen, I eulogize myself to myself—scattered, divided into two sides, as if I were two, even though I am he. My starting point is a winter that passes over me and another I will not reach. This one passes him and that one passes me. Nothing binds us, apart from my sympathy for myself.

A piercing light

On the roof at night, and alone. An intensely dark night, the stars pure white. I turn my face to the east. I don't know why I've come out alone to all of this night. And why such darkness? As if the power to the entire city had been cut.

Suddenly, a thin light appears—precise, like a diamond coming from above, to my right, piercing, drowning out everything but itself. I'm rooted to the spot, exposing my entire existence to it, anticipating it. I can't move. It becomes longer as it approaches me, coming straight at me. As it gets closer, it surrounds me with its light while passing through my chest to what lies behind me, above me, below me. I'm engulfed by an awareness of totality, as well as a new freshness, as if I'd plunged into a sea of fresh mint. I want to peer behind the barriers. I remain there for a long time and when I go back inside the room I'm aware that I'm not who I was . . .

Fear

Suddenly, I'm overpowered by the unknown.

Something will occur, will happen.

What is it? What is its essence?

I don't know.

When will it begin? From where does it start? From what direction is it coming?

I'm not aware.

From below, above, outside, inside, now, yesterday, tomorrow?

I don't know. What's certain is that it crouches somewhere, in some location—it hides, withdrawn into itself—yet at some moment, it will suddenly burst forth. It will shimmer, descend suddenly, and suddenly become complete. Gradually, it will be realized. The hardest lesson throughout my travels has been to be confronted by the unpredictable, that which defies all explanations.

Newyorkiya

The road to John F. Kennedy Airport. The EgyptAir flight takes off at eleven at night in order to cross the ocean to the coast of Europe, then across the Mediterranean skies to Africa, where we live.

In the car with Masoum, my friend and the Egyptian deputy consul in New York at the time. My wife is in the back seat. There's still time to get to the airport, to have some time before takeoff. We've spent three hours with Masoum. We're en route from Mexico to Cairo. We didn't want to stay in New York. If only I'd seen Edward Hopper's paintings at the Museum of Modern Art. If only the connection that developed between us some fifteen years later had started then, I would have lingered and stayed long enough. For various reasons as I write this, something occurs to me—the impossibility of staying in that city again. And so I will not stand in front of those paintings I fell in love with and which had such influence on me by way of masterful reproductions or books I sought to buy. There's nothing like seeing the original.

My friend's car stops at a traffic light. Next to us is a car driven by a young woman. I become transfixed by her features—fine and distinct. She's dark—a unique darkness, I've never seen the like. She touches her chin with her little finger, leaning forward slightly. She's wearing a gray dress. Her strong features capture me. Her perfect presence. I don't stop looking at her until she comes closer to us for a moment, then moves off. Wherever she's going. We continue to our point of departure, to cross the ocean.

Who will show me the way? Who will grant me the opportunity to appear before her once again—even if only for a few, short seconds? Who will guide me to that young woman who pulled up, in her car, at that traffic light on the road—whose name I don't know—leading to John F. Kennedy Airport? It was at exactly eight fifteen on that New York evening, that November evening, in 1989. Who was she?

—⁂—

Why does an incomplete work of art stir the imagination more than one that is complete?

—⁂—

I stare at the latest images of the depths of the universe taken by the Hubble Space Telescope. Two galaxies colliding. Spots of light and color. Is there not an intimate resemblance between the images of immense galaxies, vast in their distance, and images of blood cells under the microscope? When magnified and examined, does a drop of blood not possess all those details? Are they not similar in form?

Al-Kanzi

Black letters in the middle of the page, which I've started looking at recently. They're unfamiliar to me.

"Major General al-Kanzi has returned to his Creator."

I reread the words.

A few months ago—I don't know how many—he called me. He asked if I remembered him. He said he would like to meet me regarding an important matter. His voice seemed feeble, worn. He assured me he had something he wanted to tell me. He repeated the phone number twice. I wrote it on a small piece of yellow paper. The next day, I couldn't find it and looked for it in vain. It had disappeared. One day followed the next and I forgot about him.

When he asked me if I still remembered him, I answered reproachfully, "How could I forget my glory days?" I see him standing beside the Suez Governorate building, wearing his military uniform. He holds the rank of brigadier general—the military commander for the Suez area. I stand listening to him. He speaks and I hear; I don't know what's being said.

Here he's wearing his field uniform, a helmet on his head, pointing to the east.

Here I'm approaching him, raising my arm. We meet at some point, one impossible for me to locate today. We embrace. Wintry light, one of the days of January 1974, after the end of the embargo against the City of Suez and the opening of the main road linking it to Cairo.

We're walking alongside the Gulf of Suez. He points toward the east repeatedly. I can't be sure when it was.

A military celebration somewhere close to Cairo. He's wearing his service uniform, preparing to make a statement. But he comes to me, from somewhere, displacing this image and standing in field uniform at some moment in time, some place in Suez, looking away. I follow his gaze, not knowing what we're looking at or observing.

Reclining

A bed, covered by a sky blue sheet with dark blue stripes. The bed is in a room with a high ceiling with protruding wooden beams. It's the top floor of an old building, in an alley off the main street leading to Sakakini Pasha Square.

A woman's thighs, full, uncovered, parted, teeming in their vastness—their softness, oblivion, tenderness. Between them my impulsive existence—overflowing, seeking irrigation, saturation. Her thighs are the pure color of newly harvested wheat, suggesting fertility and abundance. She's neither short nor tall; she's harmony itself. To me, she has no features. The more her thighs appear before me, as she lies back, preparing herself, the more completely her face disappears. Even if she were to appear before me now, unchanged from thirty-five years ago, I wouldn't recognize her. But if she were to lie back, ready for me, the sight of her thighs would encompass everything I experienced at that moment, as if I were bringing her back again.

She has a name; I don't remember it in full. It has a *g* in it—Nagat, Nagwa, Ragaa, Gamila—it sounds like one of those. I knock on the door. It opens, and I see no one in front of me. As I cross the threshold, I turn. I see her, unencumbered by any garment, sewn or otherwise, completely naked. But she's complete: submissive, anticipating, and friendly, provoking, inviting.

She has been living alone since her husband went abroad to work in Jordan. When I first met her, he'd been away for five years. She had a friend, thin and tall, who knew a friend of mine and who insisted that he bring someone when they got together, so that she could feel at ease with him. This is how I got to know to her, and she me. Before her and ever since, I've never known the kind of affection or embraces that I tasted with her. In Morocco, they call sex *hawaa*—"holding." I can't hear this word without thinking of a woman; a man does not hold but rather is held. I never knew anyone to "hold" as she did. All she wanted was to open the door completely naked and greet me—softly, elegantly, nobly. She holds the tips of my fingers, standing on tiptoe to kiss my lips, the touch of her finger whispering to my cheek. She forces me to slow down, her music has to be answered with the correct rhythms—otherwise there's dissonance, and everything becomes cloudy.

Later, I become familiar with her; I get to know her fantasies, her imagination. She likes to walk around naked, at ease, showing off her perfect body. I can almost see her before me right now, as she moves about in the confined space of the room that has become vast, immense, broad. Slowly she comes closer. She unbuttons my shirt. Each step, each movement, is followed by a kiss. She keeps removing my clothes until I'm on the verge, as she leads me to the mattress. Although it's tidy and clean, she smoothes out the sheet and the pillow, seeking out the softness. I separate the moment in which I'm about to take her from what was before and what comes after; I separate it entirely and I remember it entirely. The joy of anticipation. Embarking on something is significant. What she utters during those brief moments soothes me and excites me. She knows the essentials of intimacy, the perfect kind of foreplay. At just the right moment she lies back, pressing against my chest with her arms, fully outstretched. She looks at me, then leans over me. I feel the erectness of her nipples, and at the moment our lips meet there comes the release. As the burst begins I withdraw. Our stars are aligned. I can't say more. The parting of her thighs is permission for the thrill of ecstasy, for crossing the borders of the borderless—where there's no first and no last, just union and separation, together.

She takes as much as she gives. She deludes me into thinking she has given up control. But she is the guide. She satisfies herself and adjusts the intensity, in full control. When she places her feet around my back, it's not an accident but a calculated move. For a long while, whenever I thought about women I'd known, she would stand out. The way she blends the maternal flood with the gentle, feminine spring—amazing.

Little by little, her features have become remote and unclear, except the parting of her thighs—their availability, their reach—until I begin to recall them for their own sake, as if they were disconnected from the person on whom I rested my head and who rested her head on me. I try to find an equivalent for the term "thigh" and the word "loin" comes to me, which suggests "calf" and then "leg." "Thigh" is associated with food, when my father would take hold of the chicken to break it up and pass it around. The thigh, the wing, the neck. I turn the phrases over in my head until I find one that reflects that shudder of longing and yearning. I focus on *them*; I see nothing except *them*. Perhaps also a part of the mattress, a stretch of the wall. I had no idea how things would end up, waking up one night more than thirty-five years after our last encounter, the last parting, her from me, me from her. The dream was clear. Distinct. Between dawn and morning. I was dizzy, with hurried breaths, seeing nothing but the two of *them* and between them, my pleasure—as if I were looking at myself from above. I was satisfied, despite my trembling. After I came within her, within the void, what I had known in life became a mere apparition. If only!

Ishtingil

Between sunset and the end of the evening, when night descends, I relax in cafés. In the daytime, cafés prepare for customers, they're extensions of the workplace. People who go there have finished with, or are about to take care of, something, or they're carrying out some task. But the night is for passing the time.

Until the sixties, Ataba Square captured an old time; it preserved the essence of the era in which the main buildings had been erected, forming a panorama around the Opera House: the Central Post Office, the Parliament Hotel, the Tiring Commercial building alongside the Parisian Lafayette Gallery, the Public Debt Commission, Ahmad Halawa's showroom, Wilson the patisserie, Charalambos Juices, small watch repair shops, narrow passages leading to bars and cafés, and bars that only served alcohol until that time in the sixties. Each time I reached the square, coming from Old Cairo where I lived, heading to the Azbakiya fence where the vintage booksellers were, then Opera Square, I would enter a time and then a place. I don't know the source of this feeling—perhaps it was the architecture, perhaps the central location of the place, by virtue of its role as a divider between Old Cairo and Byzantine Cairo—as Ali Pasha Mubarak, the man who planned and executed it, named it. Perhaps it was the traces of those who'd passed through: I'm absolutely convinced that anyone who passes through a place leaves a trace. What is its nature, its essence? I don't know. But as a result of its central location, the square took from the old and the new.

A large café beneath the Parliament Hotel that was popularly called the "Locanda." It was one of the most famous hotels of its time, the destination of the well off from the countryside and the rich from the Sinai Peninsula, before the spouting of oil. One of its rooms appears before me—a rectangular window and high ceilings. A wealthy man from our village is lying in the bed. He has had surgery, perhaps to remove a gall bladder, in Dr. Abdallah al-Katib's hospital in Dokki. He's facing me, white, flushed with red; I remember him with an Arab *abaya* made of dark blue wool. The way he's lying. Beside him is half of a flaming red watermelon with a knife plunged into it. Through the intervening space, I move between his features, the redness of the watermelon and the blackness of the seeds. In vain, I try to remember his name. He's from Juhayna, but . . . who is he? For me, someone whose name is unknown remains a face that merges with the rest—just features, with no meaning.

I sit in that café under the Locanda. Alone or with someone? I don't know, but I'm filled with joy as soon as the *ishtingil* seller appears. I watch him carefully. He appears late, by which time some of the customers are in need of a snack as they sit in the café. I first see his bright, clean, white *gallabiya*, which he holds by its hem with his teeth as he balances the yellow bamboo basket in his hands. Under his armpit is a folded wooden stand that can be closed or opened, on which he places the basket as soon as he reaches the entrance. He stands in front of it, soft *smeet* buns with sesame, round, dry cakes, tomatoes split and stuffed with garlic and parsley, pickled black eggplants, boiled eggs, white cheese, pieces of *roumi* cheese, a container of salt and one of pepper, and transparent sheets of paper. Once he appears, he catches a glimpse of some of his customers and begins preparing what each one wants, just by exchanging a look. His mastery and precision in preparing the food amaze me—his slow way of peeling the egg, choosing tomatoes next to eggplants and salted cucumber, and the leaves of green arugula with which he crowns the vegetables. He spreads out the transparent paper on top of a small piece of cardboard. He works slowly, handling his merchandise with pride, displaying his artistry in arranging and stimulating the appetite of the hesitant or one whose desire has faded. I used to order two eggs and a piece of *roumi* cheese; their combination is one of the rare harmonies of food flavors. A slice of pickled eggplant, covered with garlic, cilantro, and whole tomato. As for my favorite kind of bun, I name it after him, since that is the word he uses when calling out his wares. Why, exactly? I don't know.

"*Ishtingil.*"

What's the origin of this name?

I don't know. Those rectangular sandwiches, a little thicker in the center. There's a bit of salt in them—a special taste, especially with a bite of boiled egg and pickled eggplant. *Ishtingil* became a name for those men of graceful build who passed by the downtown cafés. The last one I saw in front of Café Riche at the end of the sixties; when he shouted "*ishtingil!*" it took me back to Ataba Square. *Ishtingil* became the name for many whose names I don't remember and a marker for the square which is now crumbling. I can't pass by or cross it without hearing that melodious cry, although I don't see from where it comes. Because it seems to originate within me, its origins—those echoes—unspoken yet significant, are features of moments that will cease to exist when I do.

Music

Afternoon, winter, Ramadan. The day is a Friday. Definitely a Friday. I only stand in the office like that on Fridays. I'm dusting books, using a feather duster with a black handle and an African carving at the end. I rearrange some sections, and rediscover titles. Just having them next to each other creates new relationships, like people getting to know each other for the first time. Stillness. Not the Friday silence produced by a lack of activity, or the fading away of noise, particularly in the suburb where I live. I don't feel the need to hear the stirring Iranian music I've spent the last few weeks listening to, in order to absorb it. In that universal silence, I have no need of music—unheard melodies welled up from within . . .

A position

After breakfast we return to the room. We'd been the first to enter the restaurant after its doors opened. The taste of coffee is still in my mouth, the light of the gray, wintry sky is dim through the net curtains. The ceiling is high; the old building still preserves its original features, its open spaces. It hasn't been divided up internally, in the modern fashion, with only the original facade preserved as dictated by the laws of the city. For this reason, I prefer this small hotel.

Between the window and the unmade bed sit two suitcases. The first is mine: large and tightly shut, containing my clothes, papers, and some books, as well as a few gifts. I packed them well yesterday evening. They're the things I've needed during a month traveling across three countries, the last ten days of it here. Beside it is a smaller suitcase made of sturdy fabric, rectangular, linked to the first moment and the last, to when she arrives in the room from the train station for our rendezvous, which may last one night or several, depending on how long I'm staying. She comes from the far north, over a thousand kilometers away, which the high-speed train covers in four hours. The suitcase is also the last thing I see of her before we part. It's her arrival and her departure.

I lie down on the bed, resting my back on the folded pillow with my eyes closed, hoping to get through these moments quickly. Not because I'm annoyed with her but out of compassion for myself and for her, for the difficulty of separation after all the delights we've experienced together, in the streets, the parks, the cafés, and the exhibitions, during our strolls—everything that we've lived. This time and the times before, it rises up again and again, arousing a melancholy and a fear of being apart and of all that can happen to two people in love, each of them in a different country, separated by space and time. Each of us accepts it because of the circumstances, content with the rendezvous that are interspersed between travels or missions or that are prearranged.

How I want to be alone. She's right beside me but also far away. After a short while, we know that leaving each other will come as quickly as the train that will take her back to her small city on the coast and the plane in which I will cross the skies to my homeland, where I've now settled. I feel her quiet breaths on my skin. They fall like a fine light—quiet, unhurried at the beginning of this winter day. I open my eyes and am taken by her look of desire, that feminine brightness in her eyes. I'm aware only of the parting of her lips, the view between. Our lips penetrate each other.

I'm not only kissing her but devouring her in order to remain inside her. My tongue explores her, and our saliva becomes mixed. I stand up with an erection. The brief moment seems to stretch out—a second equaling a day. Impossible to measure.

She turns around, takes off her long, blue skirt and her underwear and kneels down—pointing her buttocks toward me, with her head, her face, pushed into the mattress, her fingers gripping the sheet. Her act of turning is flagrant, inviting. Her apertures lead me, inviting, enticing. Ever since we first got together—those first moments in which we became one—she has lain on her back with her eyes shut. This is the first time she has invited me, by kneeling, to approach her, to come to her as I wish.

Her utter surrender shatters my desire, and I lean over the two rounded forms, desiring but unable to penetrate.

Blindfolded

At the landing of the stairs, he appears suddenly.

An unexpected place for this to happen. He's standing upright between two guards, each of them holding an arm. A man, a human being, in his thirties or forties, on the verge of corpulence. When sight stops functioning, the body takes on the characteristics of the blind: the top half leans back slightly, the entire body becoming upright as it moves from one place to another, avoiding any object that might cause harm, wary of anything whose sudden appearance is impossible to predict. The parts of the body rely on each other to cross the invisible space. The condition and the being of a blind person become one and the same thing, that seems to emerge, to burst forth. But for someone on whom temporary blindness is imposed and who is separated from his surroundings, his alertness is magnified. I slow down as I'm going up the stairs, which leads the soldier accompanying me to turn to me, silently questioning. As if seeing a prisoner, a blindfolded man, is something ordinary, not requiring a person to stop, or be surprised.

I entered this building against my will only once, at dawn, just after I was detained. Every other occasion I was summoned to explain a matter, or to deal with some harassment, or to seek some favor. Then I would be asking for protection, which would take too long to explain. This isn't the place to go into details, since I'm concerned with that brief moment from which I'm separated, at the time of writing, by thirty-five years. Despite its rapid passing, it takes me by surprise in various places. Each time, I don't know what triggers it, and I don't pause over it. I can't explain it.

At the bend, the two soldiers slow down. They don't speak but concentrate on leading the one who has surrendered to them, the obedient one. A confusion runs through the man's body. Stairs can be treacherous: they can end at any moment; their arrangement can change. Anything can happen to someone who can't see his next step, let alone someone who is expecting harm.

I only recall the first sight of him. The brief, shocking moment when he appeared and the fear and sympathy that overtook me, for nothing is as distressing as seeing a human being who expects to be harmed. I can't see him alongside me. I must have passed him, not stopping when I caught sight of him. I hesitated and slowed down, but I didn't stop going up, just as he continued coming down. Perhaps I was following his tracks with my eyes while he went down and I continued going up.

The first, brief moment erases everything but itself. All the remaining moments seem fixed, isolated from their movements. Some of their details have disappeared with time. And perhaps others, unconnected to the origin, have appeared. Only a detail, mixed with other moments. I don't recall the features of the two soldiers who held him by the arms and controlled his movements. Their places are empty, and the moment catches me by surprise. It's as if they were not there. But I'm aware of their presence from his position and the way he looks. It's as if they were two, black holes that can't be seen, only the traces of what's around them. I don't remember the soldier who was escorting me, or even the reason I was summoned. Just the building's space. And that vigilant figure, staring completely into the unknown.

Who is he? What's he accused of? Who's he related to outside these walls? What does he do? Who is his family? What's his story? Where are they taking him?

The same questions go around my mind, when the moment recurs to me at an unexpected place and time. About twenty-five years later, I'm sitting on the train to Upper Egypt, heading south. I prefer traveling by day so that I can see the Nile Valley and relive the trips I used to take with my family. I stare at the telegraph poles that flash past quickly and at the palm trees, which, for me, mean going to the deep south. With the appearance of the palms, it's complete. All of a sudden I see that standing figure, facing me—between the fields and the river, between the river and the mountain that borders the east. Behind it, the sun appears in the morning. The sudden appearance of that moment, with all that it contained, cancels out everything else. It's accompanied by a feeling that disturbs me for a while;

the source of it was my silence when I saw him, having failed to give the least support or help, either by act or word. I blame myself for my fear and for preferring to keep silent until I reach the point of sleep, while questions without answers follow one after another.

Where is he now?

What happened to him after I saw him?

Does he still exist?

I try bringing him to mind again in order to find an answer, to explain what eluded me, but it's too difficult. I'm not even able to see his blindfolded head, only his body as far as his neck—his chest, his cautious feet, the light brown color of his pants. A body unconnected to anything, being escorted to its destiny.

Missing

My friend who has returned from the Gulf for the summer vacation welcomes me. After embracing him and greeting his wife, his children surround me—his oldest daughter, his middle daughter, and his son, who is four years old.

"How are you, uncle? Daddy told us a lot about you . . . " the boy says.

As I'm leaving, he hangs on to me. "Spend the night here, uncle . . . "

I look at him, ruffling his hair. He shouts as he tries to cling to me with his small fist. "No one visits us over there, and I'm afraid here will be like there. So spend the night here, uncle . . . "

Two

From the police station in Darb al-Ahmar, two people emerge.

A police soldier, thin and short, wearing his sloppy, soiled, and overlarge dark uniform. Huge shoes. His feet swim in them. Beside him is a young man of similar height and weight, and perhaps age, in civilian clothes. A soiled shirt, shabby pants, flip-flops. Their pace is identical. They're joined to each other by metal shackles—handcuffs. The soldier is on the right, one handcuff around his right wrist, the other around the young man's left wrist. The key for the handcuffs is in the place where they will end up, where the young man will be handed over. In the intervening space, their fates are linked; they're united by the handcuffs.

After entering the side street leading to Muhammad Ali Street, they stop. It's not clear which one of them has pulled out a cigarette. The young man bends down and the soldier bends with him. He lights a match near the cigarette, which is between the soldier's lips. The soldier turns around, bending down—a half turn, a half crouch—sticking his head out to light the young man's cigarette from the burning tip of his cigarette.

They exhale the smoke and continue walking, each of their cigarettes between the fingers of their free hands. Sometimes they sway as if on the verge of stumbling, but they walk together.

Place

Where?

And the question arises, sudden and fleeting.

Where?

Where am I right now? In what location? I don't mean the small room that frames my existence at this moment, where I awake to the remnants of a dream I can't grasp or pin down.

Where in the universe? I mean what lies beyond the room and the country, the continent and the planet? What's around me seems stable, even though it's not. It revolves around its center. Around the sun. The sun within the galaxy, the galaxy around other galaxies. Place and time, always changing, and with it my existence. Where am I, then? At what point, exactly? To what reference point should I return? From my location, from where I sleep. But it's not what it seems. What's apparent is an unreal moment in the time in which I travel—to where, I'm unsure, I don't know.

A sister

A reception to bestow on the writer Yahya Haqqi an award from France. I'm contentedly heading for the ambassador's house. Happy. I loved the man and the author. I'm also happy that he chose me. He specified whom he wanted to come to his party.

Dr. Hussein Fawzi arrives. He's over ninety at this point. He's supported by his chauffeur—a young man, large and stocky. The chauffeur holds him by the arm, steering his course. He has been living under his care since his French wife died. I approach him and speak about my encounter with him in Alexandria, about the *harissa* pastry with pistachio in Raml Square. It was about a quarter of a century ago, when he was still able to walk on his own, brimming with vitality and the ability to debate. He'd bought a small piece and started eating it in front of the little shop.

Suddenly, he scrutinizes me and says slowly, "Alexandria . . . my sister's there."

Then he squints. He looks away from me, focusing. Talking to himself. "I don't know . . . is she still alive or did she pass away?"

He answers himself in a loud voice. "I really don't know."

He purses his lips.

The driver pushes him. "Hurry up already, doctor!"

Existence

Who?

The universe or me? The reality that I perceive, or myself?

Those sounds. Would they exist were it not for two ears to hear them? The same goes for the succession of dewdrops and the surge of the waves at the eye of the storm.

Those stars, those meteors. The hues and shades of color of all the elements. Would they exist without glances or watching eyes?

The smell of those flowers. Would it waft were it not for our breathing them in, if not for inhaling their perfume?

Does flavor have a presence without a sense to perceive it, to distinguish between sweet and sour, between salty and bland? During a trip, I met a friend who'd lost his sense of taste: all food was the same to him—no difference between meat and beans, between solid and liquid. He told me that he ate in order to satisfy his hunger. Not to enjoy. For him, food, in all its variety, didn't exist.

What's the fate of that little breeze without a cheek to feel it?

Would a destination exist without a traveler? Without a journey?

What does time mean without someone to define the differences between yesterday, tomorrow, and a present that does not continue? Without someone to record what happened and to predict what will be? And to try to explain its flow and understand its mystery?

When I close my eyes forever, will the darkness—of which I will become a part—prevail? Will the images disappear, and will what was become equal to what will be? Who among us reaches the end, at that point? My self, that perceives this universe?

Or the universe, which is perceived by me?

They were so green

I get on the metro carriage. Many empty seats. A quiet time to take the metro. Since I don't have to sign in and out at work, I avoid rush hours. I'm tired; I haven't had enough sleep. One of the passengers has nodded off.

Some are staring off at nothing. The seat facing me is empty. I look out of the window at what's passing by.

When did she get on?

When did she sit down?

I'm not paying any attention. Suddenly, I find her in front of me. There's nothing striking about her: a modest young woman, wearing regular clothes, humble, holding a leather purse. Her glasses are dark, completely hiding her eyes. I resume my preoccupation with what I'm looking at out of the window. After Dar al-Salam station, the number of people who are standing increases. There's some congestion.

Something happens. I don't know where it's coming from—it's indistinct, I can't quite make it out. Something in the air has changed. I turn around.

She's holding her glasses in her hands.

Her eyes are looking. At me. In their reflection the entire day changes. My fatigue disappears. I shift my position, overflowing with optimism. I've never seen such a deep green color. They're the center and the source. A face that doesn't reveal its innermost secret until the sunglasses are removed. They overflow with a vibrant attraction; at every moment, new birth and revival appear in them.

I'm seized by a zeal for things from a time that has gone. I'm torn between the desire to look and shyness. Those eyes. Beautiful. They pour over me and I'm transformed, as if they were a panacea. They fertilize me—their color is unique. I remember a woman from Ganadla Monastery whose eyes had the same quality. I prepare to stand up and go. I stare, indifferent, as if gazing from another universe, as if I were not there in front of her. She's preoccupied, utterly unaware of my evident awe. She stands up after me, and I slow my pace so that she might catch up with me and I might slowly enfold her in my sight. I turn around. I don't find her and realize that she has disappeared. When she got up, was she wearing the glasses or holding them in her hands? I go back a few steps and know for sure that she has gone. I start going up the stairs slowly, burdened by my days, my circumstances, and a nostalgia which that greenness has caused to flourish!

A flutter

In the distance between the dome of Ghouri and Hussein Mosque, I first heard of Turkish music. Beneath the dome, there was Arabic music: an amateur ensemble led by a young man, an expert at his craft. I was out with an older friend who was familiar with matters of the senses. His eyes crackled with desire and voraciousness for the pleasures of life. After his death, his widow came to me with her daughter. They had a problem they thought I could help them with. I don't remember all the details, but I'm very conscious of her eyes and her passionate glances, full of desire, like echoes of his own glances. I tried to imagine the moment they would melt into one, their intermingling and their ensuing shudder.

My introduction to Turkish music began in that distance I covered with my friend, who is always present. He led me to the music and all I had to do afterward was tune the radio at night. That same day, I made the effort and absorbed myself in a stream of invisible frequencies. From that time, I became a listener—engrossed, I would memorize entire songs in a language I didn't understand. I'm convinced that whatever meaning reached me differed little from what I got from the original. After June 1967, a classical Turkish musical group came to Cairo. I heard them at the only concert hall that was suitable for the music.

I heard a *samai*, an Ottoman Turkish piece, by Gamil Bey al-Tanbouri. He played it in the *rast* mode, a kind of scale. Sometimes I connect with a name: I can't listen to his music without him appearing before me, sitting by the Bosphorus. He merges with my old friend who introduced me to Turkish music and whom I always recall. I'm nothing but the sum of many others. Every direction I've sought out is the result of a signal from someone now passed away who left me the trace of something written or printed, or someone I was close to and who guided me with a piece of advice or simply said something aloud. If I wanted to count up all those who gave me such signals, I would be lost.

In this *samai*, the melody rose, moving from state to state—now lifting me, now descending. Throughout, I held my breath so that nothing escaped me and I wouldn't go astray. Between one transition and another, the flutter happened. I didn't know if it was an improvisation by the skillful *tambour* drummer in a moment of deep emotion, or a part of the composition, an integral part. The flutter touched me in a way I'd never felt before. It alerted me to a place deep within me, revealing previously unknown nuances. The rustle of the strings gives color to what we don't see, what we don't realize. Time. By way of the *rast* mode, I can almost take hold of time. The *samai* of al-Tanbouri or al-Qusabgi—both of them from the *maqam* mode. That modest flutter which almost didn't appear. I couldn't define it or associate it with anything. It lasted only a few seconds, yet it left me with a whisper, a breath of wind—the scent of basil, and gratitude for the man who'd first led me to that bounty, when we crossed the distance from the dome of Ghouri that day, to the tomb of Our Master the Imam, the Martyr.

The cell phone carrier

From the window of the plane, I see a special car for VIPs. It stops in front of the steps. Perhaps some minister or former official or . . . I catch sight of a businessman whose picture is in the papers and who offers his opinions on talk shows. Medium height, stocky, broad chested, firm footed. Three men with him. He shakes the hand of one and the other two follow him as slowly he begins to climb. I recognize one of them—a retired colonel whom I met during the war when he was a captain in the surveillance units. Years later the retired colonel would come to me as a sales representative for *Encyclopaedia Britannica*. His commission was his salary. I still remember his shyness and how he justified coming to me: who better than me would know who might need an encyclopedia? He didn't ask me directly to buy from him, just as I avoided showing or hinting that I didn't need it.

I watch him as he climbs then disappears from my sight through the doorway at the front. After a few moments, he reappears by the gap that separates first class from economy. The attendant shows him to his seat. Our eyes meet, we shake hands and embrace. He gestures to me, meaning: after we take off.

Above the Mediterranean, after the plane has crossed from land to sea over Alexandria, I move to an empty seat next to him, and we recall the old days and moments gone by, and each of us asks about names of people. After a silence, I say I'd recognized him as soon as I saw him. He says he works with "Mr. So-and-So . . . " and I say I know his employer only by name, as he's one of those few whose names are often mentioned and whose pictures are published alongside their news or in advertisements for projects or when signing contracts.

The retired colonel says he works in the secretariat and is responsible for this small, leather briefcase. A style I've never seen before: inside are four cell phones, two for the Egyptian networks, the third connected to a European network, and the fourth a satellite phone that can call anywhere in the world from any location, even from an empty desert. He's also responsible for answering the phones and writing down names, before passing them to Mr. So-and-So, who decides who to answer. The man doesn't dial anyone himself. The retired colonel would do it for him then pass the phone to him, except for particular names: if they appeared on the screen, he would immediately pass it to Mr. So-and-So. In addition, he takes care of the phones. He has to keep the batteries charged at all times and never leaves them except when he goes to sleep. I don't ask for any explanation, I don't utter the many questions prompted by my curiosity. I'm afraid of embarrassing him unintentionally, but he surprises me by saying, "A strange new job . . . a cell phone carrier."

I smile. After a moment's silence, I remember him in his combat uniform. His way of standing. Looking to the other side. Sitting in the car beside me. A soldier suddenly coming out of a foxhole. His gesture upward, meaning that planes are in the sky. A Jeep moving on the road parallel to the canal—a clear and tempting target.

He says it's better than having no work. After retirement, he'd been through some tough times. The hardest thing these days is to find work, he says. A close friend had nominated him for this job: the most important thing he'd said when describing him to Mr. So-and-So was that he was very trustworthy and very discreet.

On the beach

The mother keeps an eye on her young daughter. She's playing by the edge of the sea with children she has met here. Some fairly violent waves are crashing into the sand, then receding—recurring in an eternal movement. Sometimes they're calm, at other times violent, but they never stop. From time to time, she shouts, calling out to her daughter, warning her not to go further into the water. She warns her about something to let her know that she's close by, then she relaxes once again. Slowly, a pretty girl in a short dress comes up to her, with her hands behind her back. She looks at the mother for a while before asking, "They're all your children?"

The mother looks at her, surprised at her being there. "No, sweetie . . . "
She points to the girl. "She's your daughter?"
"Yes."
"She's lucky."
The mother sits up, no longer relaxed.
The girl says, "She's lucky to have you for her mother."
She corrects herself quickly. "I have a new mother now."
The mother looks at her closely. The girl seems to be alone: Who is her father? Where is her family?

She says her father is a police officer. And they live in the city, but they go to all the new seaside hotels. Her father comes with her in the mornings. He leaves her to wander around the hotel, the garden, the playgrounds.

"The manager is daddy's friend . . . all the managers are his friends . . . "

She turns to the dividing line between land and sea.

"And you always come out with her . . . "

The mother looks at her. Trying to start a new conversation, she says, "And what's your name?"

"Yasmine . . . "

"Do you go to school?"

"Kindergarten . . . "

Quickly, she adds, "Your daughter is lucky because you always come out with her."

She lifts her slender finger. "But . . . the new mama is kind."

She lowers her head, repeating, "Yeah . . . she's really kind. When I tell her I'm thirsty, she brings me a glass of water."

The mother looks at her, her eyes tender, shining with sadness.

The girl assures her, "Yeah, really . . . she brings me something to drink."

On the road

The driver is sitting at the steering wheel of the huge bus; I only see him like this. His single seat. Behind him is a dark, glass barrier that separates him from the dim, interior lights at night. I can see his features via the rearview mirror hanging in the middle of the windshield. He also looks at it. He can see all the seats. With smiling eyes, he pats the children. He smiles at the passengers. His facial features escape me completely. But the position in which he sits merges with someone else who used to drive a bus that was a similar size, on some road or other. But he used to wear a coat. It seems to me that the first one is wearing the other's coat, is wrapped in it. Many times, I've watched the drivers who spend long hours alone on the lengthy roads. When I was transferred to Minya in the midsixties, I used to go to the north of the town and flag down the trucks. In exchange for a small sum, I would ride next to the driver. Half the price of a third-class train ticket. Mostly, I would go at night, when there were more trucks and they would move in convoys—each one preceded by a police car, with another following. I met a lot of truck drivers; among them, I remember an old man who wore an old British army coat. After we got going he took out a hip flask of brandy. He raised it toward me, asking, "Drink?" I shook my head. "No thanks," at which point he raised it to his mouth, drinking one gulp after another. I started to worry. As if he realized, he laughed, "Don't worry. The road is long and we have to lighten it a bit." After a little while, he told me about the women who would come out when they heard the sound of a truck horn. He'd married one of them and had children with her. With her, he'd known the sweetest times, but marriage on the road doesn't last for long. A few moments later, I watched as his head lolled to the side: he was asleep over the steering wheel, snoring. I was terrified. However, the assistant who was lying on the long seat behind us said, "Don't worry, he keeps to the road even when he's asleep." I started watching his hand on the wheel, moving with the bends in the road, while his snores rang out, rhythmically.

Our bus driver doesn't look anything like that old truck driver. He's sharply vigilant, chatting with the passengers who come up to him. Some of them bring him a carton of juice or a glass of water or a sandwich. He politely declines every cigarette; he doesn't smoke. He arrives, then goes back the same day. Seven hours from Cairo to Hurghada. He reaches the tourist resort at half past two in the afternoon. He has lunch and lies down in a small room attached to the reception office; he might have a nap. He tells me that someone who is really tired doesn't usually sleep but stretches out to rest his body. He prepares the vehicle, checking the water, gasoline, and tires. At exactly four o'clock, he sets out for Cairo—seven and a half hours, maybe eight, as the night descends on the dangerous bends of Zafrana, which he must cross cautiously, even in the daytime at no more than thirty kilometers an hour. Of course at night he must be more careful. I think a lot about his long hours behind the wheel. He laughs in a friendly and inviting way.

"Where do you think I'll go when I get to Cairo, God willing?"

After I look at him quizzically, he says, "To Kafr al-Sheikh . . . "

The bus depot is there, at the headquarters of the Mid-Delta Company, which rents it to the resort administration. His family lives there.

"That means that in the morning you'll be coming from Kafr al-Sheikh?"

"Yes."

"Naturally you'll get some sleep and rest tomorrow . . . "

His smile widens. "No . . . I have work."

"Where?"

"I'm going to Marsa Matrouh."

He says the distance to Hurghada is normal for him: he's driven the bus further than that, when he went to Saudi Arabia during the hajj season—2,500 kilometers in one go, apart from some short stops. He says he bought a kilo of salted peanuts from a shop next to Sidi Ahmad al-Badawi, and half a kilo of limes. If he felt tired, he'd suck on a lime and eat some peanuts because the salt compensates for what's lost in sweat.

"Don't you get tired?"

"The important thing is the road. You have souls that you have to bring home safely. Look, if you think about being tired, you get tired. But if you focus on the road and the people you're responsible for, you'll get there . . ."

A dream

I recall the smallest details in dreams, on the threshold of waking. The place is a combination of Citadel Square, the buildings of Istanbul, and perhaps Mustansiriya Madrasah in Baghdad and the Old Market in Sanaa. A woman with ancient Egyptian features, untouched by foreign blood, awaits me. The wife of a famous magnate. I saw her with him at a diplomatic reception. I told myself, he knows how to choose! Here she is, looking at me, but I remain cautious: he's fairly powerful and can make trouble for me.

I keep going up the carved stone steps, but she goes before me and I continue to glance at her from below. From a particular spot, I can see all of the Citadel's gates and some of its towers. I pass very close to her. As she turns her back to me, in her dark black dress, I see the opening that reaches to the base of her spine. She leans over, as if to encourage me, to invite me. But I don't look closely. I don't stare. I keep walking, going down the wide, yellowish, stone steps that are sprouting with small weeds. I catch sight of ruby-red flowers in the corners. I cross a small courtyard to a black convertible that waits for me. She's sitting in the driver's seat; between us is a man in the hat and uniform of a Venetian gondolier. He doesn't move.

I hear a woman's voice, not knowing where it's coming from: "I can fix you two up with a house in Paris . . ."

No one answers. The car speeds off. A wall is gradually rising, suggesting the street that stretches behind Sultan Hassan Mosque and its school. But I see tombstones. Names I don't know. Despite the narrowness of the lanes, the car moves forward. I shout out a warning, but she doesn't turn to me; she shows no sign of temptation. Her inviting form disappears—her posture becomes stern, indifferent. Her features disappear. I don't know if she's the same woman I saw standing on the steps or another, unconnected to her.

Now I see her heading off between the tombstones, and there's no room for us to turn back.

A breeze

All those breezes. All those waves, traveling—but from where, and to where?

Where do those glittering gusts that touch me in the evening come from?

Where does the first breeze begin?

Where does the wavelet's journey begin? At what point does the first movement start?

Which moves the other? The winds or the waves?

I don't know where I read it or who told me about the strong winds that blow so hard, carrying sands across the surface of Mars and concealing it from the observers' view. Later, I noted the time that the winds blow there. It's the exact same time as here, the time of the spring khamsin wind. Which of the two is the source? Or, if there's a hidden, secret source somewhere, at some time, in the depths of those universes—do the winds travel through them?

Where does that breeze come from that touches my cheek as I cross Hussein Square, the moment I head toward the tomb, lulled by contentment and confidence? Accepting of every destiny. Perhaps it will carry me too, after it has stirred that affection for the universe in me—that exquisite contentment with all that destinies bring. My cheek is nothing but a stop along the way for that breeze in motion. It brushes over me, entrusting me with the acceptance of what was, and what will be . . .

—⁘—

The boy, three or four years old, doesn't stop asking questions. He's sitting on his mother's lap, sometimes looking at his interlocking fingers, sometimes out of the window. But he doesn't stop talking—everyone is quiet except him.

"Is your workplace far away, mama?"

"Yes, my love . . . "

"Really far?"

"Yes."

"That's why you don't stay with me?"

She says she has to go to work. After a few moments:

"Don't you love me?"

"Of course I do."

"So why don't you take me with you to work?"

She says she has to go to work alone so that she can bring him nice things that he likes. He goes back to being quiet—is he convinced or just pretending?

"Why does the train whistle?"

She says, "So it can go."

He turns to her gravely. "No . . . it whistles so that people can get on and off . . . " Then he continues, "Is the train faster or the plane?"

The mother says, "The plane is faster."

"It's the plane that took Daddy . . . "

The mother grows silent. She doesn't answer.

"Is Daddy in the plane for a long time . . . ?"

The mother says, "Not more than three hours."

"But why does he go away?"

She says, "He takes the plane to go to his job and bring nice things."

"I wish he'd stay with us . . . Mama . . . I don't want any nice things."

She doesn't answer.

"If the train breaks down, does the owner get upset?"

She's silent. All of a sudden, he shouts, "Come on train, go!"

"Mama . . . why is the bridge up there?"

She says, "It's up there so that people can cross it."

"OK, so why isn't it down below?"

The mother is silent. The boy is suddenly quiet.

"Will Daddy take the plane when he comes?"

She confirms that he will take the plane.

"Will he go away again?"

The mother bends down, hugging him.

"Come on now . . . won't you stop chattering?"

A letter

I see the postage stamp, and I'm delighted and apprehensive. It's the stamp that bears her nationality. The stamp of the city whose air she breathes. The handwriting hasn't changed much, despite the passage of time. I recognize it immediately. I immediately absorb her breaths contained within it. How many kinds of handwriting have I seen that reminded me of her?

Carefully, longingly, I open the envelope.

A New Year's greeting card. She remembers me from one year to the next, with all that is left behind, with what remains fixed, even in memory. That is her signature—I see it and she appears before me, perfect, complete. This is her name: names have pride of place and the utmost significance. I see the name and its owner. I have only to mention the name and the owner is there in front of me. The survival of the name means that the owner continues to exist in nonexistence. For this reason, the ancestors were careful to carve their names and to keep them out of sight until someone would come to find them, and the owners of the names would be reborn.

This is how she appears when I see her name. Her smiles come to me from all directions. Colors and everything that is visible are transformed; light flows into my depths. So . . . she still exists, breathing the air of the universe that contains us. She still cheers those who look at her, who are lucky enough to see her. I read her words again as she asks how I'm doing after twenty years apart, since our relationship ended. Of course, I don't know what she looks like now; I'm imagining her former appearance, which I don't want to alter.

She affects me from far away—a throbbing passes through me that is specific to her. It happens only when her name is mentioned or whenever I anticipate a glance from her, she who shines on my horizon. I take my time to read her words. All questions: Has my address changed? What about my hopes of long ago? How is my health? She wants to know about the man who fell in love with her so long ago and what circumstances have prevented communication.

My entire day is transformed. I become gentler, smiling at everyone I meet. I joke with anyone who calls, teasing them. I write three letters, and send each one from a different place. I don't address her by name but rather correspond with days gone by. Perhaps a trace will appear, or some news will arrive.

Inscriptions

I'm sitting on the backless wooden bench in front of the loom. I'm looking at the unfinished rug in distress, worn down.

"What's wrong?" asks Mr. Sayyid, the practical training instructor.

I tell him I wish I'd entered the mechanical weaving department, but they placed me according to the score on my certificate. I scored 126 points, missing out by one and a half points. He stops cutting the wool and evens it out.

"Forget your marks and the results . . . Look at this beauty . . . "

He says, "Is it logical to compare these colors—red, blue, yellow, and so forth—with machines and their grease? Here patterns are created between the fingers, woven knot by knot, and then smoothed out. Before that, you dye the threads how you like. They come to you completely natural—as white—and you bestow them with color, you determine the hue. What beauty! Look at the circle, how it embraces the circle. You're not weaving a rug but creating a realm—a whole realm."

I look at him silently. His voice is tender. He calms my anxiety, smiling.

"You're not convinced, but later on you'll appreciate what I'm saying."

I bow my head in deep silence. Gratefully, I recall him now.

Mirage

Coming back from my job in the Khan al-Khalili Association. The Silahdar Complex, two in the afternoon, Monday, the fifth of June. A significant time, in which we awaited each new bulletin with expectation. I heard the first bulletin at home, before I left: air strikes on the country's airports, fighting on the borders. Moments that had been anticipated for a long time. Repeated slogans from days past:

"Our forces have crossed the canal with an efficiency admitted by the foe before the friend."

"The way through the steep road is by setting free the slave" (Qur'an 90:13).

"We are expecting the first strike."

The first bulletin was followed by several others predicting the downing of dozens of planes. All were read in Ahmad Said's enthusiastic voice. We asked what we should do. Engineer Fakhri Zaki, director of the association, said we should donate blood. We should go and accompany *Amm* Ismail, who was going to the nearest donation center—that was the least we could do. He was short with a rectangular face, brimming with vitality. At one in the afternoon, he leaned over to me, saying warily, "You know what worries me is that we haven't heard any news about our forces advancing until now . . . "

Then he said, "I'm uneasy."

What he said went through my mind as I returned home, passing in front of the entrance of Sidi Marzouq Mosque. I heard the roar of a fighter plane. A plane, a plane in the sky, its long front like an arrow, its wings swept back—a Mirage. I knew its shape from everything I'd read about planes and aviation, but what astonished me was how low it was flying. And that star on its wings, in the middle of a circle. The Star of David. An enemy plane above Sidi Marzouq Mosque. By the entrance of Darb al-Tablawi. How did it get here? How?

Later, I would often recall it. Its attack position. Its yellow color. I would imagine that I caught a glimpse of the pilot's helmet inside the glass cockpit. I'll retell it, sometimes sure and sometimes doubtful, but the only certainty is that dreaded question: How did it get here? How?

Walking

The car stops exactly between two corners. The pedestrians continue crossing.

A short, stout man leans to the right as he walks. One of his legs seems to be shorter than the other.

Another man, slim, walking quickly, as if he'll never stop. He looks out from on high. His neck is long and his collarbones are prominent.

A woman of advanced age staggers as if carrying an invisible load. She stops when she reaches the sidewalk, looking back.

A young woman in a blouse that pulls away from her pants; the area around her navel is exposed. Her thin buttocks have no trace of roundness. She looks ahead defiantly.

Another man, wearing a suit and carrying a briefcase. His collar is open and his tie is half-undone. He looks like an attorney, perhaps a tax officer. He hurries along, bent forward.

A man with his pants pulled up. A beard surrounds his face, his stride is precise. He has the posture of someone who belongs to the Muslim Brotherhood. Since finding out *Amm* Ahmad al-Hagrasi, our neighbor, who has been detained several times, was a member, and since getting to know many of them, I can almost discern common traits that give them a particular look. Perhaps on this occasion it's the shape of the beard. Does belonging to a political movement or school of thought confer certain characteristics on people that are later embodied in their physical features? Marxists have a way of expressing themselves with hand gestures. Sometimes, something can be perceived, and other times, it's obscure.

A young man walking leisurely. He has his hand in his pocket, unhurried, staring at something.

A woman in her forties—according to my estimate—well proportioned, walking confidently, her bag hanging from her hand, as if she were alone on the street.

Someone wearing his shirt untucked appears: as if expecting something to come from behind, he turns around twice in the time I can see him.

Each pedestrian has his or her own particular features. Each one walks as if no one were in front or behind—either looking straight ahead or with head bowed slightly. Yet none is alike, in stride or features. Each one is independent, proceeding on his own . . .

Papers

I detest everything to do with official papers. Forms, copies, permits, certificates, receipts. I'm at my most miserable when forced to deal with an official agency, a court, or a government office, standing in lines in front of those small windows from which a weary employee looks out, grumbling about everything.

After I got married, my identity card had to be updated to a family card—to this day I still remember its number, 8166 Gamaliya. Filling out the form. The sacred seals. Heading to the Registry Office, the neglected offices, the gray walls, the offhand treatment, the waiting. I had to do it, since I had to deal with several authorities for that card. I had to have it issued in December 1976. Thank God I've never lost it: I would have had to get a replacement. To this day, it's still in good condition. My little photo on it looks as if it belonged to someone else, not me.

Whenever I hear about the national database project, I try to ignore it. It's true that the procedures are done on more modern equipment, but one still has to fill out forms and go to some Ministry of Interior office. Until this day, I don't know exactly which one: the Office of Civil Affairs? The police department I belong to? Or a third department? After the family card had been issued, all that was left was the ration card that ensures a monthly portion of oil, sugar, and rice. It's a necessity with the deterioration of the economy and the tightening of circumstances. I went to the respective office and was shocked by the line. I decided to leave and never to go back. I justified it to myself with the availability of the same goods in the union cooperative. It's true that the prices are higher, but I can't bear standing in line—all that waiting.

When I have to fill in a form or get a certificate issued to complete a process, I find out if there's anyone who can expedite paperwork. Years ago, I received a notice to collect a parcel coming from abroad, which I knew contained books. I went to the airport one day, then the following day, then a third. I didn't avail myself of a customs clearance broker—I thought the procedures for books would be easier. I had to go through the same procedures as if I were receiving a luxury car from abroad or a rare master-piece, in order to get the package released. I'm terrified of getting another similar notice. I brace myself for that day. My stress level begins to rise as my retirement date approaches. All those forms and papers until the issue is settled: papers for the savings fund and social security, for the union and the insurance. I expressed my anxiety to a dear friend, who laughed, saying that everything would be completed without my having to exert any effort. He knows someone in the administration department who is an expert and has connections and could do it in exchange for a modest sum. He would bring all the papers to my office. He reassured me and gave me his name and phone number. The matter wasn't settled for me until after I'd called him. My anxiety astonished him, as I still had ten months ahead of me. A load had been lifted off my shoulders. Then there are two certificates that I don't think about at all—the birth certificate and the death certificate.

—⚹—

Why does memory retrieve a precise moment rather than another?

Why does the wind carry a scent of a fleeting moment from the void, while moments that I was sure would never be lost have merged into obliteration?

Will we have the power, one day, to recall what we want and dispel what we hate?

Blindfolded

I don't know if I'd been blindfolded before I saw that figure on the stairs of the General Intelligence Bureau, or only afterward, along the way. During sudden flashes from the past, remembered moments exchange places. What seems to have happened in the distant past actually took place later on, despite the similarity of the situation—although the circumstances change.

The second half of October 1966. I was a number in the Citadel Prison. An inmate of cell number thirty-seven. Prison gave me a number and that became my name, my attribute, and my nickname. If I knocked on the internal door to ask for anything, I could not raise my voice. It wasn't permitted—forbidden—and shouting was grounds for punishment. Even so, voices would sometimes ring out in prayer or song, at which point the guard who was in civilian clothes would scream, ordering the particular number to be quiet.

"Shut up, thirty-seven."

"Pack it in and shut up, twenty-four."

From the song—or the groan—I would know whose voice it was. But what was strictly forbidden, what led to the worst forms of punishment, was trying to communicate by signals or words. Isolating the prisoner is a necessary prelude to questioning: he isn't left to his solitude but is stripped of anything that might help him pass the time or ward off any part of the void, however small.

The space was limited, and any new arrival had to go through isolation in readiness for interrogation. Then came the interrogation itself. It wasn't part of the Prisons Sector, so there were no uniformed prison officers or soldiers; it was part of the General Intelligence Bureau that dealt with various political cases. For that reason, an isolated and remote place was established for questioning. As it was attached to the bureau, all those who worked there wore civilian clothes. I had no fear of officers or soldiers whose rank was clear and who were in uniform, but an officer or soldier in civilian clothes made me wary, especially when the usual procedures took place, such as when someone of lower rank saluted someone of a higher position.

Food came from a contractor, since the prison had no oven of its own for cooking food. The contractor got the food from the market: loaves of bread and a few black olives. We were fed in the morning, or in the middle of the night, or at dawn. The day wasn't divided into clear work shifts or periods of time, with recognizable characteristics or divisions—seconds, minutes, hours, afternoons, mornings, evenings. Time became featureless. For the shackled, the imprisoned, the one forbidden to move, time seems short. What I noticed in solitary confinement was how quickly time would go by—no sooner would dawn break and black could be distinguished from white than the day would speed by. One could almost see it pass, day after day. In the beginning it confused me, and only by contemplation and inspection—the only two things available to me—was I able to understand something of the matter, especially that time was free of activity, from moving from one place to another, from tasks to complete. Only the journey within, navigating the self. They seemed to realize this and strove to intensify the sense of it. What would normally happen in the daytime happened at night, and things happened when least expected: For example, the cell door would open suddenly at dawn, or one would be summoned for questioning. Or the demand for returning the olive pits—if ten olives were handed out then ten pits had to be returned, which were counted painstakingly by the guard. If the prisoner managed to hold on to one each day, he would be able to invent a game with which to entertain himself. It was required to strip him of everything that would help him pass the time, to strip him of time itself, with all that related to differentiating its parts, its phases, while at the same time disrupting the power of self-preservation, paving the way for the decisive moment, to become an inmate here.

It was on the second or third day after I arrived in cell number thirty-seven—maybe the fourth day, it doesn't matter. Suddenly, a shriek pierced me through and through. It ran through my arteries like the sharp edge of a blade. It shook me to the core. The scream of a boy, maybe thirteen or fourteen years old, perhaps the result of violent contact with an unseen force—lethal, perhaps an electrical current directed to a sensitive part of his body. More screams followed, then became longer. With time, the ability to endure and express pain was exhausted. Pain requires energy to bear and to give vent to. As it goes on, the ability diminishes. The shriek turns into an audible moan, then becomes muffled, turning into a whimper. In prison, I realized that hearing pain is more difficult than bearing pain oneself. When it's done to us, it's directed against us—it becomes a part of us, merging with our inner self, and so some of it disappears. By happening it becomes lighter. For what can happen after being slapped, or kicked, or beaten with a stick or whips? True pain lies in waiting, in listening to others being exposed to it.

After the end of the first stage of my questioning, I was pushed into cell thirty-four. My name changed from thirty-seven to thirty-four. I don't know the reason for this arrangement. In the middle of one night, I heard an unusual or unfamiliar movement. For a newcomer to solitary confinement, any sound is unfamiliar. Any time that a person spends in a place makes him familiar with its particular sounds. Every place has its sounds and characteristics. New inmates had arrived and were being housed. A day or two after their arrival, the boy's screams erupted again. I needed only a few seconds to realize that it was the same pain. It was a recording, then.

I realized my time had increased. Perhaps my relatively young age lured them into lengthening my time and intensifying my pains. Perhaps!

118

This is a matter I described in detail and at length in *Kitab al-Tajaliyat.*[5] What concerns me is that brief moment in which the door of the cell is opened—the exterior door made of iron and the interior one made of wood covered in metal. In the opening stood one of them, looking as if he was about to fight. Behind him stood others, each holding a thick stick.

"Get up, thirty-seven."

He came toward me and covered my eyes with a black blindfold, just like the one on the terrified figure. I don't know how I appeared, since what happened to me was different from what I saw.

An order to run. Crash into a wall, into a step. The stick falling on my body—I don't know where the blow will come from, what I will face next. With my eyes blindfolded, vision, hearing, smell, touch, and everything that connects the inner self to exterior reality become focused on the ears—everything becomes hearing, directions blur together, it's difficult to tell above from below. Outside and inside merge.

A direction

My first attempt to visit the shrine of Abu al-Faydh Dhulnun al-Akhmimi. I know his shrine from sources, but my informed friend suggests it's in the graveyard of Sidi Uqba. After visiting my mother's final resting place, I'm standing in front of Sidi al-Layth's shrine. Under an old tree with dark roots sits a man with a gray beard. His eyes seem to be closed. But when I get close to him, I discover that he's looking down. When I greet him, he looks at me. I ask him the way to Our Master Dhulnun.

He says, "Orient your soul and you will reach him, with God's will . . . "

He says, "Read Surah Yaa-Sin and al-Fatiha and put your trust in God, and you will reach Him . . . "

He says, "When you head to the righteous ones, meditate . . . solace will arrive."

He says, "When I'm planning to visit Our Master Ahmad al-Badawi, I read al-Fatiha and I find the dervishes on the sides of the road, helping me until I arrive."

He says, "If you do not orient your soul, then you will never arrive, even if you get there."

I'm about to try to get further clarification, more of an explanation, when he makes a pointed gesture: "Orient your soul . . . "

---

5   A previous novel by the author, translated into English as *The Book of Epiphanies* (Cairo, New York: AUC Press, 2012).

119

For a white piaster

Ramadan. During the iftar meal, silence settles over the alley. Everyone is around the tables breaking their fast. The men pick this exact time to come. I rush to the window and my father chides me to finish eating.

There are no fewer than seven of them—tough-looking, tall men. Their *gallabiya*s are white. One beats the *darabukkah*, others play a oud, a violin, and a flute. The others sway in a fascinating and delightful rhythmic dance, chanting: "Twenty cakes for a white piaster."

A crisscross of *kahk* cookies in a square, little squares connected to one another like windows or openings, at least twenty of them. A "white piaster," meaning a *tareefa* or five milliemes. At the time of writing, the millieme is no longer around. What surprises me, until this day, is how large those men were and how many there were of them: an entire choir surrounding a small cart. One of them could hold the cart in one hand if he wanted—it was smaller than the round, brass table in the cafés on which a glass of tea or coffee is placed. Because of the strangeness of what I saw, it's all mixed up now. What I saw overlaps with what I heard about it, or what I imagined it could be. I recall it as if it actually was. I'm sure of the music and the singing that included the call—I can still hear it. But the number of men, the musical instruments, the dancing, the size of the cart—these I'm doubtful of, and so I look closely—hopefully, I can see.

Tea

The depth of winter flooding a room overlooking an empty space, with tall buildings on the horizon. She's sitting in the comfortable chair, looking at me with eyes brimming with sorrow. Her features are finer than expected, so much so that I fear that raising my voice will do her harm. As for her lips, they're two crescents. The touch of her presence provokes melancholy.

She married at twenty-six. He was forty-three, a talented sculptor, well travelled, and selfish in every respect. She says she was dedicated to him because she loved him and admired his art. She tolerated the hardships willingly, graciously, because she loved and appreciated him. But he didn't understand that. She stops and doesn't reveal more, doesn't expand on what she has said, and I'm content with the beauty of listening—I don't ask for an explanation nor do I take anything away.

She has lived alone since 1982, working in a publishing house, living in the quiet suburb of Maadi. Sometimes she stays at home for four or five days without anyone asking about her or calling her, except for her elderly mother who might check up on her from time to time.

She bows her head, her eyelids moisten with tears. She looks sadder. I pick up a cup of tea and let her drink, slowly. Her tears increase as she whispers, wheezing, "No one has offered me a cup of tea like this since I was a child . . . "

News

He's looking at me from nowhere, surprising me with his tranquil, sidelong glances, apparently neutral, carefree, making light of all difficulties. With his height and his slight stoop, sometimes I see him, walking past me when I'm sitting in a café or an office or crossing a road. I see him only in blue jeans and a shirt with two front pockets. His artificial hand is always motionless.

He lost his right hand while training volunteers for commando operations in 1954. He trained himself to do even the most complex movements with his left hand. When he transferred to the Department of Morale Affairs, he became an outstanding professional photographer. He would load the film, handle the camera, and adjust the settings. He was known for his accuracy and skill at capturing the moment that expressed the personality in the face of the subject.

He was close to Field Marshal Abd al-Hakim Amir. He wrote his speeches, especially on the anniversary of the revolution each year. He would point to his chest with his artificial hand, saying that he was responsible for famous phrases like "the most powerful strike force in the Middle East" and "the first Arab submarine built by Egyptian hands." After the June defeat and the struggle over the field marshal who committed suicide, he was detained for a year. He said that in the period when they were closest, the field marshal would take an ordinary taxi from his home to the office once a week, rather than the car provided for him, because he knew that a day would come when he wouldn't find it there. That is what happened after he was released from detention. He became a professional photographer and grew famous for his skill with portraits.

He married after fifty, to a relative of his whom he'd loved since his youth. She'd been married and divorced and it was fate that willed them together. He had a happy expression. I once saw them together—he was sitting next to her, stroking her hair with the fingers of his left hand, gazing at her in fascination. She was a doctor. They had a daughter. When I met up with him that morning at the corner of Sahafa Street, she must have been three. He was fond of photographing her, of indulging her and playing with her endlessly. That morning I spotted him in front of me. I lengthened my stride to catch up with him. I asked him to come and sit with me at the café opposite, where I was in the habit of spending time smoking molasses tobacco before going up to my office. He said, simply, "OK . . . I'll sit with you."

I didn't detect anything particular in his tone, which always seemed neutral, indifferent, free of any worry or care, but there was something I couldn't explain. He was either feeling lonely or hiding something.

"What's wrong?"

He said he'd just been to the doctor after feeling a few sharp pains, thinking they were from his stomach. He'd found out that there was a severe obstruction in the coronary artery. He went on to describe the medications the doctor had ordered him to take for month, as well as walking. And that he would then have to do the tests again, at which time he might be forced to undergo an angioplasty. With deliberation, he described the method by which a balloon is inserted through a vein deep inside the heart and how it's inflated to the desired width. At that time, it was a new kind of procedure. He said the doctor had ruled out surgery. His calmness was neutral; he gazed at a distant point. I said he should lose weight and he agreed, with a nod of his head. He looked indifferent, spreading open the palm of his left hand and wondering, questioning the time of life in which he'd had his daughter. She was a late arrival. He said she was still young.

I said what has to be said in these situations. He got up suddenly, waving his good hand, not looking at me. After a few days I flew to Mexico. From a town called Morelia, I made a phone call. My son told me about various things, then informed me of the news of his death. My son said he'd suffered an unexpected heart attack while he was asleep. He said everything had ended quickly and that he would come with me to pay respects after I returned. I listened silently, seeing him heading in the direction of the building after leaving the café. I notice that his head is bowed—this wasn't characteristic of him. I looked at my watch. In Morelia, it was four in the afternoon. In Cairo, it was midnight. My son asked if he'd made a mistake telling me. I said that he had to tell me . . .

A virgin

He's on a flight to Oman with me. I see him on the plane, switching seats in order to sit next to me. I know him from the café in the sixties. He used to travel to London and America at a time when traveling abroad was restricted. He came back with the title of "Dr.," though no one knew in what area, field, or subject he specialized. I once saw him on a television program, when he was introduced as a lecturer at universities in England. I recall a friend who emigrated to London in the seventies. He was a correspondent for some Arabic newspapers and used to rent an office in the *Sunday Times* building. He would introduce himself as working for the *Sunday Times*. He requested that if anyone asked about him, I should give them his address at the *Sunday Times*. He had business cards printed with the phone numbers and address of the *Sunday Times*.

I look at this doctor traveling with me. He seems calm, but there's something broken about him. Out of courtesy, I ask how he's doing. He tells me about his American wife, informing me that unlike most girls in America, she was a virgin. She was overweight, and no man had ever approached her. This was one of the most important reasons he'd married her: no one had ever touched her. He would be away for long periods of time and she would stay in London; he was reassured, content. He repeats, once again, that she was a virgin when he married her—totally intact, untouched . . .

Whatever

There she is. A beautiful, svelte Egyptian girl working in a nightclub. Energetically, she moves back and forth, communicating through her eyebrows and her glances. She gestures to this one and smiles at that one. When she hears my accent, she says, "One of my own people?"

Showing my happiness, I ask how she's doing in this city, far away from her family.

She says, "Whatever you might imagine could happen to a woman who leaves home and decides to live alone, away from her family and her country—whatever it is, whatever comes to your mind, it happened."

After going away and coming back she told me she'd met a guy who'd gone to Belgium, promising her he would send for her to join him as soon as he settled down. I can see at this moment her tall figure, but her features escape me completely, although I can see the blue glass of the windows and the door and the dim light.

Where is she now?

A photo

Framed, with a diagonal stand that forms a part of the frame. I look at myself. It's me. The main features are unchanged. I try to remember when it was taken. I'm looking upward. I'm sure of the place. I go there often: Sultan Hassan Mosque and School. I'm sitting at the base of the minbar—the pulpit—my favorite place for gazing around the eastern iwan and toward the courtyard of the mosque, as the sun rises and before it reaches the middle of the sky, facing the smaller, western iwan that is almost devoid of the decoration that fills the eastern one. The door of the minbar is behind me, its two wooden shutters covered with patterns of brass. In the photo I can't see the western wall that I'm gazing at, contemplating that vast space utterly devoid of any line or symbol and whose emptiness is emphasized by that circle in the upper third of the intricate plasterwork. There's a kind of contrast, highlighting the space, and reinforcing the space over which it hangs. There's a weekly magazine in my hands. One word of the title is visible, but not the date beneath. I once looked at the photo with a magnifying lens, but I still couldn't make out anything. However, I was able to guess at the approximate day and year.

Now standing facing me is Muhammad Abdelrahman, utterly absorbed with fitting delicate lenses and high-sensitivity film, supporting his camera with his artificial arm and doing everything else with his one good hand. He was very sensitive to any offer of help, which would bring out the old officer in him. His tone would become military, firm, leaving no doubt about what he meant. I asked about where his films ended up at the photography department, but no one could help out. I can't look at that photo without seeing him. Especially after he passed away so suddenly, but today I look at it for a while, in a different way, as if seeing it through his eyes, from no place, nowhere. It isn't his vision through which I look but the look of someone else who will look at me after I cease to exist in this life. When some photos are what's left of me, I look out across the silence, at someone looking at me. That is, if there's any interest on the part of someone with the opportunity to look at that photo, published in old issues of a few newspapers and magazines, stored in the archives. Then there's that invisible gap that has arisen between me and myself, so that when I look at the photo there's no connection that links me to myself. Facing me is someone else. I recall a difficult moment when I was crossing Bab al-Louq Square in 1978. Suddenly I stopped, sunk in a mood that was the starting point, the beginning of difficult times, nights in which I braced myself for my final exit. I saw the tram, the buildings, and the pedestrians with the eyes of those who will come after me, who will exist in a time without me, in which I will be only a memory for a few, and perhaps for no one. At that long ago moment, I stopped, seized by the intense awareness of my own disappearance. When I would no longer be my own, when my vision would be someone else's. I see that moment as the beginning of my long, continuous demise to this day. At times it's strong, at other times weaker, but it continues, it's always there. What is this state, then, that separates me from my photo, from myself?

Hellfire

My son asks, "Will the Zionists go to hell?"

"Of course."

"Because of what they did to the Palestinians?"

"Yes."

"OK . . . and what do they think?"

"In what way?"

"Do they think they're going to hell?"

A phone call

Distant mornings. On vacation. My daughter seems happy when we're all together, as joy flows between us. She likes it when I play with her and her brother. On the balcony. In the sun. My daughter loves role-play: She pretends we're in a restaurant and that she's a customer. She asks me to be the waiter and to ask her what she wants to eat. My son serves the food. She imagines she's a broadcaster. She holds some papers and reads letters from friends.

My daughter wants to have relationships, to have friends. She talks about Noha, about Hind, holding the phone and making imaginary calls; she met Hind and Noha once in the club. She says one of her friends will call her, then says, "If someone calls me, let me know." Midday and no one has called. Annoyed, she says that Dina promised to call. She keeps tabs as we answer phone calls—her mother, her older brother. Sometimes she picks up the receiver and dials an imaginary number. She starts talking, and when I ask her to put the phone down she protests, "I'm talking to my friend." One morning, the phone rings. A girl's voice: "I'm Maggie's friend." At first, when I tell her genuinely that it's for her, she doesn't believe me. She takes the phone, with joy in her eyes. She assumes different positions during her conversation with her friend.

Learning

My wife asks my son to copy some phone numbers for her. My daughter sits beside him, holding pens and pieces of paper, asking to do some copying too ("Why Mido and not me?"). She starts moving the pen in unintelligible, circular shapes, banging the table. She wants to write too! She comes to me, holding a piece of paper, saying that she has a lot of paper but doesn't know how to write. Then, hand on waist, she says she wants to write like Mido. She takes her time, emphasizing the letters:

"Teach me . . . "

Sky

I'm walking along a road. My daughter is with me.

"Did Abdelmonim die?"

"Yes."

"Why?"

"That's what God wants."

"Why is everyone alive?"

"There are people who are alive, sweetie, and people who are dead."

"Does God see us all . . . and do we see Him too?

"How is it that we see Him, Maggie?"

"When we say, 'O Lord,' don't we look up at the sky?"

Growing old

My daughter says, "Daddy, I don't want to get old."

"Why? Everyone has to get old."

"Because getting old is bad."

Then she says, "Does a person get old when he does something bad?"

"Of course not. Did grandpa and grandma do anything bad?"

Then I say, "When someone grows up, they age."

"OK, I'll stop eating so that I don't grow up."

We always tell her she has to eat so that she will grow.

"Of course not. You have to eat to become pretty."

"OK, dad—I'll eat so you don't get upset."

Reconciliation

My daughter talks about her classmates.

Sometimes she imitates the teacher's voice, calling out the names. She opens her workbook, proud of the red stars.

She says she told one of her classmates not to sit in the front seat of the car, but she did, and she crashed into the side of the road.

She phones her classmate Lotfiya and says one of their friends is upset but that she's right. Lotfiya says she'll call the classmate to hear her side of the story. Lotfiya calls Maggie again. The classmate calls Maggie.

At last, reconciliation.

Playing

We're eating breakfast in the Mohandiseen Club, overlooking the Nile. Sham al-Naseem, the spring holiday, with many children. My son sits silently, away from the children his age. He says he doesn't know them. He's preoccupied, not playing with his sister who wants to play. She doesn't know anyone. She runs in the garden, looking at children older than her who are playing ball. She turns to face us. "I'm going to play and I'll come back soon."

She goes up to them: "Can I play with you?"

They don't look at her. She says, "Are you upset with me?"

No one answers her, as if they haven't even noticed her. She says, "OK . . . I'm going and I'll be back straightaway."

She runs off and comes back. "I'm back," she tells them.

One of them comes close to her, picks her up, takes a few steps, puts her down and goes back. She runs to me . . .

"The boy picked me up and carried me away . . . I don't know why."

She puts her thumb in her mouth. She sees children her age. She runs to them, wanting to play with them, but they don't pay her any attention. She sees a girl crawling and runs to her. She tries to take on a mother's role, feeling compassion for her. The girl is afraid and her cries ring out. Maggie stands up, silent.

Friends

Maggie is next to her mother in the kitchen, telling her stories about a tall man with a long nose and long ears. She asks about "my darling Muhammad." She reinvents his world and transforms it into her world. His friends become hers. All the ones he names are in front of her. Suddenly, she says, "I'm going to my friend."

She turns to her mother. "Say 'Don't be late.'"

"Don't be late, Maggie."

She starts running, and picks up the phone. She talks to her imaginary friends.

Photo

Why did I go there?

I don't know what circumstances led me to the first floor of that building in the suburbs. I probably needed some photos to submit with some form or document, but as soon as I enter, I see something completely unexpected.

Along the wall is a huge photo composed of long panels. I notice it's composed of parts, carefully joined together. Before placing my order, I point to the picture and ask, "Who took this?"

Calmly, the man, who I would think was about fifty, says, "My father, God rest his soul."

"So . . . he was standing there."

Gumhuriya Square in Abdeen[6]—its features preserved as I'd seen them that day for myself. To the east, the palace, with a wrought-iron fence in front, separating it from the square. To the north, buildings that had been for the administration, the kitchen, and the royal guards—and which now housed the offices of the Cairo Governorate. At the time of the photo, the Revolutionary Command Council was using it as its headquarters. On the other side of the square, an empty pedestal designed for a statue presumed to be of King Fuad. But it had stayed like that until it was removed, just like the pedestal in Tahrir Square, the famous "stone cake" of the late Amal Donqol's seminal poem. At first, it had been decided to erect a statue of Khedive Ismail, but the July Revolution of 1952 had broken out. Although it was frequently mentioned that a statue of Ahmad Urabi would be erected, the pedestal remained empty until the death of Gamal Abdel Nasser. Right after his death, on a wave of public enthusiasm, the writer Tawfiq al-Hakim called for the people to raise funds for a statue for him, as had happened in the thirties for *The Awakening of Egypt* statue by Mahmoud Mokhtar. This was only a few months before Nasser and the entire period were attacked. As the criticism and attacks against the Nasserist period intensified, the idea of a statue disappeared and the pedestal remained empty. After President Anwar Sadat's assassination, some demanded that a statue of him should be placed on the pedestal. But this time, the entire pedestal was removed and disappeared from the square. It bothered me; I learned that it had been thrown in an old courtyard in the Citadel.

I don't remember the Abdeen pedestal now. There was a garden inside the square, which the traffic went around. There, throughout both the

---

6   Gumhuriya Square, formerly known as Abdeen Square, named after Abdeen Palace.

monarchy and the republic, Ramadan tents used to be erected, the Holy Qur'an was recited, and drinks were distributed. That is where we'd been standing while the photographer's father had been on the balcony of the king's office, which wasn't in use during Nasser's time. From that point, it was possible to see the entire square and the whole of the crowd. His father had been conscripted into the military police and assigned to the Director-ate of General Affairs because of the skills he'd learned at the hands of an old Armenian photographer. The picture is composed of five connected panels—a complete panorama of the square, of that rare moment. I lean forward, staring, contemplating.

"Where am I?"

I can make out the place where I was standing—we were here, just here. Students of Hussein Preparatory School. I was in the third grade. I remember our joy when we got out at the beginning of the school day—it was a break from the familiar, meaning that we wouldn't be confined to the chairs in our classroom. We walked in lines. When we arrived at the square, I saw that it was packed, overflowing. I remember the crowds, not specific features . . . just European-style clothing, traditional clothing, women, female students, flags.

I look closely and see our school flag: the triangle with the name of the school written in beautiful calligraphy. So . . . I'm there somewhere. I'm one of these people, but which one? I see only dots and small, tiny marks. I see myself without seeing me. Here I am, listening to Nasser's speech. At the time, he was a young man of thirty-eight. How could I have known, at the time, how long he had left? Twelve years. It was hard to see his features from where we were at the back of the square. I saw him in his entirety. I felt his presence from far away. He was powerful. He had charisma, a spark.

Here he is in the photo, raising both his arms. It's hard to make out those standing next to him. Surely Shukri al-Quwatli was among them. Kind features. The one who resigned of his own free will. They called him the First Citizen. A large flag hangs from the balcony: the three colors, the two green stars.

Was it taken before or after the late leader announced the union with Syria?

I don't know.

I know what date it was. It was taken on February 22, 1958. What day of the week was it? I don't know. I remember the day because of its connection with the event; without it, I wouldn't have known the date or the month. If I wanted to, I could find out, but I promised myself before I started writing that I would depend only on what I know, without documents or references of any kind.

The speech ended and the square roared. The composer Muhammad Abdelwahhab came forward. He sang for the union with Syria—perhaps the only time he would sing in public after the Officers' Club celebration in 1954, in which he sang the song "For What Was All of This?"

Was the photo taken before the song or afterward?

My gaze roams over the square. I study it closely—where am I? How many are there? How many of them have died? Who is left? Who has emigrated? Who went abroad and who came back? Who has become a father, then a grandfather? Who has ceased to be?

I can't see the details of the crowd. It blurs together, a single mass in which it's difficult to make out the details. The photo in front of me merges with my own picture, the one within me—obliterated, in both dimensions. I stare in front of me, not seeing myself. I look closely; I don't see anything. In vain, I try to find myself. From the outside and from the inside, just a mark in a crowd, a sign that doesn't show, as if seeing my own disappearance while I'm still present . . .

Present and absent

I enter the bookshop that I visit only rarely, only when I come to this part of town. There are always new books on ancient Egyptian art. The owner is behind the desk: he moves about with difficulty, with an artificial foot. There's a young woman—dark, olive-colored skin, with strong features and figure. I see her only in front of the shelves, doing some task or other, never sitting still. After exchanging greetings and enquiries about our news and turning to the young woman or pointing to a particular shelf, he asks me about our mutual friend Fathallah. The truth is that my connection to Fathallah is only casual. I got to know him when I used to smoke shisha in the Cultural Symposium Café in Bab al-Louq. He's a retired journalist. I would only see him smoking with his eyes shut, his lips pursed, his mouth completely enclosing the mouthpiece of the water pipe as if taking a great puff. He spent his life as an arts editor: the singer Farid al-Atrash would only ever put his trust in him. I don't know if he's still around or has departed this life, but each time I'm about to turn back to the shelves, the owner asks me: "How's Fathallah?"

I say he's doing well, then he almost repeats the phrase: "We never knew an arts editor of his caliber . . . "

I answer him, perhaps with the same answer: "The entire generation is irreplaceable."

"My God, that's true."

After I've finished, as I'm getting ready to leave: "Promise me if you see him you'll give him my regards."

"Of course, of course . . . "

Two people who have nothing substantial in common, or who meet only fleetingly or are bored of each other, will refer to a third party, someone absent. The conversation is about those we haven't met in years, whose affairs we know nothing of. Their news is discussed more than news about ourselves. Sometimes what's evoked is not a specific person but possibly a place, or a particular date, or something symbolic. When two people meet on a train, one starts talking to the other: the beginning of the conversation and the point of contact—most of the time—is the most general of questions about place.

"Where are you from?"

Mentioning the place leads to mentioning a person.

"Do you know so-and-so?"

The answer might come quickly: "Yes." Perhaps the attempt to get acquainted starts with recalling other names and asking about them, at which point the presence of the third person grows stronger—even surpassing those present, the interlocutors, who look at each other and cling to the one who is remote, and who may not be there anymore.

Days

I would bestow each day of the week with its own traits.

I don't know when I started doing this—perhaps in early childhood, when the differences between yesterday and tomorrow began to be defined. Perhaps the first was Friday, *al-Gomaa*, because it's the weekend, when everyone would get together. I would wake to a special breakfast that we wouldn't have on other days of the week, one that my mother and father would enjoy in complete serenity. *Zalabiya*—small home-made doughnuts fried in ghee—tea with al-Maliki's milk, fava beans from Abu Hagar, *al-Ahram* and *al-Masry* newspapers, all of us together, going to Friday prayers at Hussein Mosque in Azhar. The day of rest. After I started school, it gained a new dimension: it was the morning I could sleep in, when I didn't have to get up at a specific time. Quiet, the streets draped in a ghostly absence, especially in the afternoon. Between the late afternoon and sunset, many of the shops would shut their doors. The government offices' day off affected the traffic, especially downtown. The first half of the day would be a comfort, the second half, after midday, would be a source of hidden melancholy, especially as I set out through the empty side streets, looking up to the autumn or winter sky that would seem to be closer to the earth, almost within reach. The character of Friday was both masculine and feminine—the features of a woman and the form of a man—and frowning. I attribute this strange identification to various reasons: perhaps the feminine ending *a* in the word *gomaa*, or the quality that unites them—*gomaa* meaning "gathering"—with its unrevealed sadness and its many other hidden elements.

Thursday—*al-Khamees*—is connected to Friday and leads to it. It's the end of the school and working week. After I'd finished and gone home, both as a child and in adult life—in my studies or my work—it was like the end of a battle. I would seek refuge in a time that safeguarded me from the hubbub. When school was in session, we would finish earlier than usual. Even so, I wouldn't be happy. Perhaps this went back to Khamees, the copper tinner, who was employed at a coppersmith's just where the alley opened onto Qasr al-Shawq Street. When I went to him with his copper utensils, cooking pots, and trays, he would stare at me with his wide eyes, higher than they were wide, looking like Abu Halmous, a caricature I'd seen in a newspaper. Khamees used to wear a piece of cloth over the lower half of his body and would stand inside the great utensils, twisting his body left and right, using his feet to do the polishing. I was repulsed by him. Did I associate him with *al-Khamees*—Thursday?

Perhaps.

On another day, in the middle of the week, we would leave school early. Monday—its name fills me with delight. A bright face; it has a luminosity. On Saturday and Sunday I would look forward to it, and on Wednesday and Thursday I would grieve its passing. It would look at me from nowhere— wide eyed, brightly dressed, radiating contentment.

Sunday is mysterious—I can't grasp its features. But it's somewhere in the west. Maybe it looks foreign, European, possibly because the banks and most of the shops owned by foreigners took the day off. I don't know, I can't be sure, but my distance from it makes it difficult to determine its features and discern its identity.

Saturday is meager—it passes quickly, clutching an empty briefcase. Why? I don't know. I can't explain.

Wednesday is grim, serious, advanced in age, perhaps because reaching it means finishing a long cycle of work. Only one day separates me from Thursday, the weekend. Nothing about it has ever changed, even later when I discover that it was the day I was born, at dawn, as a wind storm arose from an unknown place to whip the rooted palms. My image of Wednesday has lasted.

I can't think of the days altogether—the severe one, the one that radiates restfulness—none has anything to do with any other, even those that are close to each other. The days seem more isolated than telegraph poles, than palm trees growing in an unfamiliar place, than me.

—⁓—

Is it possible to determine the edges of time, as we do the edges of space? Is it possible to indicate a point in the material world and say: This point separates two years, or two centuries, or two eras? Or a moment between two moments?

On a plane

A well-traveled and famous university professor was in the next seat. He appeared on television frequently. Before takeoff, he rang the call button and asked the flight attendant for a cup of juice. After the plane had reached cruising altitude, lunch service began. He began eating loudly, gluttonously. The attendant passed by with a basket of bread for those who wanted more; he took three rolls. Then he asked for a glass of water. He left no packet unopened: salt, pepper, powdered milk, toothpicks. After the plates were collected, he went to the restroom. When he returned, a strong smell of cologne wafted from him. I concluded that he'd finished off what was in the open bottle for the use of passengers.

He turned around in his seat, exploring all its features: it could bend and recline, and earphones could be plugged in to listen to the various channels. He remembered the blanket in the overhead locker. He pressed the call button and asked the flight attendant for it. He spread it over himself, even though it was still the beginning of the day and the temperature was mild. He closed his eyes, wearing the sleep mask. I caught sight of the oxygen tank in the overhead locker. I thought about drawing his attention to it: there was something he hadn't used yet.

Slump

Café Abu Rowash. Suez, during the war. Few people, empty streets, destroyed houses. I'm sipping the tea that *Amm* Khalil has brought me. He's over eighty. He has stayed behind; he hasn't left. On his own, a loner. He pays no attention to the explosions, to the constant bombardment. He sleeps in the café at night. He opens up and sprays the ground with water, sweeps the floor, sets up the equipment, and lights the coals.

A fireman comes and sits beside me. Over fifty, with country features. His chin has traces of a green tattoo. We exchange greetings. Although the café is empty, he sits next to me; only a rectangular table separates us. Perhaps he wants company or wants to talk. But he doesn't utter a word.

A distant explosion reverberates. He doesn't seem to hear it. I listen closely. The more I frequent the place and the longer I stay, I can tell the different kinds of bombs, even their direction.

Suddenly, the fireman slumps forward—a slow, heavy tilt. As if a hidden hand had pushed him while another held him back. But, at a certain moment, he collapses on the ground—a heavy fall. I look at him. *Amm* Khalil rushes over, as do two men whose features I can't now discern.

The fireman's face is calm, but frozen at a particular moment, the moment at which he came to a stop. There's a serenity in his eyes, and what looks like surprise. *Amm* Khalil bends down.

"His soul is with God."

He tries to breathe into his mouth but in vain. How did it happen? Was it a heart attack? But *Amm* Khalil, who is used to dealing with death, points behind the ear.

A very fine, thin trickle. It begins slowly, then runs down the neck, passing through the clothes, then to the floor. Shrapnel, the size of a pinhead, fired from somewhere—the fragments of a bomb perhaps. It must have been linked to the sound I'd heard, whose source and type I'd tried to work out. Mere stray fragments of shrapnel that have penetrated to the core, to that place in the café where he used to come, to the seat in which I almost sat.

The declining day

I fear entering the place at this time of day.

Specifically, at the beginning of sunset. Despite being fully aware of this fear, I sometimes seek it out—in Citadel Square, between Sultan Hassan Mosque and Rifaei Mosque, to be exact. The planning of the square has an integrity, although it dates from different eras, capturing times gone by. At times, antiquity evokes melancholy. My feet hurry toward the entrance of Sultan Hassan, as if taking refuge from one building in another, from one time in another, although all the structures are clearly laid out before me, crowded together: Muhammad Ali Mosque, imposing and fierce with its pointed Ottoman minarets, Jokandar Mosque, Mahmoudiya Mosque, the domes. The unity of the towering minarets and the entrances, the writing unified with the stone, the eternal tombs, where shadow meets shadow.

Quickly I plunge into the shade, passing through the towering entrance, and then retreat. I enter the passage and end up in the courtyard, and my experience begins. I become one with myself. I begin to be both absent and present. The height of the wall lifts me, and the decline of the day makes me disappear. As for the sounds that emerge, they move my soul in a way that is impossible for me to understand, whether they come from a dove or a passing car—a wounded cry, or the teasing of a jester, the echoes of lives which have passed, the footsteps whose owners have gone. Within, I shudder at the chirp of a migrating bird. At a time like this, the people grow fewer and sometimes disappear. I become utterly alone, as if traveling in the boundless wilderness with nothing in my way. The borders fuse one moment to the next, what comes to what has passed—the first and the last. An ancient tear glimmers within me as the meaning of *asr*—afternoon—becomes complete. I lower my eyes and recite, trying to surpass the horizon that encloses me.

"By the declining day
Most surely, man is in a state of loss."
(Qur'an 103:2)

Looking

As if seeing myself in a dream. From the outside, with the eyes of someone I do not know, who has no reality for me, I'm approaching some shore, walking, leaning forward. My hands are clasped behind my back, my vision extends as far it can, as if I were ascending the space. In my imagination, as I stand here, I transcend what I can't cross. In my eyes, a longing and a pleading to someone whom I can't define, a mysterious message waiting to be unraveled, an intention to cover a distance and a desire to build a road across the extended space to a building standing on the other side of the sea. The sea extends to the horizon. It surpasses every limit. Its blue is determined by the clarity of the sky. But this space, no matter how vast, must be followed by something, by some point, the bank of another shore that I do not know.

I'm standing on the furthest tip of the land. Sands merge with stones, the waves roll in from far away, receding to somewhere I do not know, touching my extremities. The light spray touches me. That moment exists in front of me, but the place is unknown—I can't grasp it. It's where a mainland meets a sea, but which sea? Which land? I've stood at various locations on the Egyptian coast, the Mediterranean, the Red Sea. I've watched sunsets over the ocean in Morocco, Portugal, the North Sea, the Indian Ocean, the Arabian Sea, the Caspian Sea, the Adriatic—where is this exactly?

Unfortunately, I can't identify it. All I can make out is my look—my pout, scrutinizing what I can't see, with a furrowed brow. I'm there before me, but am totally unable to name the place—some point on land that is connected to the sea, the infinite sea. The names are all relative: this is the Mediterranean, that is the Indian Ocean, or the Pacific, but the water is one. One level, neither more here nor less there. One surface, the basis of measuring, of comparing. A single spreading ocean. Standing at one point of it means that I look out over all of it. Land is just an exception to the sea's domain—isolated islands, no matter how wide. The ocean is continuous, flowing. It reaches me at this spot that I recall but can't recognize, while it also extends beyond the origin of my looking: its causes, its motives, the conditions of its appearance. Yet I know that it isn't possible to capture it fully, just as I can't capture that location, at this bridge . . .

Photo

She said, "But you don't have a photo of me."

I said, "It's better this way."

She said, "You're strange. How is it better?"

I said, "A photo wipes out memory. It limits it. If I looked at it, I'd see a symbol of you, not the reality. Let my memory preserve your features. I'll recall them from a distance; I'll see you as I want . . . as I desire . . . "

She said, "You'll only see an illusion."

I said, "Sometimes an illusion is more immediate."

A silence descended, longer than necessary. And when I said the word that gets one's attention, that connects the silent gaps during phone calls—"Hello?"—I got no answer.

Isolation

Not just telegraph poles—the rotating planets are even more isolated. If they ever met, it would be the end. Even what appears to us as integrated is the most isolated—like water, despite its contiguity. At depths that can't be fathomed, in springs flowing through plains and heights, in the succession of drops of rain. Each drop is disconnected from what follows and precedes it; the greatest isolation is from that which is connected.

My beds

A metal four-poster bed with black poles, decorated with brass, raised up. I'm lying on it, sick with measles. I'm going through the final stage—a fever, itches that make me scratch. A red *gallabiya* covers me. It's my oldest bed.

When we used to travel to Juhayna for the summer, I would sleep throughout the summer months on beds that were part of the build-ing: *mastaba*s that were for sitting on by day and for sleeping on at night. In Gurna and Aswan, I would experience beds made of *anqareeb*—palm stalks—that made it difficult for scorpions to climb their legs. Narrow beds, just enough for me; others wider, luxurious, like thrones. Beds that I've lain in for a little while; others that I was associated with for some reason. Beds on which I lay reluctantly, that were connected to wires and mechanisms: I would press a button, and they would make me sit up or lie back. Narrow beds on top of each other, in warships and submarines.

In bed, I'm at one with myself, curled up as my mother bore me— alone, by myself. In sleep, no one is with a friend or partner. As in death. We leave this world alone, just as we come into it. In bed, I'm united with myself. I journey through it, thinking about what was and what will be. In my youth, I would plan and wait for what was to come. Now, I recall what has passed. I try to retrieve what's slipping away, pausing at one moment or another. I go over my projects—what was accomplished and what was not. I recall faces of those I loved long ago and those whom my eyes have fallen on lately. I exercise the ultimate freedom. I undress this one, I make love with that one. What I experience in my imagination far surpasses what I've seen with my eyes in reality. The closer I come to sleep, the more the forgotten faces appear to me. Past moments, hidden melodies. I articulate what I do not say when I'm awake. I go where it's normally impossible to reach, running between galaxies, moving between times. I try to anticipate tomorrow. I'm apprehensive. I suffer from insomnia. I know the bed on which I spent my childhood, but I do not know the one on which I will close my eyes forever.

Lime

A young woman, Nubian, well proportioned, well formed. What can't be concealed are her proud breasts and her full, symmetrical buttocks. As for the lower part of her belly, it flows smoothly to that imaginary line that invisibly connects her front to her back.

She's standing naked in the middle of a suburban room. She approaches me as if starting a shift at work. She reminds me of when she has to leave in order to get home before her son and daughter arrive from school. In the afternoons, she works in a clinic in a working-class neighborhood. She seems tense, but just by lying down and closing her eyes she becomes totally absorbed. She moves spontaneously; everything about her contributes to the embodiment of pleasure. Even pursing her lips and parting them for a few seconds—as I recall them, despite the passage of time, a shudder passes through me. Sometimes I smile. She puts out her hand to slow me down, asking me to wait. She's afraid of getting pregnant. She takes a lime, its color something between yellow and green, bites it in two and lies on her back. She brings it close to her thighs, squeezing it hard, catching the juice. By moving her abdomen back and forth, left and right, she makes sure that it goes inside her. I watch in amazement. I've only known this with her.

Darkness

Light, no doubt. Pure. Glittering. Friday morning, after eating breakfast, I've become accustomed to dusting the books on the shelves. I make sure to do it. During the week fine dust accumulates, like flour. I dust it off with a soft brush. Slowly. I bask in the stacked books, the volumes, the daylight, the Friday morning light—the weekend, when there's no early rising, no need to go to school or work. I move slowly, feeling the touch of the incoming light that is softened by the glass of the window and the transparent curtain.

Suddenly, I imagine I see a subdued light, not really a light but a color—dark and red. I try to make it out in the empty space. I can't be at all certain, but a few moments later I see what look like very fine particles, slowly increasing.

I've never encountered this before; I have no reference that would allow me to compare these particles—especially their color, between blood red and deep black, a color I haven't seen before despite being well versed in colors and their shades and having looked at colors closely. What worries me most is what I've never encountered before, what has no reference point.

Slowly, those very fine, very smooth particles surge forward, their movement driven by an unknown source, transformed into a gentle flow. The daylight becomes feeble and retreats in the face of that mysterious darkness. I go to the balcony, the space that is draped with this peculiar color that comes from the unknown. The opposite buildings and the ones next door: all boundaries have melted, divisions have dissolved in the chromatic furnace, flowing silently, gently. I come back to the library, with its rectangular space.

The density of the color blocks the view, the partitions utterly canceled. When the colors disappear, the distinction ends—everything in existence merges, drifting into nothingness. Everything that is possible to understand disappears. The ability to recognize colors breaks down due to their absence, the absence of their existence.

I'm no longer able to see the books, the shelves, the walls. The muteness of spaces. No windows or balconies, no hand or arm, even the body disappears, merging with its surroundings. Reluctantly, I'm forced to stand up. There's no longer an outside or inside; the darkness overlapping with the deep red color is no longer present for me. I've become a part of it, no longer existing except through my perception, my realization that all of existence has become a color or an element that I can't name or define, as it has no name or equal. I'm no longer aware: am I standing or moving? I confuse my right with my left. Up with down. It's different from that night I spent in the pyramid when I chose the darkness, knowing the place and the specific time that I would be alone inside the burial chamber. That was a different darkness from what overtakes me that morning when I'm transformed into my original elements—those fine, soft particles of dust that are impossible to see after their frequent, rapid flowing, which cancels out divisions and obliterated differences.

I don't know how long it goes on. Little by little, the darkness starts to retreat. As I return, I'm able to observe the vertical wavelets separating from one another. Here and there, through the spaces, the light floods in once more.

Alone, I observe existence returning once more. I see myself standing, the bookshelves, the arrangement of the volumes, but in a different light like that which flows from some horizon in a fleeting dream.

I don't want to wake my wife and son and daughter. It's the only day they can sleep late after days of work and exhaustion. How can I ask them for an explanation while they're asleep? I go out to the balcony. The traffic on the street is normal. The cars come and go, a few pedestrians. A street in a suburb. A morning on a weekend. Nothing remarkable, yet there's some trace in the light. Am I imagining it, or am I seeing some trace of that peculiar light? I dial a number on the phone, to seek some explanation, but I don't make the call. I stand, staring into the light, doubting what I've experienced.

A dream

My beloved, whom I've loved for more than a while, enters. It's my living room, but in another house. She looks broken, dejected, holding gifts that are wrapped, handing them out here and there to people who are invisible to me, not evident. She's smiling in front of a picture of one my acquaintances, asking me about my father. I tell her he has passed away. She sits in the corner of the courtyard of an old palace I once visited in Portugal, weeping.

—⁓—

The faded, ancient gods.

Osiris of the pharaohs. For how long was he worshipped?

We know part of the answer: at least three or four thousand years before the birth of Christ. That is to say, longer than the time that separates us from his birth and twice the time that separates us from the flight of our beloved Prophet Muhammad.

Did the ancient Egyptians have less faith in their gods than we have in our faith?

Blindfolded

A spacious office. Looking through the window that ran the length of the wall, facing Mount Qasioun that overlooks Damascus. It was the first unfamiliar thing that I saw. On the way from the airport to the city, I was surprised by the gradual way the houses went from top to bottom and from bottom to top. When we look at a hill, we see the top first, then gradually our gaze moves down. Our curiosity is always oriented to that with which we're unfamiliar, which is higher or more powerful than us. As for the foot of mountains, it's closer to our view.

In Cairo, the land is mostly at the same height; only in the east—in Moqattam—is there any elevation. Since we don't see anything that towers any higher, I considered Moqattam to be the maximum until I had the opportunity to compare and I realized that it was nothing but rocky hills.

Qasioun is higher, but it doesn't tower. Perhaps what caught my eye more was the sequence of terraced houses on the slope. It was some time before I learned that Our Master, the great Sheikh Muhiyy al-Din, lies near its foot, toward Salihiya, and that his presence permeates the entire place.

From the wide window in the office of the head of the Directorate for Political Guidance. I don't really remember his first name: Colonel Idris is what has stayed with me, but I don't know if Idris was his first or last name. Usually, he wouldn't meet with any of the journalists who requested a visit to the front line, but he honored me with more than one meeting after calls from friends had facilitated my mission. One of them was Dr. Najah al-Attar, the official from the Ministry of Culture at the time—she hadn't yet been promoted—and Hussein al-Uwaydat, the then manager of the prime minister's office. Colonel Idris assigned two writers to accompany me: the poet Mamdouh Udwan and the author Riyadh Ismat, who were both doing their military service. The former traveled with me south to Deraa Governorate, where we walked the front lines. Riyadh went north with me to Latakia, via Homs, which we reached at dawn. There I read al-Fatiha for its eternal resident, Khalid Ibn al-Walid. One corner of the city stayed with me: a sweet shop that cast its light into the darkness of the night, called Natour.

Natour. Natour. Thirty years later, I stopped in Homs on my way to Latakia for the second time. I visited the tomb of al-Jalil, the noble companion of the Prophet: no part of his body was untouched by stab wounds or injuries from the battles he fought. He took his final breaths on his bed like an ordinary person, which made him scream out: "May the eyes of the cowards never know sleep!"

This phrase was carved in a monument that fused the forms of a sail and an obelisk in front of an Ottoman-style mosque. I performed the evening prayers and read al-Fatiha in front of the shrine, as if I were coming to the place for the first time, as if I'd never set foot there. Although I didn't realize it, the sweet shop was preoccupying me—to stand in front of the same shop that I'd seen three decades earlier. Just to stand there, as I was no longer interested in sweets and all their varieties. I had no choice; it was obligatory. (My companion said that Natour had been just one shop when

I'd visited Homs in wartime, but thanks to its success, it had added several other branches. There were now dozens of Natours in Homs. Would it be possible to find the right one?)

I told my companion, who wasn't from the city, that it would be difficult, so we headed out to the highway, wondering about the hidden trace of the first time I'd passed along this road and whether this time would also leave its trace. And whether I would visit the city again. Each time I learn a fact, it's as if I realize it for the first time. I absorb it and forget it. There's not a single location to which I return and find to be the same as when I first visited.

Colonel Idris. The spacious office facing Qasioun. The soft October light. One of the last days of the month that in Syria they call Tishreen. The cold started early: between Homs and Latakia, a snowstorm blew up. I was seeing its white flakes for the first time. As if extraordinary, hidden hands were tossing them in the direction of the car as it drove into the wind.

The colonel was reading some papers. Suddenly, the door opened and a soldier entered. He saluted. He was followed by a man blindfolded with a strip of black fabric that appeared to be designed for this, wearing another man's military uniform; it hung too large on his shoulders.

The colonel asked why this prisoner of war had been brought in.

He was standing still, there in the space, looking at nothing, facing Mount Qasioun but not seeing it. He was waiting for the next step from his escort. At first, I looked at him, curious, troubled by seeing someone blindfolded against his will. I didn't know his name, nor what had happened to him or what would happen to him. That he was Israeli meant nothing to me, nor did his ethnicity or religion. I watched him with an apparent neutrality and a hidden wrenching in my heart, which left me with the shadow of a pallor I can still recall each time the image appears to me across the space and time that has passed.

Ashmawi: The executioner

From the moment he showed up at the café, I sneaked glances at him, scrutinizing his features. I didn't rush to sit next to him. The waiter wouldn't address him by the usual name for those of his status and profession. They would address him as *Hagg* Ibrahim. He was retired and began to come regularly—once in the morning and once in the evening, sitting alone. He would be content drinking tea without sugar and smoking shisha. The café served only unflavored shisha tobacco; retired lawyers, judges, officers, and leading businessmen would seek it out. I called them "the tobacco party." Some of them would come from Heliopolis and others from Maadi. The last one I expected to join them was Ashmawi, whose name was associated with death, with execution. When the café was crowded, people on their own like me and him could sit next to each other, an arrangement known to the experienced staff, who were familiar with the habits and moods of the customers. It was enough to deal with a person once or twice. Due to our proximity, a brief conversation would sometimes start, that at times would grow lengthy.

"You believe it, by God?"

"There's no god but God, *Hagg* Ibrahim . . . "

He said he'd been looking forward to finishing his service in order to go back to the café, to smoke shisha. It wasn't possible while he was working—it was difficult to sit there in his uniform, and the breaks were few and brief. With a sidelong glance, he turned to me. I was looking at his long, meaty fingers holding on to the edge of the table when suddenly he said to me, "Don't imagine that the tasks you're thinking about took all of my time . . . "

He said he had many tasks, only one of them having to do with that kind of work—executing those sentenced to death, exacting God's retribution. He suddenly switched to talking about the tobacco of long ago—various exotic kinds from Iran, from Izmir, Latakia, and Aden. Some of the cafés were sought out by ladies, especially Lebanese and Syrians. He wouldn't dare to enter them, contenting himself with passing in front of them and watching. His limit was Fishawi Café. The tobacco of long ago had disappeared; its aroma used to waft out, perfuming the street in front of the café that served it. Only this café was still committed to the real thing, maintaining the standard of tobacco and beverages. Its owners were true artisans, worthy of the name. He fell silent all of a sudden. I got used to his silences; it was hard to resume a conversation with him. I almost believed that he was talking to himself, but he would trick his table companion into thinking that he was engaged in conversation, while saying only what he wanted to say. Over several days, I learned a few things about the first Ashmawi. His successors didn't carry the same name, but the first to occupy the position had bestowed his name on all those who'd followed. The first Ashmawi seemed like a myth to those who came after him. He'd married four wives, siring so many offspring that he would meet some of his grandchildren in the alley and not recognize them unless they told him. He was compassionate with the condemned, whispering prayers in their ears. His hands were models of delicacy and dexterity: he was skillful in placing the hood over the condemned, in helping them climb the steps, in pushing the lever that controlled the little stool. They said that the pulse of someone in his time of service didn't use to last more than a few seconds, while he said that for some of them now their pulse would last more than five minutes: when the heart stopped beating, the attending physician would pronounce the death. But with the first Ashmawi, the matter used to take just a few seconds. Why? He wouldn't disclose this to anyone. A secret of the trade!

When he smiled, a space showed where the left canine was missing. His smile suddenly appeared and then disappeared without him saying anything, but sometimes he elaborated.

He once stared ahead as if talking to someone who was invisible to me and said, "There was that strange, young beautiful woman, more delicate than *rimsh al-ayn* fabric. She was a crime reporter on a famous paper. She always attended the executions. She would ask beforehand, and confirm the times that were always confidential. She had powerful connections in the Directorate for the Execution of Sentences and with all the prison officers. If the execution was at three in the morning, you'd find her there in all her splendor. While she was there, she never failed to do two things: first, to accompany the full committee as it went to the condemned's cell. It was out of the question to inform him of the appointed time; this is one of the meticulously observed rules that are never violated. She always made sure to be present for the opening of the cell and seeing the condemned when he realized that the time had arrived. The second thing she never failed to do was to go down to the pit underneath the platform and take the pulse. God Almighty, how strange are his creations! I heard someone who detested her saying that she never got married and raised cats only in order to strangle them—but only God knows!"

I listened silently, looking in the same direction in which he was looking. Without looking at him, I let slip the question that I'd been holding back: what cases would he never forget?

He didn't shift his position. In the same voice, he answered, "The first is a man who wasn't yet thirty—healthy, well built. He killed his mother. I heard a lot of talk, God forgive me. After hearing the question "What do you want?," he asked for a cigarette. The police chief gave him a Belmont cigarette and lit it himself. He took one puff, a puff that finished the entire cigarette. He exhaled through his nose and through his mouth, and after he'd finished it, he looked at me and said, "Do your job. I've taken my share of this world."

"The second was a tax officer, calm and respectful—clearly from a good family. Calmly, he dictated his will. He instructed that his kidneys, liver, heart, and corneas be sold. Of course, he'd already written a letter, so that the doctors were ready to transport the body to the prison hospital to obtain the organs. He repeated his instructions in the will to allow the committee to hear. The truth is, the strangest thing I ever heard was the reason."

"What was the reason, I wonder?"

"To complete his daughter's trousseau. She was preparing to get married, and he hadn't left her a thing."

After a few seconds, he said, "The third was a young woman, and what a woman! Magnificent—long, silky hair hanging down her back like a sesbania tree. She was a work of art. What a chest, what a waist! How mighty is the Creator! Her beauty could have got her out of the noose! I sighed when I put the hood on her. If it wouldn't have got me into trouble, I'd have cried when I put the rope around her neck. God preserve us! When I went down to check her pulse, she was fluttering like a dove. As I carried her body up the stairs, I felt something I hadn't felt for anyone that was alive!"

I looked at him. He was biting his lower lip, his eyes closed, totally absorbed by the woman who'd died, the one whose body heat still flowed through him, as he put it.

Fear

Once again, this mysterious fear catches me unawares. No specific time, no particular place. There's something hiding, lying in wait, which I can't define or put a name to. It makes me stop if I'm walking, or sit if I'm standing. If I'm on the verge of falling asleep I become alert. A recurring fear, each time taking a new route or a different aspect, as if catching me for the first time—honed, sharp as a blade, as mysterious as a prophecy.

—୭—

The electron revolves around the nucleus of the atom, the moon revolves around the earth, the earth around the sun, the sun around the galaxy, the galaxy around galaxies. Rotation is a principle of the universe. Around what does the universe rotate? Everything rotates—around what?

Definition

Al-aan—"the now" . . .

Now, time itself, the present.

For philosophers, it's the end of the past and the beginning of the future. With it, each is separated from the other. In this sense, it's both a divider and a connector, a common border between past and future, through which each connects to the other. So the now relates to time just as the point relates to the line that is infinite in both directions. Just as there's no point without an intention, there's no now without a supposition. Otherwise . . . what's required is a part that can't be divided without an external presence. With this presence, it's possible to determine a now. When we say "now," just by uttering the word it becomes part of the past. It's not possible to differentiate between what has passed and what will come except through consciousness, which is linked to the presence of someone. For this reason, I say, "I am now" and "Now, I am."

—∞—

The ancient Egyptians built the pyramids. They raised extraordinary pillars from the granite of the south. They carved out obelisks and moved heavy boulders. But . . . despite undertaking all of this construction, they didn't build bridges across the Nile. Why not, even though I'm confident that they were able to do so?

—∞—

The seed is buried in the soil and so life develops from it, and the green emerges. The human is buried in the soil and decomposes into its primary elements, merging with it. Some day, will part of me be part of a flower? Of a plant? Of a newborn human or an animal that is not present now, not alive now?

A dream

I'm waiting on some sidewalk, in some city, heading for an airport the name of which I don't know, in order to board a plane heading to an unknown, indeterminate point. Beside me are a few suitcases belonging to me. A bus stops, with writing on it in an alphabet I don't know. I have a fear that I'll be late, that I'll miss the plane that is heading to no particular point. Carrying my suitcases, I rush between people whose features I don't make out. One suitcase at a time into the luggage hold, the doors of which have opened automatically. I start with the first suitcase—a blue backpack. I find it open, with things inside that I'm not able to identify. I go back to pick up the second, and the third. I thought I'd brought seven suitcases, but each time I go back to the sidewalk, I find additional suitcases, all of them mine. I begin to fear that I won't catch the bus—that is to say, the plane. I quicken my pace, but there isn't enough time. The bus doors close automatically and it starts to move. There were more bags on the sidewalk than I'd brought—all of them mine!

Salaam!

That same look . . .

This time I observe it in my own eyes—lingering, searching. It has its own existence, separate from me. It seems clear and distinct. I'm not terrified of it but receive it calmly, with that calmness that emanates from my eyes when I look at others, when I address one of them sharply during a discussion.

A look that I discovered about a quarter of a century ago, when I recalled it after my father passed away—the last time had been in my father's eyes as he looked in my direction, when I was about to travel. I was in the habit of visiting my parents before any trip to say goodbye and to make sure they were all right. On that morning, my father seemed calm, gentle—in harmony with all that was around him and all that he saw, with all that he concealed and all that he displayed. I'd never seen his face so peaceful before: he always looked sad. He might suddenly laugh at something that occurred to him and his eyes would well up, something I inherited from him. He asked me about the countries I was heading to, so I told him my expected stops: Rome, Paris, and London. He repeated, "*mashallah, mashallah*"—"how wonderful what God wills for us!"

His eyes didn't blink, his stare didn't waver, but rather remained fixed in my direction, calm and gentle. Afterward, when I sought out what was left of those fleeting moments, with nothing to ascribe them to except their embodiment in my memory—stable, polished—with no connection to what was before them or after, this look remained with me. Not because it was a mark of a particular border, for borders unite and reveal, as much as they divide.

I took my family to see my mother the night before I was due to travel. On the following day, I was planning to go to Malta with some friends and colleagues. At dawn, the phone rang. It was an omen. Only a few hours had passed between the visit to my mother and her sudden death. However, this time I didn't need to recognize her look, especially at her two grandchildren—my son and daughter. She'd attracted my attention by the way she supported her cheek in her palm and her easy, gentle look, especially at my daughter. Even though I recognized that look and might have known what it meant, I've never compared it to my father's calm look, which flowed to me until after he passed away. When I stood in front of her deathbed, before her expression of suffering and the blueness of several places on her face, seeing her complete greyness— I'd always seen her in a headscarf—I recalled this look and was convinced that there had been something . . .

This is what I observe in myself.

As if it were a continuation, a connection to what was severed by their absence. I don't need to make an effort or investigate the time. This is my look, their look—from me toward whoever I'm looking at, posing mysteries that eluded me. I lean forward, staring, scrutinizing. No, it's not my exhaustion, not my fatigue, but something else. When I was invited to that conference, I expressed my fear to my friend that I was tired, exhausted, but he insisted. He said he'd announced that I would be coming. The attendees would welcome my presence, and in any case, the Khan al-Khalili Association was like my own family and I could leave when I wished.

Six years and some months ago. My doctor, who was very experienced, warned me: "Don't be shy—when you feel tired, don't go on."

However, I was disposed to an old shyness. With the passage of time, I realize that what wore me down, and what has burdened me intermittently—the sole cause of misunderstandings—is this shyness. Not just over petty matters but rather extending to the most important issues, the essential matters.

During my participation and my presentation, I don't feel tired. I'm not surprised by what I call "the pull," when all that's present liquefies and all that has to do with me dissolves, when I'm about to scream, pursuing someone who will stop my slide into the abyss. Yet most times I brace myself. The push doesn't come from outside me but starts within me.

None of this happens to me. Neither while I'm talking nor listening. I'm calm, except that my movement becomes slower. I figure out that it's the rhythm. Each movement or action is accompanied by a certain rhythm: calm, anxious, or cautious. There are endless ways to describe it. It's determined in accordance with conditions, some of which appear and most of which are difficult to understand. Yet the matter seems different—moving in another direction—when I begin to review the conference on video, especially when I was speaking to the others.

I don't look but communicate by looking through a stream of calmness, as affection and peace emanate from me, as well as the desire to disclose that which can't be perceived or absorbed. For the third time, I perceive it—but this time, from me and to me!

Contessa

Jean-François lives in an old house with a wooden, spiral staircase that creaks with each step. We're descending with Jean-Francois, my wife ahead of us. We go through the interior door, then the front door, to the side street that branches off from St. Denis, one of Paris's red-light areas. Some artists and intellectuals have lived here since the seventies. The rents are high; only those of high social standing can afford it. Corners, stone sidewalks, little entrances, women of different nationalities—Eastern, Western—standing and waiting. Once, while I was heading to Jean-Francois's house, one of them opened her fur coat. Her nakedness was complete, the color of her body reflecting the pale light of the vintage streetlamp. I was alone. I felt afraid; the unfamiliar is frightening. Jean-François said the area is considered safe and that incidents are rare. The pimps are tough: their mission is to ensure the safety of the clients who need quiet and security, as there's no sex without a sense of security. Likewise, they guard the women who could be exposed to various kinds of violence, some of which could be sudden. When I was visiting Jean-François with my wife, I warned her as to what she would see; in Cairo, such things exist only in secret. The time of openness in Cairo ended in 1949, when the parliament member Sayyid Galal won the Bab al-Shaariya district. He was self made, influential: he started out as a simple man and sacrificed his life in the service of the people. They trusted him and elected him without serious opposition. He was behind the law to put an end to organized prostitution. It used to be concentrated in Darb Tayyab, branching off of Clot Bey Street, downtown, near Cairo Station—the starting point and destination for the railways. The prostitutes would obtain a license to practice their trade from a hospital specializing in sexually transmitted diseases, near the tomb of Umm Hashim, or Sayyida Zaynab. It was named Houd al-Marsoud. It seems that the name *houd* came from a stone or marble basin surrounded by legends. *Marsoud* means "monitored": genies and the souls of ancient ancestors protect it.

We walk through the narrow alleys that immediately remind me of the shadows and passages of Old Cairo. They're preserved with care. Jean-François says he has chosen a restaurant that serves dishes from the south, a regional restaurant—that is, for the locals of a particular region. Most of the customers are from the neighborhood. No one comes from far away unless they're looking for it, seeking it out. This reminds me of the cafés in Cairo, where in the best ones in a particular area the customers know each other; if anyone is missing, they will send someone to ask after him. A stranger is easily spotted. The patrons' tastes are well known: when one of them appears, the waiter's voice rings out to signal that his particular drink should be prepared. This is the opposite of roadside cafés—the ones on the highways—where the afternoon patrons may not come back tomorrow, and today's patrons will perhaps never return. For this reason, less attention is given to preparing the drinks. Jean-François says that this restaurant is among the best in the district.

An old gray facade. Entering an eating place with companions is one of the things that arouse joy and intimacy. In Cairo, it's rare to eat in restaurants—it's always linked to some occasion, to an invitation from a friend or a dear one. However, in Paris in particular, and in France in general, it's different. The restaurant is a part of daily life—going there at lunchtime breaks a long day. In the evening, it's a source of companionship and joy, especially with wine. Perhaps there's less intimacy in our restaurants in Cairo due to the rarity of drink. I don't know . . . there's much to say about food, so I will be concise. But before we enter the place, I have to say that its location has escaped me; it's now impossible to identify. At the time, I don't have the habit I begin later on, of noting the addresses of places I come across and which will leave a mark on me. Perhaps I will go there again—whether it's a hotel, restaurant, or shop.

A generously lit hall. Now, at the time of writing, the source is those old lamps, hung from the ceiling, with a house plant coiled around each one. Apart from that, through my gaze back at that moment whose presence elapsed some twenty-three years ago, I see nothing except her. Her presence cancels out everything else.

The way she walks toward us while we're waiting by the entrance is the essence of welcoming—she was born to welcome, to host, to radiate gentleness, comfort, reassurance, and generosity into the souls of those approaching the place, whether familiar or unknown.

The sight of her seizes me: how could this nymph be so delicate, as if woven of glittering tulle, or transparent *rimsh al-ayn* fabric, with a promise of calm? Her smile approaches, forthcoming, not pursuing nor lingering—always moving. As for her footstep, it's the touch of the shadow of light on the surface of water.

Her blouse and pants are gray, with black shoes. Her hair is smooth, framing features that I'm not sure of, that I'm no longer able to recall or examine. Only her presence lingers with me, her evocative gestures. For she's only a signal, a signal only a mark, and a mark only a symbol, an indication of something—perhaps present, realized, or remotely absent.

The moment she enters my field of vision, I wish I'd counted the years leading to her and those that would pass afterward, during which I would hope to recall her or reach her once more. Recalling her is possible by virtue of remembering, that utmost melody and the most sublime possibility.

I don't conceal my captivation, neither from Jean-François nor from my wife, nor from anyone else—whether known or unknown—after she leads us, leaning, bending, inspiring all the joys, to the place where we will eat. A table, a mere table, but also an observatory, a watchtower—an abode. I don't conceal my captivation: I tell my wife and Jean-François that she's a contessa. I don't know exactly what the title means, but I find nothing else available in the depths of my conscious, derived from early readings of translated novels about nobility. Among them were those who held the titles of duke and count, duchess and contessa. I want only to elevate her to a lofty position.

Her bearing, her step, approaching, returning, walking on the tips of her toes. Her waist is an axis, her buttocks a model of perfection, her breasts soaring, firm, unmistakable. Gray—what's linked with her is the color gray. The night envelops everything except her. The more I listen to the music, the more I drift toward her, not knowing, unable to explain the connection. Logic doesn't apply. No connections explain. No height clarifies. No plain—fertile or arid, with crops or without—explains. She remains there, in that location, in that place to which I was led to her. I will never recover it, never know it no matter how much I try. Jean-François informs me that the restaurant is family owned—she and her husband and no one else except for a cook who prepares the dishes and whom no one sees apart from when he occasionally comes out to greet the patrons at the end of the night. The number of customers and the precision of the service and the authenticity of the welcome—I no longer have any idea, except for the lines embodied in her presence. Only the shadow of her figure—soft, lacking form, without perceptible features. But the merest flutter of her within me suddenly compels me to silence if I'm among others, inducing me to move if I'm sitting down, not moving—alerting me to the possibility of alleviating my great distresses and finding an escape from my troubles and cares!

Footsteps

The name of the city escapes me.

It's on the other side of Lake Balaton, in the middle of Hungary. I leave the train station. Houses of equal height, two stories, with Slavic facades. The dominant color is yellow, with a touch of deep, subtle red. The windows are framed with plasterwork patterns of plants. Closed doors, windows with draped curtains, decorations filtering the light. At the intersection, I start out on the uphill road. I stick to the sidewalk, paved with old stone. The passengers who leave with me scatter and I climb the street on my own.

She emerges from a green door and turns to start walking. I don't see her features. She's two paces ahead of me. I slow down so that anyone who sees me from near or far away doesn't think that I'm following her, that I'm on her trail. It's an old habit of mine that started in Old Cairo—not to appear as if I'm pursuing a woman, due to some shyness.

Tak, tak . . . tak, tak . . .

A regular, confident stride. I look at the shoes—narrow high heels, black. Two legs bursting forth. The moment I notice them, what comes to mind are the words "a perfect sculpture." My eyes linger. I see only them, moving forward, one after the other. Whatever originates in such a firm, coherent, and coordinated way will only lead to the same. I don't linger on her confident buttocks, but there's something about her legs that grips my being. I try to keep it in my eye, in my memory. I hurry so that only two short steps will separate me from her, unconcerned that anyone will notice or what she might think. She must have noticed me when I left, known that I was behind her, already walking before she appeared. I reached the road, the sidewalk, before she emerged.

Tak, tak . . . tak, tak . . .

Nothing is left of that trip which lasted just one day, the purpose of which has slipped from my memory. Perhaps some museum or a landmark; I remember nothing of it now. But that stride comes back to me, her legs appear in places she never visited and doesn't know, places that I will never revisit. They come to me in my rest, while I'm lying down, during those fleeting moments that divide waking from slumber. And so I'm alert, amid a raucous din. Her appearance within me cancels out everything outside me—that stride that appeared on that corner . . .

A boxer

He sits next to me—solidly built, a kind look. Despite the cold weather, he's wearing a short-sleeved shirt that shows his solid muscles. I look at him—a coarse neck, prominent jaws, and a snub nose.

"Where are you from?"

The question we always ask strangers. Perhaps followed by a question about someone who doesn't exist. The important thing is the flow of conversation.

"Kenya."

"Nairobi, then."

"No, a small town in the south."

"What do you do?"

"Boxer."

"Are there matches in Tunisia?"

"Yes . . . worldwide qualifiers for the Olympics."

He radiates friendliness, a hidden smile as he talks.

"Is Tunisia cheaper than Egypt?" he asks me.

"About the same."

"So, would I find something for the children at a decent price?"

"In Cairo, there are nice things, and cheap."

"Unfortunately, I'm returning via Rome. I spent one night here and didn't even see the pyramids."

"So . . . you have to come back."

"I don't travel much . . . this is my second trip. The first was to Addis Ababa."

He says his wife is a teacher. That he's a professional boxer, earning some money from local matches. He doesn't have another job. He asks me if I'm a father.

"Muhammad is studying engineering and Magda is in secondary school."

"Only two . . . "

"Thanks to God. And you?"

"Four."

He extends his fingers and bends them back: A son, fifteen. A daughter, thirteen. A son, seven. Another son, only two years old.

"Wonderful. Isn't that enough?"

"Yes."

"You have four wives?"

"No, only one."

"That's enough."

He laughs loudly, holding his arms up high, as if he's preparing to fend off a punch. His laugh is pure, fluttering, with a childlike quality, despite the awesome build of his body. I hear it once again when I say I love boxing, that it's the only sport that gets me to sit in front of the television. I once entered the ring in preparatory school and received a punch that had me seeing stars in the middle of the afternoon. From then on, I stuck to the spectators' seats. After a short silence, he asks me, "How much does a girl's dress cost in Tunisia, for example?"

"It depends . . . but let's say ten dollars. The important thing is to bargain. If they say 'ten,' you say 'five,' without hesitation. Of course, you, specifically, are not afraid of anything."

He laughs and laughs.

"How much is a dowry in your country?"

"It varies . . . but generally, marriage is expensive. And in your country?"

"A dowry for us is in cows. For my wife, I paid four cows." He says he loves his wife a lot, and that she's very, very pretty. He spends time with his children every day. He hadn't been with another woman during his marriage—not out of fear of the AIDS that is widespread in Kenya but because he loves his wife and she loves him. She satisfies him and he satisfies her. Some women send him flowers, but when he's traveling he shuts the door firmly. A very beautiful Ethiopian woman almost raped him in Addis Ababa.

"Is it true in your country that a woman has to be a virgin when she marries?" he asks.

"Of course. What about in your country?"

He smiles, shaking his head. His features become serious again when he says, "Of course, in the Rome airport it's not possible to find anything cheap for children."

Oblivion

The first thing I see of Aali Nasr is his way of sitting—on the lookout, as if about to pounce, as if suspended in midair, unsupported by anything, neither standing on a firm surface nor seated on a chair or tree trunk or some edge. This position is associated with my first meeting with him, which took place after the martyrdom of the leader of the thirty-ninth combat platoon, Brigadier General Ibrahim al-Rifaei, after a fierce battle on Friday, the nineteenth of October, south of Ismailia. Even though I'd seen him during my meetings with Ibrahim al-Rifaei, for me his features are always associated with that visit. I can pin down the location in a general sense—north of Cairo, perhaps in Zaytoun or Heliopolis. When I met him on my own, it was a difficult time: the war had ended, the platoon had lost its founder and leader, and everyone was waiting for what would be decided for them. All the indications were that their platoon would no longer be required, there would be no reason for it to continue to exist. Perhaps due to all of this, Aali Nasr seemed worried, anxious, tense—his conversation unreserved, brave, and unafraid.

I used to pronounce his name "Ali" and a close friend, connected to them, would correct me with "Aali." The name seemed unique to me—strange and unfamiliar. Before I met him, I'd heard about him. Just as he returned to the naval forces from the US, the June defeat happened, Egypt's loss in the 1967 Arab–Israeli War. He'd been sent to the US to study diving medicine. He was originally a physician before enrolling in the naval college to specialize in this rare field. However, the June defeat weighed heavily on him, as was the case for every one of us who lived through that period, including me. We all did our best to adapt or find a way to keep things together. That was when Ibrahim al-Rifaei began to form the combat troop and to prepare it for precision missions characterized by a high and exceptional degree of valor. The people needed these kinds of missions to communicate confidence and to regain control.

How did they gravitate toward each other? There's much to say about this. They developed a connection from their first meeting in 1967 until Aali Nasr's return, bringing Ibrahim's corpse from south of Ismailia. As I expected, a decision was issued to dissolve the platoon. I started asking after the situations of the men I hadn't met in person, or whom I hadn't seen during my visits to take part in the marching drills they went out on, or the exercises I did in preparation to accompany them during combat missions. For this, I was not destined.

In one meeting, Ibrahim al-Rifaei was standing in a simple office, hands on hips: a way of standing unique to him and, for me, a position not associated with anyone else. A long strip of successive photos of the enemy's positions was on the table. I didn't look, nor did I examine them closely. An officer was sitting at the table, with his back to me. Perhaps it was Aali Nasr, or Wisam, or perhaps Khalifa Gawdat. I only saw Ibrahim. Only what he said recurs to me: "We don't walk a lot during the operations, but we need a very high degree of concentration so that we have an effect."

After the war, after Ibrahim had died, I began to get to know those who'd accompanied him, who'd fought with him—investigating and writing about them. Perhaps I would do something to counter oblivion, the forgetting produced by changing circumstances. In Alexandria, I was going up to the third floor of a building, the location of which has slipped from my memory. A naval officer came out—one of Ibrahim's assistants. He asked me to remove my shoes, and I walked across the carpet in socks. He seemed reserved, his eyes looking at me, his hands on the edge of his seat.

In Bahari, the working-class neighborhood, Abu al-Yazid was holding a huge dog's leash. He said he's going to become a diver somewhere on the coast. Which coast? I don't know.

How do I know that Aali Nasr went to France? That he worked in the south as a diving instructor? How do I know that he didn't make it? That he returned to Egypt and had no job, spending his time in the club? I don't know and I can't figure it out. However, the interest in a person comes through with news of him. Direct links may be cut off, time may be scattered; friends and acquaintances may disperse. But news leaks during a fleeting encounter. Someone gleans a detail. An image of a person met only in passing becomes complete, and obscure details fall into place.

Aali Nasr visited me in my office. How different one bow can be from another! In the first, there was eagerness and alertness, a hidden discontent, a severe tension. In the second, a visible defeat, a storm beneath troubles. He said he was suffering from the effects of a blood clot in the leg; the anti-coagulant medications were tiring him.

Right now, I don't recall the context in which I gave him the address of a tailor with whom I used to deal at some point. His shop is near Azhar Mosque.

Aali Nasr looks out at me from among lines written by a colleague he knew well. This is how I knew about his passing away, from the news-papers. In one picture, he's wearing a military uniform, in that meeting the location of which escapes me. He looks out at me from his final visit. Situations change and merge together, sources of news are cut off, the known and the hidden.

A dream

I was invited to accept a prize in London. A foggy sky, with accommodation in a two-story building. I examine the spacious, Moroccan chamber. The building is in London, but the room is in Marrakesh. Despite its breadth and the vastness of its area—to the extent that its walls appear far apart— I'm puzzled, because it will not be big enough for me.

—⁂—

The train crosses the night. The city lights are weak. Which crosses which?

Annette

She's sitting on a bench under the glass shelter that protects those waiting from the falling rain, the cold, or the sharp winds. She's wearing a white leather jacket; underneath it is a woolen pullover with a high collar. I hadn't seen her in anything like it before. Her pants are light blue. I'd always seen her in the jacket and pants she used to wear in the restaurant, in the early morning before lunchtime or before and during dinner as she would greet the patrons. I've amply described her luxurious appearance, her quiet movement, elsewhere; he who desires should review it in the third notebook, devoted to *Streaks of al-Hamra*, as Annette is only a distant streak, a passing ripple.

I'm standing in a bus crossing Boulevard Saint-Germain and heading for the Institut du Monde Arabe. I'm going there to look and to watch: there's an exhibition on horses in Islamic painting. A good opportunity for me to see the original Shahnameh Tahmasp miniatures. I'd seen them previously in Prince Sadr al-Din Khan's collection in the British Museum, even though I have several good quality books on the subject, in which I often study their colors and intricacies, and yet . . . there's nothing like seeing the original, exploring the breaths of artists who bent to the task so creatively hundreds of years ago, who left a trace between their lines and hidden colors.

The sight of Annette—sitting with her only son beside her, their shoulders close, touching. I don't know what conversation they're having. In a little while, they will leave Paris, leave the building in which the restaurant is located. The floor on which they live belongs to the restaurant. I stare in her direction, and when the bus moves, I lean to follow her until she leaves my field of vision, sure that I will not see her again, apart from in my memory—a moment among moments, a shard among the shards that wander the horizon of my soul.

When I arrived in Paris this time, after I'd arranged my things in the old room, I went downstairs, kicking off my stay us usual by heading to the restaurant of Annette and her husband Simon. The restaurant was next door to the hotel; I called it "the Belgian" due to the variety of Belgian beers they served that were unavailable in any other restaurant or café. I would take refuge in its intimate space, its antique mirrors and the broad, crowded bar. I made a habit of sitting at a table facing the bar. A young waiter approached, with black, bushy hair, whom I'd never seen before, though I realized he was of Tunisian origin. He made me remember my friend Gamal whose Algerian father had named him after Gamal Abdel Nasser. He used to struggle to speak Arabic. But each time I showed up at the restaurant over the course of the past years, he would come to greet me warmly, attentively, bringing me my favorite drink without me saying a word. Despite the short intervals between the times I came back, I would never find what I was used to; there was always a change. A change in circumstances would always surprise me, even though I've known so many changes in people, places, and situations that nothing should surprise me. But I thank God that I'm still capable of being surprised and unable to accept change. I waited anxiously for Annette, for her surprise appearance, coming from upstairs or from inside. Until that point, I didn't know exactly where she lived. It wasn't just her figure and the purity of her glances— which made her a streak of al-Hamra—but also the way she would appear so smoothly, suddenly, from the unknown.

I could only see strange faces. I hadn't seen any of them before and none of them knew me. Simon, Annette's husband and the owner and manager of the restaurant, didn't show up. He used to wear a white apron: at first, I thought he was one of the staff. Among them, he was the simplest in appearance and the most active; he never stopped moving. Perhaps they were on vacation somewhere. After some time had passed I got up, forlorn. I felt depressed and out of sorts at first; I hadn't found what I was expecting.

When I came back after eating in another restaurant on Monsieur-le-Prince, perpendicular to rue Racine, I met Richard, the hotel's night receptionist. Richard studied at university by day and worked at the hotel at night. He always sat behind the desk holding a book. He was widely read; he'd read my books in translation and discussed them with me, making observations. He also asked about some things in the novels of Naguib Mahfouz, whom he spoke about admiringly.

I asked him about Simon and the restaurant, about the new faces. What had happened? He made a rapid downward gesture with his hand and said, in English, "collapse." Simon had been forced to sell the restaurant. It had happened only a week before. A new owner had taken over.

Early the next day, as I was leaving the hotel, I met Simon in front of the building next door. A few seconds later, Annette came after him holding the leash of a huge dog I'd never seen before. It was in front of this door that I'd met her one evening with her son two years before. She'd been wearing a fashionable, tight-fitting coat that clung to her body. I hadn't seen her looking as tall and proud as she had that night. I hadn't known that they lived above the restaurant and that the residence was meant only for the manager and his family. That night, I gave her a bottle of ambergris oil, which I made a habit of carrying in my pocket, dabbing a little of it under my nose throughout the hours of the day, especially before I went to sleep. Perfumes are one of life's secrets and blessings. During the brief conversation that we exchanged, I found out that they lived upstairs and that the entire building was one unit, just as it had been since it was built in the eighteenth century. How nice she'd looked on that day off, accompanied by her son. I was looking at her, suppressing everything that might show my fascination, my attraction to her, abandoning myself utterly to those hidden feelings, not expecting anything except the pleasure of seeing and the gentleness of recalling.

I asked Simon what had happened.

He said he'd settled his business affairs in preparation for moving to Saint-Malo, where he would start a new project. He didn't tell me that he was bankrupt, that he was going through some difficult times, forced to sell the vast restaurant and leave the house. While he was speaking to me, they stood there, touching—each of them looking at me in the same way. As for the son, he kept quiet. He stood next to them, not looking at me but facing life and the difficult situation. I said that I hoped to see the two of them again—in France, or in Egypt. I said I would leave them my card with all my addresses.

I asked where I should leave the card.

I pointed to the restaurant. Simon raised his hand in objection, repeating: "No . . . no."

I said I would leave it with Richard. I said that places are the people in them, and that I wouldn't be able to enter the restaurant without them being there. They looked at me with frozen expressions. I wasn't aware of the impact of my words on them, on the silent son. I didn't know how he would remember me in times to come.

She's wrapped in a white jacket, a wool pullover with a high collar and blue jeans. A conversation between her and her son about which I recall nothing. They're waiting for a bus to take them somewhere. How would they appear if I didn't know them—if I hadn't met her and didn't look forward to her appearing? Hiding my elation at looking at her, at her smile. Where will she go, and where will I go? When each of us is in a place far away from the other, will anyone know what went through my mind, what filled that final moment? I'm sure it's final. Early one autumn morning, at that bus stop: my gaze from within the bus as she waits, her intimate conversation.

The Ali Basha Madrasa

At that time I used to smoke shisha, and because Istanbul was one of its sources, I was eager to find a café where I could relax and exhale authentic tobacco smoke. The hotel designated for me was in a European-style neighborhood close to the Bosphorus, with a mountainous landscape. Its streets rose and descended, with varying heights. The building resembled many hotels: modern architecture and clean lines, all with similar windows and balconies. The rooms could have been anywhere. Old Istanbul was on the other side of the sea. I still remember the first time I went to Istanbul with my wife and son Muhammad—on the way back from Varna, the Bulgarian summer resort—when my son, who was two years old at the time, got lost in the blink of an eye. I don't want to relive that.

This time I'd arrived in the early morning, after a stormy night. Although I hadn't had any sleep, I spent the entire day wandering around the markets and passages, not remembering whether I noticed a café or someone smoking shisha in front of a shop or a certain place. But I do remember the answer of a Turkish man in the Egyptian market, from whom I bought some frankincense with a perfumed scent called *rahat halqoum*, who said that the cafés that served shisha were very few: the people who smoked it were the elderly.

Because I was staying a whole week, I decided to try and find one of them. I started asking around, investigating. Now, some fifteen years later, I don't remember who led me to the café. Despite having written memoirs before, I've committed myself, in writing this, to record what occurs to my memory directly, without the assistance of any papers, or audio or video recordings—not out of laziness but out of a desire to record the fleeting moments and what they've left behind, as they appear through those traces which pour over me when I don't expect it and which come to me at mysterious, fleeting moments. I have no explanation for what drives this or what power animates these traces!

"Ali Basha Madrasa."

At first, I didn't understand. I looked at my interlocutor. I don't remember his features now, or in what language we spoke, but he was definitely not Egyptian. There was some emphasis in his pronunciation of "school"—*madrasa*—as if the *m* was more rounded and followed by a long *a*. He said it was a famous place; it would be enough for me to mention the name to any taxi driver.

The car stopped in front of a gray wall with a narrow door. A wide street with mysterious gray buildings, similar to most of Old Istanbul's buildings leading from Galata Bridge. Another reference point: the domes and minarets of Muhammad Ali Mosque in Cairo's Citadel. Although Istanbul and its buildings are considered the origin of mosque architecture, for me Cairo is my fixed reference. What I've first seen, and become accustomed to, has set the standard; the offshoot is the measure, not the original, since I'm temporarily passing by the original while the offshoot is where I permanently reside. Now I'm almost certain I will never find that café again—and perhaps never return to Istanbul. Each city has a dominant color associated with it: gray is appropriate for the spaces of the former Ottoman capital. I looked at the door; it gave no indication of a café.

A long narrow passage with marble tombstones planted in the ground on either side. Some of them stood upright, some were leaning, touching each other, or intersecting as if in a duel. The columns were made of marble, with a verse from the Qur'an in Arabic as well as Turkish writing on each one, linked with a year from the Islamic calendar. Clear numbers like those used in the East—Indian in origin, as some say, or Arabic according to others.

As a foreigner, I might well have been fearful. When I travel, I'm always vigilant, anticipating risk, wary of surprises. A foreigner is always weak, even when he's in a group. But what comforted me was the smell of tobacco—strong, piercing, and, despite the space, authentic. I wanted the smell of smoke, especially shisha tobacco from Aden, Latakia, or Iran. No longer, of course, to the point that I now have an aversion to any fragrance. But in that twilight I took pleasure in it—each step brought me closer to the center of the place.

On the right of another small wall: what looked like a small dome standing on columns. Perhaps a sheikh lay below, surrounded by followers who looked out, across the silence, through the tombstones. Perhaps he was Ali Basha himself and that was his school. Even in eternal rest, there's a hierarchy: in Gurna, west of Luxor, lies the Valley of the Kings; nearby is the Valley of the Queens, and in the next hill are the tombs of the nobles, ministers, and royal court; then, hidden away in a small valley, are the tombs of the artisans and workers who did the carving, drawing, and coloring. In Marrakesh, I stood at the Saadian Tombs: the kings in the middle, then the ministers, the high officials of state, and the retinue—the lower the rank, the more distant the tombs.

At the dome, I stopped and looked in amazement.

A rectangular courtyard with what looked like iwans at the two ends, with stone benches furnished with carpets decorated with typical patterns. Bold colors: red, blue, yellow, white, black. The green was green and the ruby was ruby, nothing else.

Opposite was a pavilion made of glass, revealing the people sitting inside; in one corner was a place for preparing drinks. The shishas came from somewhere that I couldn't see clearly. Meanwhile, a man with whom I spoke later made his rounds, wearing a loose shirt and baggy pants—a Kurd from Diyarbakir, who knew some Arabic phrases. Tea was served in small glasses, slender at the waist, the like of which I've seen only in the old Fishawi Café in Cairo. Red and green tea. I also came across them in Iraq, where all the cafés serve tea in such glasses. They're called *istakan*.

The shisha in the café was perfect in all respects: easy to smoke, with a nice design, its parts matching each other, from the glass bowl filled with water, to the metal waist, to the clay head on which the moistened tobacco was placed, slow burning with a luscious scent and a warm flavor. The hose was covered with colored wool fabric, like an old rug without the pile.

Each day, after the seminars and discussions, I settled in the café. At five o'clock, I would take a taxi from in front of the hotel. I crossed streets from the modern areas to the older ones. I walked through the passage and greeted the tombstones with a look or a touch. They didn't end at the courtyard entrance but were spread out, distributed, throughout the iwans, behind the pavilion. And because I would seek out the same place I'd settled in the first time, I would come across a cylindrical tombstone that had writing on its edges and was crowned with a stone turban that seemed to be looking at me constantly. A dialogue took place, but I can't be specific or remember its details or thrust. I recall my time there and feel certain that a dialogue did take place—between me and that stone, or the remains of the one lying below, with the intertwined letters. On the following day, I feared that my place would be occupied, but I found it free. I clung to it until the day I left.

It's my habit to stick to the same place: if it changes, I'm seized with anxiety—whether at home or in my office, or in my favorite cafés in Old Cairo. If I find someone sitting in my place, I circle once or twice, passing the time until the person occupying it leaves. Sometimes people get involved, whispering and gesturing, so that customers get up and move somewhere else. But it's difficult for me to accept that; I don't like disturbing others and also because of my chronic shyness. This is how I'm in the city where I live. But if I'm staying in a place for a short time or a time with a beginning and an end, my connection to it doesn't become firmly established until I've settled in a place from which I can see and observe people, and with solitude for me or for whom I like—I will then feel a familiarity in the place, it will become part of me and I a part of it. I will even invite some friends as if inviting them to my home. The matter becomes complete by establishing a connection with people of influence, whether the place is a hotel or a café or a restaurant. In this way, I make acquaintances in the countries and cities I frequent. Sometimes, after being away for a year or more, I will find the intimacy and welcome I would find from my family when I visit my own birthplace.

I invited some friends who were participating in the seminar to the place. The Kurdish man looked kind, wanting to show me respect in front of them, even though my acquaintance with him preceded their arrival by only three days. Yet I knew something of him and he knew something of me, especially after I told him that I'd listened to a broadcast in which I caught the name of his city—Diyarbakir. I'd also mentioned to him that I'd visited Iraqi Kurdistan and that its mountains and villages were among the most beautiful I'd ever set eyes on. When he saw my friends, he insisted on bringing tea and coffee from the pavilion, although his job was to bring the coals for the shisha smokers. He began to come over at frequent intervals and ask in Arabic, "Do you need anything?"

A friend who was with me from Egypt said, "You're sitting in a cemetery."

He pointed to the looming tombstones that looked out at me across the years dividing us, the round tops with which they ended. I've forgotten all the customers I looked at, with whom I exchanged glances—even that Scot, accompanied by his beautiful girlfriend who was so devoted to him and who'd asked me to teach him how to smoke the shisha because he got dizzy with the first puff. I advised him to take it slowly, to take short puffs, at intervals, although he seemed dazzled by the discovery. I can't recall his features, only the way he sat. Even the Kurd with whom I was so friendly— his features have disappeared. Only his gait, the way he handed out the coal, how he arranged it on top of the tobacco—his form could be that of any other person, with any name. As for those tombstones, they seem to look back at me from a distance—with their positions, their proximity, the way they intersected, with all the distinct Qur'anic verses and unknown names, the years of absence, and the references to lives gone by. I now know none of them at all.

An explosion

A European city, perhaps Rome or Budapest. What's certain is that the street is wide and the presidential palace is on it. The street is congested— cars following each other, with narrow spaces between them. Suddenly, a young man wearing a helmet and leather jacket speeds through. He's crouched over a huge motorcycle, swerving between the cars.

A black car is in front of us as we're stopping at a red traffic light. I'm startled by the way the car stops suddenly, and a woman wearing a black dress gets out. She seems to be in a state: gripped by a kind of ecstasy, per- haps because her hands, as well as her face, are raised toward the heavens. She's barefoot. She undoes the buttons on the dark dress and with a quick movement throws it on the ground. Her body erupts, filling the air with light. A female form, perfect, a glowing presence. The roundness of the flagrant buttocks across perfect mounds; the breasts soar. I see her from different angles: from the front, from the back, as if I'm hovering above her. She doesn't just appear but rather bursts forth. It lasts only seconds. Hands stretch out—just hands, pulling her inside. She resists, and with her resistance her firm, wayward body assumes positions that make me dizzy.

164

Her disappearance is complete; she vanishes inside the car. I don't know if a hand stretched out to pick up the dress that lies in the street. What I do know is that she has become a sign for me, a light within what can't be verified.

A breeze

It's deep evening—heat, humidity. Despite my annoyance with the resulting sweat and insomnia, I listen to the emptiness. I follow the rhythm, until it blows—a gentle breeze, with meaning. Its significance comes from its rarity, from its singularity. I follow it, erecting places and observatories for it, wondering about the place from which it started traveling toward me, about its course and where it would come to rest. It's not a breeze exactly: it's a herald of the small breezes that will arrive with autumn, a preliminary to winter. It comes to me, touches me, alerting me to the continuity of the cycle, close on the heels of the summer heat. It's truly a whisper of the universe, for anyone who understands, who observes . . .

Winter

It's truly winter. I listen to it approaching, to its arrival. It's the gray light, that silence that comes from a remote sequence. It's an awareness of an ancient space, a consciousness of the cycle of the stars, of inevitable oblivion and the end of the cycle which drives us slowly, slowly, to forgetting, to nothingness, to disappearance. It leaves us for others. Nothing calls attention to change, to transformation, to shifting, to anchoring, to completion, like the approach of the seasons. That polished tranquility—its whispery flow overtakes me. If only!

Prayer

Norham Park—tidy, relaxing, fertile. All the hues of green. A rapidly flowing brook runs through it. I gulp the pure air. A man and woman in sports clothes, running. Along the sides are rubbish bins.

Unexpectedly.

A powerful wave of anxiety washes over me, enfolding me. My daughter appears, walking: at some moment, in some place, alone and confused. I'm afraid for her of the unknown—that her brother will emigrate, that she will be on her own. I recall the others who were left alone after the departure of those close to them, the children of the same womb. No sooner does life unite than it disperses. I mourn my absence from her, though I'm still around; I feel pity for her because of my eternal exile from her, though I still exist. In this place, far from where she lives, I pray to God that my two children will stay close, that they will not leave one another.

A saying

Before I boarded the high-speed train, a saying that I'd heard one day came to mind. I don't know where I'd heard it. Perhaps I'd read it. I can't be sure, but it's present and clear to me:

"To travel, in order to lose yourself, you must abandon yourself to the road. Your journey is only complete when you're lost."

A letter

The brief moments between dawn and sunrise. Awake, hoping for sleep to return, but filled with the expectation of the arrival of some letter—a letter of mysterious content from someone unknown, uncertain that I will receive it. I don't know by what means it will arrive. A letter from me, to me. I don't know, but this vague expectation revolves around something, ambiguous in some way. It makes its way toward me. I don't know how long I will be in this state of expectation. Its arrival will end it, but it doesn't arrive. I imagine that I'm both the sender and the addressee, ignorant of what I've sent, that what I will receive will be vague, in that moment when I break the seal, when I will find out.

A letter

I tell my sister that I'll drop by tomorrow. She says she'll wait for me: she won't go out but will stay at home. I don't stay long anymore. I can't say that I make visits but rather brief drop-ins whenever I'm passing by or in her area. Tomorrow morning I have an appointment at Ain Shams University. I'll be near Nasr City; it's convenient.

Before I ask how my brother is doing, she starts talking to me, because she has found an old letter to my father.

"From me?"

She says she'd been going through some papers she'd kept when she found this letter. Twenty-eight years since it was sent. It's very moving. After the phone call, I start contemplating time gone by. What letter?

From where? Why?

My father—God bless his soul—was never able to read. Circumstances didn't grant him the opportunity to complete the education for which he yearned, and for which he saved the money. I elaborated on this in *Kitab al-Tajaliyat*, whoever wants may refer to it. I don't recall writing to him, sitting at a table and writing to him with my own hand, addressing him. How could I have written to him while he was only able to distinguish one letter from another with difficulty?

When did I have the time to write a letter to my father?

I'm not able to pin it down or figure it out—it would have been the first time I had written a letter to my father, a letter about which I don't know anything. Nothing can stimulate my memory cells to recall a past moment, one that had ceased to be. I can grasp nothing of it.

When? Where?

My sister said the intervening period was twenty-eight years. In other words, written in the midseventies. I now understand the total erasure that has happened to moments I experienced and situations I lived through and suffered. The times I went through and that went through me, but which are no longer present—whether near or far—in my memory, as if they belonged to someone else and thus stir nothing for me. The issue began years ago, with the forgetting of people's names. Sometimes I run into them: I recognize them, but I can't recall the name. At times some of them ask: do you remember me? Out of honesty and amiability, I say "Yes, of course," hoping to bring the situation to an end. But some of them follow the question with another: "Who am I?" When this began to happen, I would resort to evasion, but when it continued, I became unafraid of being honest and asking for clarification: "Could you remind me, because I've forgotten?"

It's natural, with the aging process and the accumulation of fleeting moments, for erasure to affect names, but to be met by a letter written in a particular situation—this is what seems strange. How could I write to my father when I was sure he wouldn't read it? Was I counting on others to read the letter? Just as my uncle's letters would come to him from the village, dictated to those who'd mastered writing. My uncle was barely literate; he could write a few words. Hamid's son knew how to read and write. The people would dictate their letters to him in exchange for a handful of dates or half a *keddah* of corn or wheat, or a cone of white or red sugar, or a couple of eggs—whatever they could afford. The end of the letters was always the same; it didn't change: *Now then, all of us here send you our greetings, and all they lack is to see you. Al-salaam khitaam*—"signed with salutations."

Such a letter had to be from somewhere far away. There had to be a strong motive that made me write, but I'm unable to recall those fleeting moments, the conditions in which I wrote my words, or the motive. Defeated, I put off the matter until my visit to my sister the following day.

My sister returns from her room holding the envelope: she says that she'd been tidying up her things when she found it. I'm unable to get a sense of her feelings precisely. She's smiling, but there's a hint of sadness, perhaps under the influence of nostalgia. She's now nearly fifty-three, living on her own, after good fortune deserted her. This is a delicate matter, so let me put off talking about it.

The envelope is open from the left-hand side, the stamp is Iraqi, issued on the occasion of the Anniversary of the Revolution, but it's not clear which anniversary, which year exactly. A fifteen fils postage stamp.

Issued in Sulaymaniyah.

Northern Iraq, then . . . 1975. But I'd never been to Sulaymaniyah, only passed close by. Surely I hadn't entered the city. I'd been with the military units at the time, in the nearby mountains, in order to report on what was happening in the Kurdish north. I was crossing the mountains and staying at places perhaps no one had set foot in since the beginning of time. Unspoiled mountains, abundant greenery, and peaks covered in snow throughout most months of the year.

Maybe I'd asked one of my companions to mail the letter for me, which would explain the city postmark. I certainly don't have any indication whatsoever that would confirm anything like that, nor to whom I may have entrusted the letter.

I only remember an officer escort from the Department of Political Guidance, the equivalent of the Department of Morale Affairs in the Egyptian army. However, there was a great difference between the two. The Iraqi Department of Political Guidance was under the authority of the governing party, and the party was utterly hegemonic and had the final say. My escort combined both aspects, as he belonged to the party and was an officer with the rank of major. He was called Sharaf. He was kind and loved to have a good time; he joked around a good deal and was always mentioning his five children. The majority were girls—perhaps three girls and two boys, or four daughters and one son. His features aren't clear to me right now, only the generalities of his appearance: he was of medium height and slightly rotund, with a ready smile. I was with an Egyptian friend who lived in Baghdad: after he left Egypt, he'd ended up there and settled down. He specialized in documentary film. We were communists. At that time, the Iraqi Communist Party and the ruling Baath Party were allies; among the conditions of the alliance was that no party—with the exception of the Baath—was to work in the army. In the mountains of Kurdistan, the armed groups loyal to the Kurdish Communists would fight alongside the army units. Later on, the state of affairs changed, the situation was reversed, and the confrontation occurred. Our symbol for the Baath was the orange, and the apple stood for the Communists. That became the source of jokes throughout the voyage through the mountains of Kurdistan. Sharaf would repeat that Egyptians love to joke. What worried him was dying in the war, leaving his children orphans. "They're still uneducated," he would repeat. Later, I followed his news and found out that he'd been injured during the Iraq–Iran War and was moved from the front line. After that, I lost track of him.

Did I give the letter to Sharaf to put in a mailbox?

Perhaps.

Yet he hadn't left us the whole time.

Slowly, I take the letter out of the envelope. The words were written with a pen. It had been written in Irbil; I stayed in the old city for two nights, I don't remember writing it. During my travels, I only write down observations. If I have to write a letter, I'm concise to the utmost. I prefer postcards.

Smiling, my sister says, "The date is March 15, today is March 15—it's the same day." I look at her silently. Surely not. It was me who'd determined the date of the visit, who'd got in touch the previous evening and told her I would stop by. A strange coincidence—on this precise day, twenty-eight years ago, I wrote this letter. What was the motive? I don't know now: I can only think and guess about a situation that I went through, and which went through me. Although the matter is linked to me, I'm cut off from it by forgetting and by erasure. Severed, as if I were mining my missing origins and roots, which do not show, trying to find the signs, to read what appears in them and infer what might not be seen even though it's in front of the eyes.

When I embarked on that trip, I didn't know that my father would depart to eternity five years and seven months later. But I can explain the motive. When I went to Irbil, in northern Iraq, I was far away from him. Across the distance, I was seized by feelings of guilt and inadequacy toward those we love and to whom we belong. I'm like this when I'm about to go on a trip; before leaving, I take stock of myself and give expression to what I've been concealing—or hiding from.

169

No doubt something was worrying me in that remote place, fraught with dangers, which drove me to address my father in writing. This was rare between us. Perhaps for this reason, I began by referring to the distant place from which I was writing in order to fill his heart with compassion toward me—he who was always compassionate. Among the traces that have escaped erasure is the moment he came to see me off on my first trip, the first steps of my departure, which happened more frequently in subsequent times.

My father must have been sad for some reason. A misunderstanding must have happened. After talking about the distance, I assured him of my profound love, my deep appreciation and pride in what he'd done for us, even if the circumstances hadn't allowed us to tell him, since our emotions are profound—stronger than speech.

Did my brothers read to him what I'd written?

I don't ask my sister, fearing that she'll say no. Let me keep the possibility open, especially since I suddenly have a sense of myself, as I read the words with my eyes, as if I were addressing them to him there and then, to the eternity of which he'd become a part . . .

A voice

It comes from somewhere within me, it must be from over the fields. Thick palms, a canal with rapidly flowing water. A wooden bridge nearby, the smell of figs and grapes, perhaps sesame not yet ripe, the sound of a *tambour* raising the water, operated by hand, an arched back. The sound is deep, gurgling, melancholic:

O basil leaves, why are you withered?

The eye is black, and the eyebrows lowered.

Cry for me and trace lines of grief in the sand,[7]

Cry for times gone by, that won't return.

Outcasts

An airport. Preparing to enter the checkpoint leading to passport control. A yellow dividing line. The young female officer takes the passport and opens it. A quick glance during which she compares the photo in the passport to the person standing before her.

Next to her, a poster on the wall. Colored photos of five people—four of them male, one young woman close to them in age. Outcasts, wanted.

---

7   In Upper Egypt, tracing crossed lines in the sand is a custom that signifies grief or mourning.

Another poster alongside it: photos of the people facing forward and photos in profile. Although I don't speak the language, I grasp the matter. They must belong to the group demanding the secession of the western region of the country. There's always news of explosions and occasional assassinations.

Their features are different but similar. The young woman is beautiful, as if her photo had been taken head on, while she was running. Her eyes stare at the onlookers, perhaps indicating some familiarity. But the people are presented here as rebels, terrorists—the source of danger that must be prevented. Outcasts at the gates of departure and arrival. In their region they're considered heroes, some people sympathize with them, give them help.

Through the eyes and the hunted features stolen from fleeting moments, I try to understand what's not visible, what's not announced: concerns, motives, hidden pulses—what the police photos don't disclose. After various stations of perception and anticipation, I've learned not to be quick to condemn, not to take one side against another without knowing—to inquire into the subtleties of the most violent and the cruel among humanity.

The sound of the stamp hitting the passport pages. I leave the small window, accompanied by the wanted faces, wondering where they are now.

—⁂—

The sequence of my names breaks off after my seventh great-grandfather.

I wonder—if I were able to find out my full name, back to the first originator, how would it appear? Pharaonic, Syrian, Babylonian, Assyrian, Himyarite, Phoenician, or something we will never know? How many names will bring comfort, and how many will arouse anxiety? How many will make one proud, and how many will bring about a desire to conceal? Is it possible to determine the first name, before which there's no name? Is it possible to determine the name after which there's no name? Is it possible to determine the name of the name? Can I—can we—determine the name of the name?

Samarkand

A sunset with a dense presence. Despite spending a long while looking at the enormous mosques with their striking blue tiles and soaring entrances, the most prominent thing I see now is a long path bordered by a row of magnolia trees—slender, graceful, and tall. Here and there the spaces between the tiles are dusted with fine weeds. The domes: as if I were looking at them from above, although I never flew over them. A market, with rows of vendors. All that's left are balls of white cheese, their taste closest to what we call Halloumi cheese. The features merge together: two wide eyes, a coarse nose, a bushy mustache. Each belonged to a different person, but I see those features in a single face. A high wall with a structure on top for a telescope, pointing to the sky—the Ulugh Beg Observatory. Ulugh Beg was interested in examining the effects of the stars and the planets and tracking their paths. I see the base, but I'm not certain if there's a telescope. Inside the observatory, I spoke with a young man wearing a coat. Who was it that mentioned the name of Tamerlane? I don't know, but I remember his answer distinctly: "Our liberator and national hero."

I looked at him in surprise. Tamerlane was a slaughterer, he built a pyramid of skulls. I didn't say this, but I wondered: "Your liberator from whom?"

Sharply, he said, "From the Arabs."

Someone we think of as a destroyer, a killer, a pillager, is considered by his people to be a national hero. Once again, through my travels and the many conversations I have, I get a sense of how relative things are. I always conclude with the realization that what I consider east is, for someone else, west. I'm aware that what remains are specks; one can't recall a conversation exactly as it happened. The sentences are muddled, the places are switched, the phrases transformed. After a while, perhaps, what was intended disappears entirely. As for the scenes, they follow each other in fragments—frozen, with no movement within them. At times, I focus on recalling a moment from a road congested with vehicles. The cars surge by at top speed. I glimpse only still images, like those in projected films. I focus on that path in Samarkand. Despite everything I've seen of towering buildings and the abundance of colors, I hold on to that path. Not the length of it, precisely, but its tiles. Not its tiles, exactly, but the patches of earth interspersed between them, as if I'm seeing them close up. I can almost count them.

Texts

A restaurant overlooking the Nile. At the front, a French writer and academic. Next to him is his wife. The names of both escape me. They have me sit in front of him, directly facing him. He speaks fourteen languages, including Arabic. He says that some of them are ancient and obsolete, not in use anymore, like Latin or ancient Egyptian. I ask him about the relationship of a human being to a language that's no longer spoken. He's taken aback a bit. Changing something in the tone of his voice, he says, "The language dies, but the texts remain alive. As long as a text can be read in its original language or one in which it has been translated, even if the original language has disappeared completely, it means it's alive, active. This is the vitality of texts. It's the texts."

Flamenco

An evening in a building overlooking a meadow. I'm seated at a table, accompanied by Egyptian and Spanish friends. An old playhouse that started operating in the forties, although the structure itself is older. A stage with a small area, raised a little, with tables in rows around it. Reservations get priority, and because I've followed the advice of an experienced friend who has lived in Madrid for a time, there's very little space between us and the stage. This is where Blanca del Rey performs. In the world of flamenco, she's the most famous. She has danced in many capitals of the world: before the Japanese emperor, at the opening of the Olympic Games.

The performance begins with the entrance of the dancers and the musicians. The singer sits beside the guitarist. Poems of unknown origin mingle with poignant voices, full of suffering, beseeching someone absent, unknown. I don't know what they mean, but the voices pierce me. Perceiving the obscure enriches more than absorbing what is manifest. Sadness pervades the Andalusian musical rhythms: I don't know precisely what has flowed into what, like the Portuguese singing known as Fado, which, it is said, originated with the camel driver, the plaintive song that urged the camels across the desert. After the singing, the guitar playing starts up. The first dancer shifts, fidgeting as she readies herself. We realize this through the movements of her fingers, which touch her knees, through the swaying of her body, from her sidelong glances, which begin to be directed toward us, from her fixed gaze at some indeterminate point; she transcends the confinements of the cramped place. She stretches out her arms and flexes her fingers as the sound of the guitar rises. Each dancer is a particular circumstance that is not repeated: a dance with roots extending to India, Andalusia, in a "no place" that does not even contain the traveling gypsy. Customs and cultures, both extinct and extant, are merged within it. A dance containing arrogance, anger, rebuke, coyness, and tenderness. In it is the spring breeze, from it comes the storm. An attempted closeness and a bending toward, then a sudden movement away. Advancing and retreating at the same time.

One dancer forthright, another mysterious, a third who inspires, a fourth who is joyful. But all are merely a preparation for Blanca la Coronada. She must be over sixty, but she still gives it everything. As she spins rapidly, we glimpse her thigh. So quickly does it disappear again that we don't know whether we'd seen it or not. Her energy is extraordinary. With her dance, she imitates nature—at one moment, a fine cloud, while at another, she seems to be a predator. But throughout, she's the woman who's difficult to fathom. The eyes can only feel weary with the difficulty of following her. She never stays in one position. The perfect dancing, flowing from within, changing with the pulse, with the rhythm of breathing. Always the inner core, difficult to understand. At certain times, even bodies are transformed into apparitions. We're totally absorbed in a dialogue with a party we can't see—hidden, not showing, and at a particular moment, we don't see the dancer herself, although she moves within our sight, within our hearing.

Music

All music is an echo of another hidden source, whose melodies only hint at the deepest secrets. Some of it tells of distant horizons that vision can't make out. Through it, I cross distances for which there isn't yet a measure. Successive generations have not been enough to cross them, but the sound of a melody suffices, quicker than the blink of an eye. Some chords suggest lofty skies—not those that we can see with the naked eye or with the aid of binoculars but those that are hidden, concealed, there in the no-place, one sky followed by another. What we see from our earthly location is limited; it might be seen as earth by someone looking from a different part of space than the one I occupy. Particular rhythms indicate the succession of moments, imitating their diffusion, their transition from one time to another. Yet it's time that we don't know; it's the time from which our time began. It has its progressive and successive melodies. The modes—the *maqamat*—flow, following one another, suggesting water in its various states, flowing so quietly that its sound is not heard, scattering its droplets, persisting through the ages to wear away the most resistant of mountains, and continuing. Nothing can stop it—the murmur of streams, muffled in the cool shade. The states of water are but parallel signs—only through them is music complete. The courses of the melody multiply, and so perhaps it indicates some element, while at the same time suggesting an underlying state, something hidden in the depths, possibly revealing a forgotten moment considered for long to have been lost forever.

The music follows successively in its various forms and compositions, its shades and shadows, coming from a tune from which all melodies originate, and where all compositions, movements, and paths end. All compositions originate from it and return to it: a tune which one would vanish into, should it begin to be perceived. For in the tangible universe, there's no one with the power to absorb even a glimpse of it . . .

All melodies are in motion, are always with us. What the composers write down are but discoveries of their distant echoes. What we listen to, what stirs our inner depths, is but a far-flung shadow of what lingers where our perception may not grasp—that distinct, essential melody.

Floating

When I'm traveling alone, I yearn to float, to break habits, to sever bonds for a time. As I arrive at the departure gate, alone, I hide behind myself—rather, within myself. I'm careful not to get into a conversation with anyone beside me or anyone who looks at me. Even if someone recognizes me, I gather myself up quickly, taking refuge in a polite and dissuading smile. Sometimes while waiting, I prepare to retreat within myself. I begin by drinking a glass of beer or wine—neither of them taking me over the unseen border between consciousness and unconsciousness. The best time is while I'm waiting for takeoff, or settling into the seat, which I always prefer to be by the window. The sipping helps me to reach that point of ecstasy. My hidden yearnings come to the fore; all that's buried becomes visible in me. I retrieve all that is lost. I'm about to reach everything that I've missed. I don't lose myself completely, for I must remain alert so that I know what to do, so that I don't lose my way. I'm closer to a state of deluding myself about what should be, about what I hope for and not what is.

I imagine that I've taken the shape of a bow—flexed—although this is not my natural state. I look carefully at anyone who enters my field of vision, whether nearby or far away, although I don't examine their features but rather question them, asking for clarification, rendering distinct all that's hidden and what's apparent, what's revealed and what's implied. I bide my time with their questions and listen to their answers with deliberation.

My heartbeats quicken, they separate from me. They come from afar. I nod to someone I don't see, who warns me repeatedly not to drink before boarding. He says that it's one more burden for the heart to bear, "So do not cause it stress. Be kind to yourself." I flaunt my disregard, my swerving from the path, until I've righted myself and found a balance.

—m—

A hair, just a hair hanging down before the eye. Does it not block out the sun's mass?

Persons unknown

I wake up to his complete features. Down to the color of his suit and his tie. I was getting ready to board a train. A station with a stark appearance, as if dedicated only to military trains: everyone within it disciplined, not turning around. Except for this towering man with a wide jaw and full lips. He stopped, suddenly, and began gazing at me, without looking away. I was taken aback by his staring eyes. He was holding a bag; I don't know what it contained. The way he stood and the way he looked aroused an odd fear in me. I was rooted to the spot, unable to run. I began to try, and as I struggled, I woke up, breathing rapidly. Between waking and sleeping, as if he were still present in front me. I sat up in bed, my sleep finished, and drank a glass of water that I always keep close by.

Who is he?

From where did he come, to see me in my dream?

He wasn't anyone I'd once known and who was now far away, whether in life or death. There can be no place to meet them but in dreams; he didn't enter my field of vision by coincidence. I'm sure of it. But then . . . where did he come from? From what dark region?

But he's not alone. Perhaps I'm struck by how distinct he was, since the dream ended abruptly when I woke unexpectedly. In the course of dreams scattered throughout my slumbers, many people I don't know have come to me, visited me. Some of them have talked to me, in different situations. They moved through the reaches of marvelous colors, woven reaches of outer space—as if they were tents of a material unknown to me, pitched under water. Features I'd never, ever encountered in my waking world. The effect they have on me exceeds that of people I've known well when conscious. Among them are women who aroused my senses, with whom I experienced every wonder. Sometimes I see their features, clear and distinct, before they change into others as we begin to hug, kiss, and make love. They may fade away entirely the moment I ejaculate. At this point, I wake up cheerfully, willingly, listening to the growing dampness near me, wishing the moment would last. If only it would go on a little longer. I make an effort to recall the women's features, the way they looked. I'm surprised at how their origins are unknown to me. From where did they come? I don't know. I try to remember how many times I spilled my sensual fluid unintentionally because of a woman I don't know, and whose features I can't recall. How can the material result from the immaterial? How can something that can be felt and measured by the senses be produced by the imagination? At this point, I stop to ask: which of the two is real, and which is imaginary?

Sometimes, features I don't recognize surprise me from the unknown. I try to assemble the different elements of their owners, to recall their names, but I'm unable. Do those features belong to dreams, or did I visit them or see them in passing? I observe a galaxy within me. I can't define its location, or its depth. It's crowded with features, with moments I've experienced and utterly forgotten, erased. Did they remain in that hidden place? Do they come to me where I don't expect them, and can't return them or drive them away? I can't choose whom I see in my sleep. Yet I know the physical effects that some of them have stirred in me: fear, crying, the dread of awaited terrors, and the ultimate pleasure in which I pour forth and awake in ecstasy. This is precisely the state al-Sheikh al-Akbar attained, which he considered to be the border between the worlds of the tangible and the indeterminate, or the point of their connection. So people seen in dreams are from the imaginary, while ejaculation is from the concrete world of the tangible.

Those countless vanished moments—and the features of those people from whom we've grown distant. Will they be reshaped somewhere, so that the characteristics that are hard to make out will come back to us? Why do I imagine they will come to me? Why am I not the one to go to them, to meet them, according to a logic that I find difficult to define now, so that those meetings take place and those features come back to me or respond to me, stirring those feelings—including the confusion that prompts these confusing questions: To what world do those people belong? Do they also ask this question? Does my image come to them while they sleep? Is it their sleep, or mine?

In between

I'm about to cross between two years, if there's a between. The moment doesn't last; it elapses just as one becomes aware of it. The year doesn't concern me—those are illusory signs. What I know is that every transition brings me closer to my end.

After sunset, I spend some time alone. I prepare the stage—that is, I organize my papers and notebooks on the desk. I get rid of papers it's no longer necessary to keep, though I'm one of those who find it difficult to get rid of papers. I go around the study, straightening things up. I turn over books that I haven't touched for a long time. I choose a book through which I can cross the dividing line. It has been with me ever since the days I read *It Is What It Is* by Our Master Jalal al-Din al-Rumi. Over the past few years, I've been reading more than one book at a time, under the influence of my increasing hunger. I have a deeper and more intimate connection with some of those who have written those books a few or many years ago than with people I've known in flesh and blood.

I look at the organizer that holds the phone numbers. Tomorrow morning I'll begin going through the numbers, crossing out those who have passed away, those with whom my connections are broken, those I met briefly, whose numbers I wrote down and then forgot. I stand in front of some of the names, trying to recall what the person looked like.

I come, I go, with my eyes fixed on the clock. The hour is almost upon us. Little remains before the waning is complete. The television stations switch between world capitals—the squares filled with men and women, colored paper, golden hats, bottles of champagne, yearning for a moment in which the shouts, the laughter, the meaningless noises will rise up. I smile in amazement. How do those approaching their end celebrate? Birth is death—with the emergence of the newborn begins the countdown. The passing of a year means that the past grows nearer, hastening toward passing. It requires reflecting on what happened and what will happen, straightening things up. If only . . .

Once

A light chill. Signs of autumn at the end of days of heat that have lasted so long. The portents of winter are not hidden, especially at night. The father and son are in a taxi. The son is a little drowsy, having accompanied his father since the beginning of the day. They've visited the uncle, the engineering officer: very quiet, never married. He got out his calculators and other electronics and began to explain to his nephew how this one and that one work. Then he showed them pictures of his last trip to the United States. After visiting the uncle, they headed to a children's book and toy fair. In a few days, it will be the son's birthday. The father bought an airplane for him and a doll for his sister.

They go out to the street, to a spacious café with high ceilings. The son looks at his father silently. From time to time, he asks about the parts of the shisha, how the smoke passes through the water. He looks at his father, afraid to say anything or ask a question, or do anything that will anger him. The father is quiet for a long time.

"Are you angry with me, Baba?"

The father looks at him. There's melancholy in his eyes, the shadow of a tear hanging at their edges.

"No, my love."

"But why are you silent?"

"I'm thinking about something."

The child's eyes are full of questions, but he's quiet, not speaking, afraid of annoying his father. He bows his head silently, seeming for a moment beyond his years. The father stands, the son stands. They go to the theater. After listening to different styles of Arabic music—*adwar*, *muwashahat*, *taqatiq*—they leave. At the theater door, the son says, "I like Arabic music."

Then he says, "Do you know why?"

The father looks at him.

"Because you like it."

In the minibus, the son holds on to the package containing the plane. He asks about some details concerning the toy. His questions grow further apart. As the vehicle rocks, he becomes drowsy. He rests his head on his father's knee. On the way, in the dark of night, the son wakes up. Hurriedly, as if speaking in his sleep, he says, "Baba . . . I wish we could go out together more."

"Hopefully. *Inshallah*."

"I wish . . . even once a month, Baba."

The means[8]

Water—we see it, we sip it, we take refuge in it and purify ourselves. But we're not able to take hold of it. The air—we float in it, depend on it. If it were cut off, it would mean our certain end. We feel the breath of its tiniest breezes on our cheeks, or we listen to the piercing of the wind as storms begin. But we can't see it. Time—we see its manifestations, yet we do not grasp its essence. We're born as it passes, we die, we arrive, and we pass away, youth passes us by, we grow gray. Feebleness

---

8   "Means," as it's used here, occurs a number of times in the Qur'an. As well as signifying ways and means, it can refer to reasons and goals.

creeps up. The planets pass by and the stars flicker, erupting suddenly. Another vanishes—we don't know the source, the final destination, or the trajectory. We're ignorant of all things linked to the means of our existence, and we're unable to take them in or absorb them—however trite or majestic!

A reprimand

The girl flips through the photos of her parents' wedding. She kisses a picture of them on their own, as they cut the tiered cake. Suddenly, she turns to her mother.

"Why didn't you take me with you?"

The mother asks, "Where?"

She continues, "Of course, madam, you left me home alone."

"My love, I . . . "

A lament courses through her voice.

"Aren't I your daughter?"

"Of course, my love . . . "

"So why didn't you take me to your wedding? You went together and left me by myself!"

Friends

The young girl says, "Why is my brother older than me?" She looks angry, gesturing with her little hand as she addresses her mother. "Why didn't you have me before him?"

She continues, "I would've been in school, and had friends!"

A voice

The father is watching a beautiful Turkish singer. Her voice comes from nowhere. The daughter rushes in, her hand on her hip.

"You like that lady?" the daughter says.

"Yeah."

"So you don't love Mama?"

"I just like her voice."

"So you don't like Mama's voice?"

She raises her little finger in warning. He recalls his own finger, when he warns or threatens.

"You like mama's voice, and only hers!"

180

Play

The daughter is trying to play on the slide. An older boy pushes her. She says, "You think you can scare me? I've got an older brother who'll teach you a lesson!"

She runs to her brother who is of similar age to the boy, but taller, his chest broader. She shouts, "That boy over there is bothering me! He doesn't want me to play!"

Her brother approaches the boy slowly. He stands in front of him, his legs apart, his hands clasped in front of his chest.

"What's going on, captain?"

The boy moves back, withdrawing. When he's several steps away, he starts running. She goes back to climbing the slide. She looks at the boys and girls and shouts:

"All of you get back!"

A phone call

A continuous ringing—an overseas call. It's late. Who is it? From where in the world? I pick up the receiver. Although I haven't heard from her for ten years, I recognize her voice as soon as she starts speaking. There's a ring, a melody to every voice. Hidden features frame it, setting it off, differentiating it from others.

She says, "You haven't forgotten me."

I laugh. How could I forget her, around whom time was organized, on whom all breaths hung?

She says she'd read an article in which my name appeared. She wanted to let me know since I wouldn't see it. And if I received it, I wouldn't know what it said, since it was in an unusual language.

A moment of silence. She says she wanted to hear my voice after all these years.

I ask her to explain. She says she has a son with her husband, with whom she's been living for seven years.

Her voice restores an era for me that is no longer, a voice of joys and longings. What I suppress and conceal, that with which I live. How distant everything seems—remote, difficult to comprehend. Her voice doesn't bring us closer but rather makes her more distant. I make my questions more precise:

Where is she calling from?

What time is it? Where is she? Now. At this moment. What's the temperature? In what position is she? Is she sitting? Being stubborn? What's she wearing?

I long to cancel out the distances, the times that divide—uniting the times, merging them, banishing the details. If only!

A bridge

Rocky hills in the background—rising up to the clouds, sloping down toward the sea. A beach, low clouds. I cross a wooden bridge connecting the shore to a ship. I don't see its features clearly. I cross a temporary bridge, not fixed in the ground. I cross a bridge . . .

Longing

That café has slipped away. Attached to the old hotel. A source of elegance and simplicity. I pass by it on my way from the hotel or heading back there. In the morning, it's open only to the hotel guests having their breakfast. Despite the narrowness of the place, it gives off light. The dominant color is ruby red. The bar counter is wide and curving. On each table lie small jars of jam and honey, tiny blocks of butter in metallic wrappers, a little bowl with cubes of white and brown sugar and small packets of sweetener. In the afternoon, I pass by: it's open for lunch. The menu selections are limited but expertly done. During the time I spend there—either going to an appointment or coming back to the hotel to get some rest—I always long to sit, to look through the glass facade, to have lunch on my own, so that I would get the chance to see those passing by and the building opposite that has came down to us from the eighteenth century, to contemplate the features of the people sitting around me, whom I don't know but with whom I share the space. Every day I tell myself: I'll stop by tomorrow. I must have lunch here tomorrow. Specifically lunch—not tea or coffee or a beer in the afternoon. There's something joyful that stirs up feelings of familiarity and the desire to stay a while. When I stop by early the next morning, I look at it, at the facade. One of the guests is having breakfast, reading the newspaper. I'm on my way to the airport. As I anticipated, my days had become busy, the opportunity was lost. I don't have the place to myself. I tell myself, next time the first thing I will do is seek out this particular café, making sure I'm alone, with the place to myself. What I fear is there will not be a next time.

Someone I don't know

I attend funerals and weddings in which I have no connection to the families they're for.

In Upper Egypt, in a village located between Luxor and Qus, I seek out a friend of mine. After sitting with him, as the sun sets fully, he tells me that his house is my house and asks me to wait for him to return from an appointment he has to keep: someone distantly related to him has passed away after suffering from an illness. I'm shy of staying alone in his house. It's true that he's on his own, but I'm not accustomed to it. So I go with him to pay my respects to someone I've never met and whose relatives I don't know. We arrive at the *mandara*, the place designated to receive guests and strangers.

Every family that has the means has a *mandara* or, as some call it, the *madyafa*, or guestroom. In the old days, a stranger would stay for three days, during which he would be served food and drink. On the morning of the third day, after breakfast, he would be asked who he was, his destination, and the country he was from. I remember Moroccans who crossed the desert on foot on their way to Mecca. One of them would suddenly appear in the village, carrying a small skin-flask of water and wearing a burnoose, perhaps holding a manuscript through which he would tell fortunes. The cries of some of them come back to me repeatedly—not just in Upper Egypt but also in Gamaliya: "I open the pages of your future."

A spacious *mandara*, lit with dim lamps. In the dimness, features intermingle and shadows grow deeper. I shake hands with the men. Woolen *gallabiya*s with wide sleeves, turbans, and more turbans. For me, nighttime and the remoteness of the place lend the people dimensions that are impossible to categorize or determine. I sit silently with the silent ones. A man of stature, advanced in age, makes the rounds, greeting everyone.

"Thank you for coming."

Those who enter don't shake hands: each of them contents himself with raising his hand to everyone, in greeting, and proceeds to stand in a free spot, in his turn, to greet the newcomers. Their movements and their shadows appear before me still. I don't ask my friend about the departed. Until this moment, I've been thinking of him as a man—why not a woman?

This is one of the funerals I've attended without knowing the departed or their relatives. If I went into detail about each of them, it would be too

183

much—but I'll describe what happened in Istanbul, when I attended a wedding where I didn't know anyone.

I'm on my way to Moscow when the plane is grounded in Istanbul, necessitating an overnight stay in a hotel close to the airport. After checking into my room, I go out for a walk around the hotel. I can see a mosque in the Ottoman style, from which arise two minarets. I'm scared to get too far away; it's a place I don't know, one of those hotels built for emergency situations, customers in transit. I've known many like it during my travels. I follow some men and women, dressed in all their finery. They're entering a large hall, with wide, round tables. At the front are the bride and groom. A small stage on which a band is lined up—the qanun, the oud, the *tambour*, the flute player. I'm delighted; it's the first time I'm seeing and hearing a Turkish band in its native land. My passion for it is deep rooted and well known among my family and friends.

I stand outside the hall, looking at the stage. The music begins as a prelude to the woman singer's appearance. That I was moved and affected must have been obvious in my features. A man approaches me, wearing a black suit and white shirt, neatly attired. He invites me to come in. I nod in thanks, but he insists, leading me to a table close to the stage. I greet the seated people and sit in the empty seat. When the waiter comes to turn over the plates, I nod to him in thanks. I reassure the one who invited me, when he comes over, that I've already had my supper. The singer begins, brimming with vitality. Melodies that I know, lyrics the meanings of which I guess. When she leaves the stage, she approaches from one side or the other, at which point the people who are seated greet her with spontaneous, enthusiastic applause. She approaches me twice and I clap for her for a long time. She singles me out with her eyes. At a particular point during the evening the guests start to leave, shaking hands with the groom, kissing the bride. In this way, I find myself facing her. I kiss someone whose name I don't even know. My sense of smell is permeated with cosmetics, my sense of touch with the smoothness of well-groomed skin.

I'd encountered something similar in Toledo, Spain—a bride of stunning beauty preparing to enter the church, holding a bouquet of flowers, leaning on the arm of her groom. The two of them standing to take some photos—every passerby approaching them, shaking hands, and kissing. I approach the newlyweds in Istanbul, and as I did that night in Toledo, I shake hands and kiss and congratulate people I do not know.

Antique

Sicily, on a trip for which the reasons or motives are no longer clear. Each step scheduled, planned with care, a detailed program. Beautiful young women in gray reminding me of girls' secondary school uniforms in the sixties—elegant, welcoming, reserved, attending to their tasks precisely as required.

One of them leads us to a period building, preserved with care—sweeping windows, rooms, halls, large spaces with elegant furniture, curtains that screen and filter the light, oil paintings, carpets with Oriental inscriptions, interlaced geometric patterns of Turkish design, bedcovers of Florentine weave. I know the crooks and whorls of those patterns.

Who used to live here? I don't know; I don't remember. Perhaps the young escort said something which now escapes me. Where is the building located?

It's impossible for me to pin down, despite how the light appears to me, and that enigmatic, hidden component which defies perception, which embodies antiquity. I recall the apartment of a foreign woman, who was unknown to me, whom I didn't know and never saw. I was able to enter her home one day after she passed away—to see her unmade bed, containing the traces and secrets of her final moments. My friend, whom I'd accompanied, was charged with making the inventory. She had no inheritors, so the state intervened, as represented by that department with its unique specialty of inheriting from people without heirs. In that apartment, and in other places, I sensed that enigma, closer to conjecture than understanding or full realization. It's not limited to such closed, confined places but is also there in paths, corners, and passages. Where is the distinction between a corner in Old Cairo and another in Mohandiseen or Maadi? In Istanbul, around Topkapi Palace or the modern area on the Asian side? In the Latin Quarter and the La Dèfense district in Paris? Where, to be precise? Why does the antique appear so? From where does it derive its antiqueness? Why did I experience this certainty—in that Sicilian apartment—that I was in a different time from the one in which I live and which is within me?

Honor

After we ate lunch in the fertile green farm—under the shadows of aged trees, near canals in which the water flowed, seeking out the whorls of the land—the head of the host organization approached me and said he was inviting me to shake hands with the lady who owned the farm. This was the custom when guests came—for a representative of the guests to be invited to enter the house and shake her hand. He smiled, saying, "There's another reason. The lady lived in Egypt in her childhood. She was the daughter of an important official in the Suez Canal Commission before it was nationalized." He said that she lived alone in the house and was served by Martin, who'd prepared the lunch himself.

I said, "The onion tart was wonderful, as was the red wine."

He said that the wine was local.

We entered the double doors—a wrought-iron door, the inner door made of the wood of ancient trees uprooted many years ago, then polished and trimmed. The hall was heavy with shadows. Over there, beside the door leading to a balcony overlooking the other side of the farm, the lady was sitting in a bamboo chair with a raised cushion. Her dress was loose, narrow at the waist, with a lace bodice and long gloves up to the elbows. Her right hand was bare, holding the glove in her left in preparation to shake hands. From the position of her head and the way her eyes stared off in one direction, I immediately realized that she could not see.

He bent down to her left ear, shouting my name in a voice resembling a shriek. She didn't seem to react; her hand didn't change its position, she didn't extend it. She showed no reaction. I initiated the handshake. The reality was she didn't shake my hand—rather, I took her hand in mine, then I retreated. Her lips were pursed. I imagined that this was a result of her head being turned in one direction. The man continued to shriek in a French I couldn't understand. He bowed deeply, kissed her hand, and turned around with an almost military gait. He pointed to the door, holding my elbow.

"Go right ahead, please. Your name will be recorded in the special register for madame's guests . . . "

An attempt

It's him—trying to stop a taxi, waving his hand, bending down to speak to the driver. The car pulls away without him. He steps back, looking for another. His general frame is still the same, although he no longer fills it. His bearing is suggestive of his old age. He seems determined, looking ahead, despite his thinness and his stoop and the plastic brace around his neck, which restricts his ability to look around.

I met him during the first days of my detention, with his confident stride and his quiet expression in the face of my fear of the unknown. As for him, it was as if he'd moved from one home to another that was just as familiar to him. He would arrange his belongings on top of his *bursh*— the thin mattress placed directly on the floor—holding his yellow towel striped with black, like prison bars. Laughing, he would say that it was very suitable, as if he were a longtime resident, as if he were to spend the rest of his life there. He overcame my introversion, coming closer to me and saying that the most important thing for me was to make sure that I left in good health, without any illness that would stay with me for the rest of my life, to learn to form a bond with things: with this cup, with that wall, with time—with the imprisoning emptiness, if need be.

By chance, I came across him again in Beirut; I knew he'd been in the Palestinian resistance. He'd joined them after 1967. He was decisive, firm, and determined, and he knew his way. I came to Beirut in 1980: the civil war was at its height, every movement was calculated. I took a shared taxi from a point near Corniche Mazraa, sitting in an empty seat beside the driver. As soon as I settled in my seat, after closing the door, I was overcome by a feeling that someone was looking at me, enfolding me in their gaze. I turned around and was startled to see him. He was looking at me, smiling—cautiously warning me. I understood. I shouted, "Hello!" I didn't mention his name, neither the real one that I knew nor the *nom de guerre* by which he was known. I accompanied him to his modest apartment in West Beirut. His movements were just as I remembered from the difficult times.

He doesn't know who has been watching him or has observed the many things he has been through, and they in him—until this moment, when I see him trying to stop a taxi on the street opposite the British Embassy in Garden City, leading to Tahrir Square . . .

Speech
Basically there's nothing silent in the universe, everything in it speaks, expectantly!

—⚏—

I'm fully aware that I won't read all the books I want to read, all the ones I've bought. Despite this, I keep buying new ones or tracking down rare ones. And spending what I have on them. Why, when I'm sure that I will leave them, and they will leave me?

—ᗰ—

In ancient positions of rest, the deceased was laid out with his feet touching his chest. Why was he placed in the position of the fetus in the womb?

—ᗰ—

Is there a place that holds the departed?

Will there come a time when we can determine a precise location where those who preceded us reside? In which it will be possible to train our faces toward it, to reach it, so that we meet, and reminisce?

A dream

I'm lying in a locked room, completely naked. My eyes are fixed on what's above, my father lying beside me, also naked. This is what I think—joy at being close to him, sadness because I don't speak to him and he doesn't speak to me. Each of us looking at a point that doesn't intersect with the other. Each of us alone, completely isolated.

A dream

My mother is standing somewhere, I can't see where. Some place with no features, whether it's on the earth, or in space, or underground. A faint light is shining, cold and strange. She's wearing a dress I haven't seen before. I approach her, eager to enjoy her company, but as I get closer, her wailing rises up and her whimpering deepens, crying passionately, for my sake. Why, since I was granted the chance to be close to her? I hadn't seen her since she departed forever. What's happening?

"Why are you crying, mother, just as I'm coming to you?"

She shivers. I see her tears, pouring, overflowing.

"Mother . . . I'm staying with you. I won't leave you. Why the tears . . . why?"

Those books

I'm sure—sure that I won't read these books, that I won't recall what I want to read once again. I'm conscious of the lack of time, the lack of space. Why do I hold on to them then? Why keep them close to me? Why allow them to fill the space? Why do I get agitated and feel threatened if I find that an author I've been keeping for a while has disappeared?

What I know is that these books are an extension of me. Every morning I look at them during the brief moments I stand in front of the laden shelves. I hold the ones closest to me, I brush off the specks of dust. I turn the pages, recalling the first time I looked. Sometimes I bring a book with me, placing it close to my pillow. It spends the night near me. In the morning, I return it to its place on the shelf. Of course, the meaning is not in the paper or the print but in those realms and characters I got to know, in the expressive texts. I know that those books are simply my existence—my frame, from which I look out, and my core.

I worry about where they will end up. Within my son's hearing I once said I would leave them to a library. He became upset, saying that the books would end up with him, that he would take good care of them. I told him that I really didn't want to leave them with a burden: most of the texts are from the Arabic heritage and have nothing to do with his or his sister's interests. He looked at me sharply and said, "It's enough that your breaths lie within them."

Spinning

Just before the end of the day, Galaa army camp, with my colleague the photographer. We're walking toward an English-style, one-story building. A soldier holding his key, numerous beautiful houses, all of them empty. It was the headquarters for the English forces until 1954, when the evacuation took place. The army camp became empty after 1967, as it was within the range of fire of the enemy who would hoist their flags on the eastern bank. Mutual bombardments, raids by the special forces, the air force. The commander of the second division said that sometimes shells would fall on the buildings, but the bombardment wasn't targeting them. It was known that the camp was empty; there were no troops there. I decide, with my colleague, to spend the night in one of the buildings. As he inserts the key, the soldier says, "This building has not been opened since June 1967. It was designated to house someone of high rank." During the night hours, I think of the sudden shelling—without warning, the direct injuries. Soldiers and officers say that when a shell falls it has someone's name on it—the name of the victim.

We enter a spacious hall. The smell of a stuffy place; it has not been aired for a while. We open the windows, leaving the shutters closed—it's better to keep it dark. Any light could be detected. My colleague, who entered the inside room before me, says, "Come here . . . look."

A fan in the ceiling, spinning with a faint noise.

"It was going around when I came in."

Astonished, the soldier says, "It might have been turning ever since the place was closed up."

Then he adds, "No one has entered except you two."

A boy

My friend, the director of the presses, told me that he had a skilled worker named Rida who fell as he was climbing a ladder. Everyone gathered around him and found that the fall had killed him. There was no sign of life. Rida had married many times in order to have children, without success. He died heartbroken, without a son of his own. As his funeral was setting out from Sidi Ahmad Abu Hurayba Mosque, a woman approached, carrying an infant who'd just died. She was coming from the hospital, holding him to her chest, not knowing what to do. Her husband had gone abroad, and her family was far away in Upper Egypt. She said, "Take him with you! Bury him out of charity with this decent man." My friend said they lowered the two of them into the grave together, and the infant lies next to Rida now.

A visit

On the morning of my birthday, I head to my parents' final resting place. It isn't a visiting day. The living visit the departed on Fridays and on special occasions: the middle of Shaaban, the beginning of Rajab, holidays. I want some solitude, to sit close to them, to talk to them in silence. I don't need to speak; I communicate with thoughts.

When Abdo, the gravedigger, sees me, he hurries to bring me a chair. Over the years, he's grown accustomed to leaving me alone. Today, he doesn't leave. He looks hesitant, confused, asking me if I know anyone in the Hospital for Pulmonary Diseases in Abbasiya. He has tuberculosis, which he caught from the dust caused by digging graves. He's spent many years here, but the big bosses only have time for someone who is healthy and able. Before he leaves, the boss appears and looks at him quizzically. "You didn't tell me that the gentleman was visiting." Abdo looks bewildered. The boss says, "May you live and remember."

The boss then asks if I know any official in the governorate. He points to the northern side, saying that the owner of the neighboring plot is an influential official. The man has decided to build a high wall that would block the window, he says, pointing to the window in the middle of the northern wall. He says it will block the air coming into the plot. The official is threatening everyone with his influence, and he will not be stopped except by a governorate official. The boss asks, "You wouldn't be pleased, of course, if the air was blocked and denied to the departed?"

A retreat

A mineral-water lake—olive green in color, a thick consistency, bordered by wooden platforms, posts supporting balconies. Hands clinging to the edge. The body must be immersed for specified periods of time. Around the lake are the buildings: the hospitality rooms, a reception area—seats, tables, faces of various nationalities.

The lake is outside Budapest. A road ascends, almost mountainous, leading to it. I'm here to visit an officer from southern Yemen, sent for treatment.

Who is he?

I don't know anymore.

What's his name, what does he look like, why did I come to this place to visit him?

Not a sign, no indication—I don't know a thing. I can't find an explanation for that visit. I can't pin down a precise date, although it could only be one of two: I visited Hungary twice, the first time in 1979 and the second in 1983. Which was it? I don't know.

I stare and see only the brown color of the wood—dark brown. I breathe in the piercing, sulfurous smell of the water, as if immersing my whole body in it, now, right now, at this moment. But why I was there and who I visited—this I don't know.

Loneliness

The main room of my friend's home in Paris. I'm sitting facing a beautiful young woman, the wife of an avant-garde playwright. Her eyes are wide, staring at me, even as I write this. Do glimpses remain even after they're over? Perhaps the eyes, and what they communicate, are the last to vanish—just as sounds are the first to be obliterated, utterly impossible to recall.

The fronts of her knees are round, full. I present her with a letter her husband has sent with me. She puts it in her handbag without reading it. She asks me how he's doing. I say I'm not close to him, but I see that he's doing well—his performances are well received.

"Didn't he talk to you about me?" she asks.

I try to find something to reassure her. I say some broad, generic things. She looks at me. How piercing her eyes seem. I avoid eye contact with her. I try not to see the female in her despite the tenderness, the fullness of her knees and the enticing position she takes when she moves away, leaning back in the seat. A message appears in her eyes. I try to avoid it. Her association with someone I know prevents even the thought. She takes her time speaking, saying in clear English, "Can you give him a message of two words?"

"Of course . . . of course . . . "

"Tell him that I'm lonely . . . very lonely . . . "

Then, after a moment's silence, she says, "He never calls me, he doesn't write, he doesn't ask about his daughter."

Then, sharply, she says, "Tell him that I'm alone, utterly alone . . . "

Reveille

Three female students—an Iranian, a Syrian, and a German. They arranged to host me in the house where they lived, during my visit to the University of Bonn. They were friendly and caring, making sure I was comfortable. They lived in an old house, in an apartment with high ceilings. One of them gave up her spacious room: there was nothing in it but a table, the surface of which she cleared of books, and an old cupboard, the contents of which I didn't know. As for the bed, it was a luxurious mattress in the corner facing the door, with a pillow and a cover.

There are very few times that I've slept deeply and woken up feeling sufficiently rested. Few and rare enough to the point that after all these years I can't recall them—among them, my days in the training institute located at the end of the street perpendicular to the sea in Sidi Bishr, in Alexandria. That was at the beginning of the sixties. Despite the passage of some forty years, I can hardly remember that time without being overcome by the comfort which came from the rest and deep sleep that I knew in those vanished days, as if recalling rest induces it, even at the height of my disturbed sleep. That is to say, since my school days I've never managed to get enough sleep. My life has always been split in two: daytime for study or work and the night for my own pursuits, for what concerns me—reading, writing. This has become all the more true as I've grown older and my preoccupations have increased. This would take too long to explain, but what I've noticed is that my sleep intervals have grown shorter over the past twenty years, so that it's possible to say that I've never slept for more than two consecutive hours.

That afternoon I made an exception. I curled up in bed and went to sleep. I sank into a fine, soothing slumber from which I awoke only by the delicate insistence of the young Iranian. She bent down, touching my shoulder, saying—kindly and respectfully—that the time of my lecture was close and that we had to leave now.

I looked at her, trying to take it in. I made sure to smile, not showing any irritation, so that I didn't trouble her. They observed everything I might do with interest, mindful to fulfill any request. However, I couldn't rid myself of the feeling of a sleep interrupted—deep sleep that I haven't known since I was a breastfeeding child, that quick, fine light that pushes the inner self to distant depths I never reach. How would it have been if I'd awoken without her touch, her timid call? Despite the passage of nearly twenty years since that night, I can't recall my forced waking without two things recurring to me: the first is the exhaustion that overcame me, and the other is the regret prompted by sleep I hadn't experienced before, or after . . .

Vanilla

Vanilla, O vanilla . . .

When I taste it, what's within me flowers and reaches distant horizons. I cling to the echoes of the aroma and try to follow its traces within me as well, to a space in a bygone time, which leads me to my childhood alley, framed by a sorrowful melody, repeated through silence.

Hagg Nassif's bakery, in the very middle of the alley. The space was redolent with vanilla. No Eid cookie or pastry was without it. I didn't know at the time that the wafts of it would grow, settle, and persist as I searched for it whenever I missed it. I would wait in front of the bakery, with the youngsters at night, in order to get the empty baking trays. There was heavy demand and they were few—those black, rectangular trays that would stay propped up the whole year long, until the final days of Ramadan when demand for them increased. No matter how long we waited, it was one of the joys of the time for making the cookies. Breathing in the wafts of vanilla added a tenderness and a sweetness to our waiting. It was the most powerful moment—nothing equaled it except the arrival of the baking trays, covered with freshly baked cookies. When Owais the baker entered the narrow room, lifted them down, and settled them in place, I would breathe in their aroma. My mother would start arranging the cookies slowly, carefully; she mastered making them in Cairo, as she did the Ramadan *kunafa*. I never tasted anything like the ones she made, no matter how many I tried later. It would take too long to elaborate.

But I'm concerned with vanilla right now. In Dokki, the first place I practiced my profession, by the Galaa Bridge. In 1962. The neighborhood was quiet, the acacia and casuarina trees lining the surrounding streets promised mysterious joys. The back road leads to Vini Square. To this day, I don't know the significance of the name, whether Vini was a man or a woman. It's still there. Although the traffic was at its heaviest, my walk back from there was one of the joys of my day. Perhaps one reason I liked it was because the name was similar to "vanilla." But also because of the smell of vanilla that hung over the road. A European bakery: as I came alongside it, I would slow my footsteps, my soul inundated with its aroma—powerful, lingering, permanent. I would glide through it, never entering the bakery. I never bought anything there, yet I hold on to the scent as a distinguishing feature.

In a building overlooking this road, on the floor opposite my office, two window shutters opened at precisely eleven fifteen. For some reason, I turned around when I heard them crash against the wall. I was startled to see a dazzling woman—totally nude, with full breasts and dark eyes. I could see as far as just below her navel; the rest was hidden by the wall. It was only a split second before she closed the shutters. Every day afterward, during my time in that office—for four years and some months—I would anticipate her appearance, that revelation. It never happened, until I began to doubt myself—had it really happened, or had I imagined it? Was it a mysterious apparition? For some reason, I associated the woman and her nakedness with vanilla, perhaps due to its wafting from below at the moment of her appearance. If the scent had a color, I would say it was precisely the color of her skin—white, tinged with yellow.

The ice-cream cart showed up in the alley in the afternoon, long enough after lunch, when many people go out for a breath of fresh air. The vanilla cookie was rectangular or rounded at the edges. Various colors: yellow, bright red. Eaten with ice cream. There were cones full of it. I licked it with pleasure, taking my time, speeding up the instant I'd devoured the vanilla cookie—melting quickly, the spreading of its delicate flavor, its remnants lingering. For many years, I didn't taste it—I stopped standing in front of the ice-cream cart. During one of my trips to Paris, a friend who was living there invited me to an old restaurant. He said it specialized in traditional southern cuisine. When dessert was about to be served, he said he would choose for me: their specialty, which the restaurant was expert in preparing. I was surprised when it was served with round vanilla cookies—smaller than those I used to devour with ice cream in the alley, but the taste was close. When my friend noticed me taking my time, my lapsing into silence, he asked if I hadn't liked the special dish. I smiled. I told him about the vanilla. He told me he would take me to a restaurant café that served only vanilla products and natural vanilla pods, which I'd tasted mainly in the alley. Vanilla is a plant that only grows in particular places in the world, like Mexico and Indonesia. As demand for it grew, its price rose and an artificial flavor was created; of course, it was different. My friend said the restaurant café was very near the hotel where I was staying in the Latin Quarter.

I took my time getting there—to the alley of my childhood, to the times of vanilla. I stopped in front of the shop window. The plants were displayed in different configurations: dry, circular pods—brown in color, closer in appearance to carob. The carob has its own special quality—if I start describing it, I'll never stop. Jute sacks with small, black seeds, some from the Comoros Islands, others from Madagascar, or Mexico. I entered the place—a small room with adjoining tables. On the walls were pictures of vanilla trees in Tahiti, with creeping plants clinging to the trees. Everything the restaurant café served had to do with vanilla: different kinds of tea, desserts, dishes of food that were served from eleven thirty until two thirty in the afternoon. On small shelves were vanilla products, ground seeds, small bottles of extract. As for the young woman who worked there, she too was connected to the lands of vanilla: her complexion was dark, blending together the redness of dusk, the approach of night "and all that it enshroudeth" (Qur'an 84:17). Her smile was a brightness, an incomparable optimism, as if she were formed from the bouquet of vanilla within me, wafting from the bakery, from the ice-cream cart, from the street leading to Vini Square.

That precise street, with which so many things were connected—the trees were deep rooted and towering, the light of ten o'clock in the morning, that flowing tranquility. A kind of elegance, its source unknown, the smell of vanilla that added a hidden dimension as if linking the street to the distant horizon—to what I knew of vanilla breezes, to my soul's breeze—coming out of that small, faraway restaurant.

—⁂—

Why do aches grow more intense at night?

Remnants

When her movements grew heavier, and her remaining alone began to worry the children because of the risk, she yielded to her oldest daughter's pressure. She began to give away her possessions: her middle son took the chairs and sofa from the living room, the youngest moved the china set and carpets to his house. She dismantled the bed and the cupboard and asked that the bedroom furniture be kept in its room, that something had to stay behind in the house. She didn't mention that she wouldn't allow anyone to sleep in her late husband's place.

I say hello; she seems shy. She moves cautiously, as if she wants to hide. I realize that it's difficult for her to leave her house, her home, so I show her a warm affection, to dispel the feeling of estrangement. She has brought only a few items with her—a necklace of pearls adorned with diamonds that she inherited from her mother, two antique fans made of ostrich feathers, her clothes, and a large number of photos. The color of some of them has turned to brown from age. She kept them close to her.

A Hungarian

A room for listening to music in Haram, in Giza. A dance troupe from one of the Balkan nations. Three female singers wearing traditional dress. One of them is slim, her mouth a delicate flourish. She sings. It's the strongest and deepest of voices, as if it will not stop—starting, never to end. I imagine that her eyes meet mine. I'm only a listener in the hall, in a country foreign to her. She sings in a language I don't know. I don't understand its vocabulary, but I get a sense of the general meaning. This is how I am with songs, when I don't understand the words because I don't know the language.

She doesn't know me. I don't know her. But I know her voice—she sings and I listen.

She evokes unconscious images and mysteries in me. She may go back to her country tomorrow or the day after, and I will remain here. She may go before I do, and I may go before her. She is there and I am here, I am there and she is here . . .

Names

The professor—the one who has organized the conference and arranged its activities—tells me that he will show me something that none of the other guests will see. He and the other members of the department are proud of my visit to Lady Margaret Hall, at Oxford, which is hosting the sessions.

Silently, he precedes me down the corridors where I walk each day when I leave the hall of residence on my way to the meeting rooms. I catch sight of the tables in the cafeteria that serves breakfast. We pass by, turning onto a long, shaded path. We enter a darker passage. He stops by the middle of a wall, pulling back a light curtain. He takes his hat off, holding it in both hands. I'm not wearing a hat or anything on my head. I stand, watching. I'm unhurried in my movements—I don't ask, waiting for him to explain. I don't want to commit some blunder or do anything that might be misunderstood, especially since he has told me how significant the place is, the most sacred part of the college after the chapel.

I grow accustomed to the dark. I can make out names written in an organized way, precisely arranged. After looking closely, I can see that every name is accompanied by the dates of birth and death in parentheses, with a gap before inscriptions such as "In loving memory," "For the good life," "For boundless giving."

I try to memorize some of the names. It occurs to me to take out the little notebook in which I write down observations, but I'm prevented from doing so by his raptness. Once again, I fear committing some blunder. The professor shakes his head and gestures to me with his hand to walk in front of him. He draws the curtain. When we reach the familiar passages, he says that the names I'd seen were of the greatest professors the college had known over the centuries since it was founded. It's one of its most deeply rooted and greatest traditions. I nod, showing that I'm moved, wondering what the names mean to someone who doesn't know the course of their owners' lives or what they did. Is it enough to say the name in order to breathe life into the unknown, to restore something that once was, or to evoke the essence of a meaning I didn't know?

—⁂—

If I was able to trace the languages that my ancestors spoke, how many would I encounter? How many accents? How many consisting of mutterings and signs? How much would I know of their etymologies, their meanings, and their opposites? How many silences would I not grasp?

Ago

Right now, here. A second ago, there . . . For an hour, I've been following the red band of news running across the bottom of the television screen, as the speaker asks about the situation of Muslims in the United States after the latest regulations in 2004. The Mahdi Army is pulling out of Najaf, the destruction of ten houses in Rafah, preparations for the G8 Summit, the threat level is still yellow, yet there are possibilities it will be raised to orange.

Twenty-four hours ago, I entered the café. I caught sight of a good man sitting on his own. I nodded in greeting, although I wanted to be alone. If the doctor treating me knew that I'd started smoking again, he would have exploded: "This is suicide!" Once a week. What I went through last year had been tough. And yet . . . this didn't justify resuming a deadly habit. The waiter asked me, "Something to drink?" I said tea, no sugar.

A month ago, I was sitting in Opera Square in Munich, taking my time drinking a frosty beer. I watched the bicycle paths. They appeared from behind the cathedral with its two high towers: men and women surged forward, bent over different styles of handlebars. Their number increased, then diminished, bit by bit. Their movements resembled soaring flocks of birds before sunset—heading in one direction, unswerving.

A year ago. Where? Where? I won't check in any paper: perhaps I was in Luxor, stretched out in the large room in the house I used to stay in, near the Valley of the Queens. Looking at the ceiling made of palm fronds, wondering: can scorpions slip through?

Ten years ago? I don't know. I can't determine—the sights are intertwined, the remnants intermingled. Twenty years ago, thirty, forty, fifty, sixty—I don't know for sure. I stare at length, yet I see only shadows of someone else. Now here, now there. What links me to myself?

Soup

A house surrounded by a garden. A small village in the south of France. Annette, the cultural director of the city of Agde, is accompanying me. The owner of the house is a friend of hers, a pharmacist. He lives with his wife. They don't have any children. They welcome me. I look at the room I never expected to come to and to which I won't return in all likelihood. I'm preoccupied by those places that hold me by chance, that I won't return to. I never knew I would come to that place close to the sea. What catches my eye in the library are the art books, especially two: the first about the German Lajer and the second about the Swiss Balthus. I copy the name of the publisher and the address in my notebook. For a while, I look at a painting of a nude woman with a wound, dripping blood. Before we arrived, Annette had said that the man was a Jew who'd lost his parents under the Nazi regime. Throughout my travels in Europe, I've got used to meeting Jews. Religion doesn't concern me as much as a viewpoint. The man seems friendly, tending to silence. His wife looks young, with a lithe figure despite being advanced in years.

198

We gather around the table. The wife brings a silver, rectangular pot, covered. She says that she has cooked a soup of small crabs for us. The crabs appear for only two weeks a year, and only a small number are caught. She ordered them a few days ago. She lifts the cover and the marine aroma wafts upward, reminding me of the Egyptian coast—Port Said, to be precise. The small crabs lie, bite sized, in the soup; one can chew them, grind them up, and swallow them. I recall ones like them in Cyprus: they were fried in oil—scaly, their flavor alluring.

I take a sip of an exquisite white wine, following it with some soup. The taste flows slowly to the distant cells. As we leave, I'm seized by a coughing fit—sharp and dry. The weather is cold, and the stars are shining intensely. I'm transfixed by the constellation of Orion; the wine brought me close to it. The man—whose face and name I don't recall—is wearing only a shirt and a sleeveless vest. He insists on opening his pharmacy, which is normally closed at night. He gives me some syrup and pills, advising me that it's necessary to start by taking some of each. The cough is still in its beginning stages but to ignore it would be dangerous. I lose him as I say goodbye. I don't know his name or the name of the village. Even Annette—I've lost track of her.

Those traces

I don't know, and will never grasp, what drives those traces from their resting places and thrusts them to the center of my vision, my gaze. Isolated moments, incomplete phrases, vague, delicate smells that I can't grasp by sight or by touch. And yet they evoke eras and phases and perhaps lost times about which only speculation remains. A face may appear from afar, sending us a message from oblivion: long after we thought something had ended, disappeared—suddenly someone appears. I talk about him to friends, or I tell a story, a saga or tale to which he was linked. As for those moments that spread out suddenly—sometimes like showers of comets or renegade shooting stars—as if suspended, unmoving, disconnected from what comes before or after and from what's below the earth. All that is past is silent; it does not move when it's remembered. We recall a scene while those who appear in it do not move at all—they have no voices or fragrance. Scents have their own paths, each of them retrieving a past moment and its details. But a single detail will not bring back a scent. Only the visible and tangible moves; as for what has gone by, it appears only frozen, fixed, neither coming nor going, still, because it's united with nothingness.

Despite its absolute silence and its transformation, we do not cease in our attempts to retrieve it. Its nonexistence in the void signifies that we're still here. The fading of its fragments in our memory of it is a confirmation that we're present now, that we only have what we've experienced.

—◊—

A light—I see it in the heavens, emanating from a distance of a billion light years. Is its source still there? Or has it transformed into a black hole, devouring all that exists to the point that even light can't escape. Then . . . what light do I see?

Crossing

The officer at passport control—with quiet features, a compassionate face—asks me, "How long will you be in Cleveland?"

"I hope I won't be here more than a month!"

He looks at me, his humane gaze reaches me. I recall his tone.

"I know what you mean."

He repeats it twice, wishing me a pleasant stay, and a speedy recovery.

—◊—

Why are sighs of pleasure and groans of pain just the same?

O Lord

In the hospital's hotel rest house, Ali Sabri, previously the head of the Egyptian Arab Land Bank, who is seventy years old:

"Who will perform the operation?"

"Dr. Cosgrove . . . they say he's the expert in this type of double surgery: mitral valve repair and artery bypass."

He looks at me silently, then says, "Pray to God . . . "

I scream from deep within myself:

"O Lord . . . "

Alas

What's behind me seems more than what's to come; what I've left behind is more plentiful than what I approach. I repeat my desire, my impossible wish to be granted the opportunity to live again, to be born anew, but in different circumstances. I would come, supplied with those insights that I acquired in my first existence, which is almost reaching its end. I would be born knowing that flame burns, that water will drown someone who doesn't know how to swim, that this glance means friendliness and that one means warning, and that one is a sign of malevolence.

How much time did I spend in order to grasp the obvious, deciphering the alphabet? How many matters will pass me by without my grasping their inner meaning, without comprehending their specifics? I grasped what concerned others and didn't comprehend what had to do with me. "Alas for mankind!" (Qur'an 36:30).

—※—

Why do possibilities seem better when situations are worse?

Borders

I came close to those invisible borders that divide what we know from what we don't know, life from nothingness. This happened during the war, when colors reverted to their origins, characteristics became clear, hindsight grew stronger, approaching the essence. Of course, what a vast difference between a situation that a person chooses for himself—especially if it's linked to an entity larger than him, connected to his community, his people, his nation—and a situation he's not expecting, when he's thrust into a situation he has not chosen, coming from within, even though the essence of those borders remains linked, united. At which point I stare at that which is connected to me, around me, within me.

Numerous are those borders at which I stood—detained against my will in the face of enemy shelling, aerial bombardment—a heightened state of affairs, at their climax. But in all of this, I had the choice—I could decide, even with the blockade. As for the damage coming from within me, from my core, it's a different matter, on a different level. As I grow frail with the deterioration of my body, I arrive at the borders, but on a different path: visions have become sharper, moments more valuable, sensations more clear, impossible to conceal. Sight can almost discern a part of it . . .

Nostalgia

Stirrings of energy course through me. Despite some differences, it resembles the state in which I approached the front, the battle lines at wartime. A state of readiness, the senses on alert. Despite all the shades of melancholy that accompany my weariness, and my illness, I'm overcome by nostalgia— a brightness that distinguishes the presence of things from everything else around me, as if all existence had been freed of impurities.

Nostalgia comes with an awareness of approaching the crossroads, the significant moments. Nostalgia for places I've known, for people whose company I've enjoyed, those I've accompanied, who've offered me help, who've guided me. I showed them—and they showed me—deep affection. For foods I've tasted and which became reference points to which I later gravitated. For moments gone by, for texts I've read and to which I became attached; I've kept some of them close to where I slept. For moments of extreme lucidity.

Illness is not all misfortune: it locates us somewhere contrary to the ordinary and the familiar, so that if we lose what's ordinary and circumstances divide us, we're aware of how much time we've squandered, how we've failed to do justice to our loved ones, how much we've failed to comprehend all this beauty . . .

—m—

Why does death happen mostly at dawn?

My pulse

I turn to my left, to where my ear touches the pillow. I'm surprised by my heart, with its clear, distinct movement, its uninterrupted pace, its constant throbbing; within its continuity lies my existence. A mysterious fear and a strong curiosity overtake me, so I don't listen for long. I try to monitor the faint beating, where the damage appears. I turn the conversation to the one curled up within me who's facing a silence. I don't know when its time will come, despite his attachment to me—the core of my depths, the center of my being.

The beats follow in succession, eluding understanding and explanation. At times, I feel a different beat—why? There's no answer—just like determining the reason for the first beat. What force propels it? What preceded it?

Did the ancient Egyptians know its secret essence?

As the corpse was embalmed, they would empty the body of all its contents: the intestines, the stomach, even the brain. They left only one organ intact within. The heart. At the time of judgment, immediately after which

202

the eternal fate would be decided, the heart would be weighed. It would be placed in one pan of the scales and, in the other, the feather of Maat. The heart determines fate—it has an independent existence, its own nervous system. It's the one organ that doesn't rest, from the beginning of creation until a person departs this world.

The brain rests a bit during sleep, transmitting its contents—what troubles it—by means of dreams. All the limbs, the organs, operate at a lower capacity than the heart. It's called the heart—from the same Arabic root as the "fickle," the "changeable'—because it transforms from one beat to another, from one state to another. With that beat, it's not what it was before nor what it will be afterward. Sometimes I talk to it, though it's a part of me, myself. I tell it my secrets, although it's a part of me. I'm cautious with it, since I'm not able to push away that delicate entity that eludes the eye, which was penetrated that distant day in my childhood. Something of which I wasn't aware: I didn't find out it had happened until later, after many long years, when the doctor told me that it was affected by a fever long ago. I said I didn't remember; he said the symptoms are similar.

I listen to its beats, seeking forgiveness for burdening it with my longings, my desires and my sufferings, the implications of what I lived in the imaginary, going beyond the felt reality, my yearning for all that isn't within reach. It never let me down—it followed me and I obeyed it. It didn't harm me; I'm the one who caused it harm with my excesses and my joy, the harshness of my distresses, the weight of my silence, the intensity of my fear, how easily I was swayed by every breeze, the gleam of every light, and the trembling of any star—my quivering at every dispatch that reached me from the blue of the sea, from the breezes of basil and the emerging of flowers.

—∿—

What would be, if what was not actually was?

The surface of Mars

I'm delighted by what I've heard on the radio; the news puts me at ease. Scientists at the NASA observation center have succeeded in solving the problem of communicating with the computer that operates the rover and its systems, which has now settled on the surface of Mars. After it landed, it broke down. It took twenty-four hours to fix: commands and communications sent by humankind over the distance of millions of miles.

The broadcaster says the rover will be moving soon.

It's eleven o'clock here. I wonder what time it is there. Is it the same moment on Mars? Or does each planet have its own existence? I empathize with that rover as if it were flesh and blood, a person like me. I imagine it in its loneliness over there. I recall the images—that surface, tending to red, those rocky boulders. When were they formed? When did they settle into these shapes? Was it lava that solidified? Did it fall from distant space? This is its state now—until when will it remain? When will it change? What will be its fate?

Bird talk

Marrakesh.

Dar al-Basha Palace. A wooden bench in the garden. I'm sitting beside him—olive skinned, tall, his features straight. His *gallabiya* is Moroccan-style. He doesn't cover his head with the *silhab*, what we call a burnoose in Egypt. It hangs down his back. He's sitting facing three goldfinches, conversing with them, making sounds—short, prolonged, numerous tones. The birds look at him, he makes a sound, then the birds come closer. One of them flies up and lands on his shoulder. Another sound, then all of them fly away. At that point, he turns to me, saying, "It's the goldfinch. This is its time: it comes at this time."

When the first flocks begin arriving, he goes out in order to be the first they see in the city and its surrounding area, the space ending at the Atlas Mountains. He not only speaks the language but also knows some of the birds themselves, especially the leaders of the flocks. From them, he asks about certain matters and seeks explanations. Not just the goldfinch but other birds as well. I saw him in Aghmat, when we went together to visit the tomb of Muhammad Ibn Abbad al-Mutamid, and his wife and children. I was with my friend, a resident of Marrakesh, Si Jafar al-Kansousi. Two other people were with us; I remember what they looked like, but their names escape me. After we sought out Sheikh Mustafa Salitin in his retreat, and before the resting place of al-Mutamid, we turned off into open country with trees and grasses, flowers and birds. Our friend got out with a smile, gesturing to us to stay and not go with him. There were only about four meters between us. A group of starlings faced him. I couldn't count how many of them there were, since they didn't stay still but moved from one place to another. I also noticed how a number of them obeyed him and looked at him, and began to converse with him, at which point he returned and said, "All is well."

He was telling them how he was doing, and they him. Si Jafar told me that he talked to passing flocks and birds, not imagining that, one day, it would be possible for them to stop flying in order to alight on a person's hand. There was no bird whose language he didn't know, whether it was from Marrakesh or migrating to it or the Atlas mountains. He would ask and answer, advising of what was hidden if asked. Sometimes, he would treat them for aches and pains as only he knew how.

He appears before me wearing glasses with thick lenses. I don't know if he was wearing them on my first visit or if I'm mixing things up. What I'm sure of is that when he's with the birds, he wasn't wearing them or looking through them . . .

Mars

I go out to the small balcony that's connected to my office and my bedroom.

Here is Mars—gleaming, round, almost the size of a tennis ball, or slightly larger. Shining, illuminated, even though it's a planet and not a star. But the light of the sun is reflected from it, just as it is from the silent, cold, and lifeless moon. It's a good intermediary for the light that emanates from the deep remoteness of the sun.

Here it is before me, facing me, taking approximately the course of the sun and the moon itself, from the east to the west. After a month, it will disappear from sight but will remain suspended in its orbit. We think of it as stationary, but it's retreating, moving rapidly away from Earth, hundreds of kilometers per second. If some creature were to look at Earth tonight from out there, how would we appear? What I know is that our planet would appear twice the size of that luminous globe, and if the creature were provided with a telescope like the one I looked through that night, it would see a blue planet, its deep color wrapped in white clouds. When we photographed Earth from afar, with its deep color and its clouds, it seemed the most beautiful, the most intensely pure. When my friend the astronomer invited me that night, at about ten o'clock, to look through the telescope for the first time, I saw multiple hues of red, a cap of white ice crowning the circle, with scattered white spots. I saw in it the shape of a loaf of *baladi* bread, perfectly round. Here it is before me. If I had a telescope now, I would investigate and inspect it, but I content myself with looking at it, drawn to it. Today, in the morning, it approached the closest point in its orbit around the earth, a point it reaches only once every sixty thousand years. That is to say, all the features I see now will not be there next time. I don't know where my fragments will settle. Will our planet still be in its orbit? I can only ponder, yet I stare, trying to absorb all that these moments bring me.

Wednesday night, the twenty-eighth of August, the third year of the third millennium since the birth of Christ. For the next two weeks, this glow will continue, this continuous, circular light. For years, stars have been disappearing from our city's sky due to the intensity of the light emanating from it, which obscures the stars, the celestial bodies, the meteorites, and the comets. For this reason, its presence is close and powerful. I probe it for as long as this rare opportunity lasts.

Today, at exactly twelve fifty-one our time, Mars and Earth came as close to each other as possible. The last time they were as close as this was in 57,617 BC, when Mars reached a point 55,720,000 kilometers away; the same distance separates them today—at twelve fifty-one, Wednesday afternoon. Several times, as I look up, I repeat the time. It was a moment of sunshine in our abode; the stars couldn't be seen due to the earth's position at the time. The closest point to Mars would be in the southern hemisphere, in the Pacific Ocean, in Tahiti and the desolate Australian desert. There, Mars was intensely clear and bright: when there's no pollution, its reflected light appears to be red.

Earth is in orbit, Mars is in orbit: sometimes they come close to each other. The proximity recurs every fifteen Earth years. A second level of proximity occurs every 284 years. But what happened today only occurs approximately every sixty thousand years. I don't know my location as I look out from the balcony, just as I don't know my ancestors who perhaps looked out from their caves at the sky, whether one of them understood this exceptional appearance as I see it right now. I wonder . . . what crossed their minds? Were they afraid? Did they chant any spells, or were they satisfied with enigmatic mutterings? Did they perform certain rituals?

What space does my vision transcend now, in order to see the planet?

What dangers am I witnessing?

Cosmic rays, the asteroid belt, meteors—the remnants of the original chaos, a chaos governed by an eternal, universal law. Would a disaster be more likely with such a short distance?

The usual distance is about 78 million kilometers; at the closest point, it reaches approximately 55 million kilometers.

I asked my friend about the speed of both. He said that Mars is now moving away at a speed of twenty-four kilometers per second. The Earth moves at a speed of sixty kilometers per second. If we know that a bullet travels at approximately seventy-seven meters per second, we can imagine the speed at which each of them swims in that oval orbit. The orbits of all celestial bodies are oval. Galaxies are oval. Is the egg a symbol of the universe?

I'm influenced by my belonging to the human race. What does the proximity of Mars to other entities signify? I pause and call to mind those dogs that run and bark before an earthquake—is it not possible that these planets have a language? Perhaps a conversation takes place between the red, the blue, the yellow and the furthest celestial bodies in the sky. Why not? Will humankind master this language? Why not? Did I not see the man with the telescope in Marrakesh speaking to the starling, seeking answers from the goldfinch, asking the turtledove to leave, then calling it back, and listening to scores of secrets that the nightingale tells him? If I'd never seen him or listened to him while in the company of friends, I would never have believed it. Why do I deny the possibility of such a conversation in some language, of a vocabulary between the celestial bodies?

Time passes while I'm transfixed, looking at the sky. If there's someone out there, he must be in the exact same position as me. I'm looking out as he's looking out, but each of us is staring at the other. After sixty thousand years, I'll be merely the potential of my existence on earth now. I gaze at those human beings who will exist in the time to come: will there be anyone related to me among them? Will he know anything about me? Or will he be utterly ignorant of me, just as I'm ignorant of those who looked out like me, on a night like this sixty thousand years ago, whether they noticed, whether they realized . . .

Sunrise of sunrises
It's Baona in the Coptic calendar—the month of June. The peak of the heat. I used to travel south, perhaps because of the associations with returning to Juhayna during the summer vacation. Now I've come to Gurna. I wake up intending to go out, to have a walk before the heat becomes intense, before having breakfast.

The orb doesn't appear far away—several stages will occur before it burns, which will also accompany its setting. Just like the stages of ancient Egyptian architecture—as well as in their narratives, in drawings, in sacred books. I carry a thin stick, just as my father used to when he traveled between the small villages, in order to drive away the dogs in the road. Here, I'm afraid of dogs and scorpions. I breathe in the odor of the earth, the palms, and the old sycamore fig trees. I turn my head toward the east. The road ends at the river. I enjoy the view of the vivid green of the fertile plants that stretch around the two statues of Amenhotep III. They've been known as the statues of Memnon ever since their restoration during the Roman era. In ancient times, before their restoration, they used to emit melancholic melodies between dawn and the rise of the sun's orb.

I lengthen my stride. Suddenly, I stop. The entire open space is concentrated on that crescent—rising leisurely, determined, purposeful—that no one can stop. But I can almost see it moving, the beginning of its journey across the sky toward the place where it will set: an allegory of the cycle of human life and of the universe. We see it every day and we pay no attention. What begins, ends—who is aware?

The orb is yellow, tinged with a kind of green. Around it is emptiness, a vast void, free of any trace of clouds or fog. An absolute void to which I try to cling. I try to dispel all my knowledge of the matter: I put myself in the position of the ancestors, striving by way of their knowledge, their visions, even though I don't need to recall any situation, merely to imagine it. A clear and distinct sunrise: I recall a sunrise that dazzled me when I opened the shutters of a balcony overlooking the Nile in Minya. But this is different, as if it were a different sun, its movement foretelling the orbit of the planets, the movement of the celestial bodies in outer space, the succession of time, crossing dimensions that can't be perceived by the senses: all of these materialize before me as I stand, dazzled, before this sunrise of sunrises.

A universe in my heart

I'm lying on the white, rectangular table while the young, energetic doctor puts the wires in place, after painting my skin with a viscous substance that resembles *balouza* pudding. Another stage is about to begin in the attempt to find out what has been happening inside me, to my heart, since the aches began. Pains are symptoms, merely signals—many hidden secrets that, for the human being, are linked with the body, the self, like the secrets of the vast universe, the dimensions of which we haven't yet discovered.

Twice I saw my heart in detail: the first via the ultrasound and then after the echocardiogram had been inserted and scanned it from up close. Both times, I saw the lines indicating its movement. But I saw it from inside when the two branches of the catheter entered it, and its beat changed with the threat of a foreign body coming into contact with its core. The screen was facing me, and I was asking about the location of an old injury to the mitral valve, after a bout of fever that I don't remember at all. I was trying to make out the locations that were affected by joy and grief, by passion, by loss, by silence in sorrow—beginning with the loss of hope at being able to retrieve an intimate moment, to the collapse of a relationship that was always dear to me.

Here it is, beating—expanding and contracting. A unique movement, starting in the womb, the first sign of the unborn coming into existence. An encounter with which I'm not familiar: between me and myself, between what's shown and what's hidden from me. On the screen, the veins and arteries appeared, large and small. They looked like a small tree, connecting and branching out according to the logic of the uninterrupted sequence of branches and the arrangement of the limbs themselves. A tree stripped of its bark, of the earth's clay. I see its essence.

Here are the sounds—in the beginning, unfamiliar. I can't separate them out. Little by little, they become clear through the beats. This is the whisper of the ocean wave at the height of a storm, as the wave reaches its peak, then its trough, and the droplets it reveals.

As the apparatus moves to another location, quiet winds blow, flowing into a thick jungle, but permeated with a special light. I make out the rustling of trees, the sway of branches carrying fruit, as a soft trilling emerges like the stirrings of passion.

A different location, and thunder begins. Lightning bolts follow the sounds of the roiling universe, changing from something resembling whispers into something unfamiliar. As the device moves locations, I hear what I haven't known before, what my ear has never caught. I try to distinguish it, to get acquainted with it, inside me.

—⁓—

In what ways are the ocean and the desert similar? Why do the same feelings overtake me each time I stop at the edge of each of them and gaze? Could the difference be only in name?

A dream

I'm giving a speech—perhaps on a roof, or on a hill. What's certain is that it's a resort village for journalists. I gesture in warning, alerting them that someone is plotting to rob them of their resort. The village looks utterly empty. Dense clouds nearby. The sound of distant waves crashing and retreating. I can only see the windows and doors, and the solid walls.

A dream

A dream of an earthquake about to happen, a dream of losing my shoes during prayer, a dream of appointments I can't make as there's not enough time. A dream of losing my way in a distant country. A dream of losing my passport in a strange land.

The room of heavenly silence

In the city airport overlooking the sea, the conference coordinator awaited us. She welcomed us. Her wide smile, her even teeth, her welcoming features filled me with familiarity and joy. What I remember of her is her smile, how quickly and gracefully she would turn around. She led us to the parking lot. My colleague sat in the back seat. He didn't respond to my invitation to sit beside her, saying that he didn't like seat belts!

When the car crossed the road leading out of the airport zone, she said that she was sorry to inform us of a matter she hadn't wanted to happen. I prepared myself to hear the worst, despite her broad welcoming smile whenever she talked and whatever she said. She said we would be spending the night in the city of Sète, near Agde, as the hotel in Agde was fully booked until the following afternoon. The next day at eleven, she would come to accompany us to the place where we would stay for the duration of the conference.

I asked how far it was between the two cities. She said about seven kilometers, not far. My friend said we would see another city. I said its name was an ancient Egyptian one. She said that Seth was the origin of the word for Satan in Latin. I asked if she knew the ancient Egyptian language. She said that in France they study the basics in secondary school. I turned around and exchanged a meaningful glance with my friend. I recall this brief moment and all it contained. I was telling him and he was answering me, in silence: in Egypt, we know nothing about the language of our ancestors. Only specialists do.

At night, it's difficult to make out features, no matter how bright the lights. I saw a canal: the city extending along its banks; small boats were anchored. I recalled Dubai's docks: the old-style boats at anchor, the boxes of goods on the quay. Boxes of different size. The Indian sailors with their lithe bodies. The boats in Dubai are medium sized, made of wood and powered by motor. I saw similar boats in the port overlooking Shatt al-Arab in Basra, which sail under the power of the wind, crossing the Arabian Sea and the Indian Ocean with the same nautical methods that Sinbad used on his seven voyages. Nineteen seventy-four—the year I visited Basra. I was amazed by the continuity of the ancient boats, the orderliness of the ancient routes between Basra, Oman, and the ports of the Emirates and Bahrain, regularly sailing to and from India. I can barely recall the port of the French city of Sète, and the moored ships, without them being followed by the ships on Shatt al-Arab, and Dubai's docks, and Oman's coast—perhaps because of the resemblance between the canal and the docks, and perhaps due to the size and similarity of the ships. I don't remember the large ports I arrived at on massive, multistory ferries. Things trigger similar things—whether in appearance, dimension, or meaning, or in humble glances. But the hotel didn't recall its like: neither in the entrance, nor in the building, nor even in the room. An old, rectangular door, whose glass pane showed nothing through it. After about two minutes, we heard an old, tired voice speaking French. About three minutes later a key turned in the door. The shutters parted, and a hallway stretched before us. Everything on which the eye fell was antique. Crossing the threshold led to a different time. It didn't separate two places but rather two different times: the design of the wallpaper with patterns in relief. The lamps were dim and hung from a high ceiling whose decoration I didn't see until the following day. The thin, old lady appeared to be a part of the place which preserved a different, special era, so that I imagined that if she were to go outside, she wouldn't register in anyone's vision, whether moving or still. One could only see her in this space.

We went on to the office that was covered with a layer of green felt, resembling the surface of billiard tables. She handed us papers that we filled out with the usual information. She didn't ask for passports, having confidence in our escort. She gave each of us two keys: the first was small, with a little piece of brass with the room number hanging from it. The other was long and thick, with a head shaped like a heart. She said this was for the main entrance: if any of us left during the night for some reason, he should lock the door and open it when he returned. She wouldn't hear, as she was going to bed. She said that breakfast was from seven thirty until nine. She wished us a good night and a good sleep. Our escort asked if we needed anything; we thanked her. It was late, and my desire for sleep was increasing. I hadn't followed my usual ritual whenever staying in a distant city for the first time, arranging my things and then going out to get to know the surrounding streets. I would associate the location of the building with a specific landmark, especially if I took a side street. I would get to know the facades, looking for a café or a place that served drinks, where I could take refuge. Wherever I stay, I form particular habits no matter how short the stay. I start by arranging my things in the room: my clothes, my medicine bottles—which are kept in a small bag—my shaving kit, the books I'm carrying. If the room has two beds, I choose one of them. If the bed is wide, I favor one side, not the other. I can only sleep if a connection develops between me and the place, no matter how short my stay—even if it's for just one night, like this.

I didn't go out. Our trip had taken a while because there were two legs: first from Cairo to Paris, with the Air France plane taking off early, at seven in the morning. In Orly Airport, we waited a long time, about five hours after the transfer from Charles de Gaulle Airport—from the far north of the city to the south. Then from Paris to Montpellier. The cities of the south are packed tightly together. As for the sea itself, I was used to standing on its opposite shore at the furthest southeasterly point, on Alexandria's singular shore. While the sea doesn't begin in any one place, for me the Mediterranean and its flow begin at Alexandria—of this I'm sure.

I didn't go out to the nearby streets at night. I would get to know them in the early morning, before my friend woke up. The city was small, and the ships were docked directly in front of the hotel, stretching into the distance, one after the other.

Before climbing the wooden stairs, I saw the keys on a board above the desk. With the exception of the two suites, all the keys were hanging there. Only the eight smaller-sized room keys. This vast building contained only those rooms; the presence of the keys here meant they were vacant.

Our escort bid us farewell, after leaving us with a trace of her broad smile. I wished my friend a good night's sleep. He went up to the second floor, directly above my room. Mine was number two, his was six. I'm always careful to memorize my own room number and the number of whoever I'm with, or the way to contact reception. I fear a sudden crisis, that a sudden illness will overtake me. Years ago, I didn't use to take this into account, nor was it part of my arrangements or included in my rituals.

I opened the door. The ceiling seemed lower than that of the story itself. I turned the key twice. I opened the suitcase and began to arrange my clothes and the rest of my things. The room was quiet—a sterile silence.

The window looked directly out at the canal, with glass, a net curtain, then a thicker Roman blind operated with a double cord. I moved the net curtain aside. Scattered lights—it was clear from the difference in levels that the other side of the street was elevated—the landscape wasn't flat. We would see in the morning. The boats weren't moving; they appeared to be fishing boats. When I lowered the blind to shut out the whisper of light leaking through the framed space, I became part of the room, and it became part of me. A confined space covered with wallpaper, or old fabric, dominated by patterns of plants and the color of the sky.

"If all the keys are on the board, why is my friend not staying in the next room, or on the same floor?" Merely a fleeting question. I didn't follow with another.

My obsessions don't follow each other, one after the other. I didn't think about the size of the building and the small number of rooms or the space behind the low ceiling. I hadn't felt as embraced as this in any other room I'd stayed in briefly. I was covered by the color blue, which enclosed me with bare branches and scattered leaves. I wondered about the many eyes that had looked out from precisely the same spot. Numerous questions followed each another but didn't linger: who'd lain on the same bed, who would come after me? If I were in another room, one of these same questions would preoccupy me, as would other related questions. I felt in that room a familiarity, a closeness, as if I'd been there for many years, as if I'd taken refuge in this hue of color for nights too numerous to be counted, as if this weren't the first time. The color stirred me, it became rich and familiar—a special kind of familiarity that flowed from those walls and ended with them.

My usual obsessions don't trouble me, whether old, or new and unexpected, after the beginning of my illness and my fear of suddenly dying in a strange land. The confining walls and the enclosed space in which I move so warily bestow a degree of distance I've not known before, as if I've reached the utmost point of the inhabited world, a place that no soul has set foot in before me. A degree of continuous silence—still, undisturbed by any whisper. I haven't felt the same in any other place I've stayed before, nor since. I don't know where the building is, and when I want to recall the degree of light and the decoration of the room, I close all the openings in the place I'm in, I exclude all sounds and I close my eyes, at which point the decorations appear to me, and the color of the sky flows, peaceful, pacifying . . .

Books

I'm looking at the books on the shelves; I'm not searching for a particular title. I've got used to this. Once or twice a week, I stand in front of a particular corner and look over the books, perhaps trying to remember them. Sometimes, I'm taken aback by the presence of an author whom I've forgotten buying. I haven't made a catalog. Throughout the years, I've depended on my memory and the general classification: This for poetry, that for Sufism. That one's history, those are novels, those are favorite works. As one ages, memory dims—it grows heavy, the dark places broaden. Looking in this way, standing like this, helps me to remember, especially since I don't read everything I buy, but keep it for the moment I need it. Perhaps what I've read exceeds what I own, by way of borrowing from friends and public libraries, especially in the early years, when means were limited and didn't match up to my desire. Every book bears three of my signatures: the day it came into my possession, the day I started reading it, and the day I finished it. If I've read it twice, the signatures come to five. I take pleasure in books when I look at them, when I turn their pages, when I read them. The pleasure may exceed what I find in people. Those volumes speak by their silence: their presence is powerful by the absence of those who wrote them, printed them, or bound their pages. The one who is absent is not restricted by borders or limits, like someone present before us, who interacts with our senses. There's a mysterious intimacy of which I'm aware, and which is aware of me, a mysterious continuity with those who belong to distant eras—times in which I wasn't present. But their breaths are repeated through those lines. At times, I read lines through which the author speaks about himself, or feelings about what he experiences, so that I can almost see what he looks like—his way of sitting, the look in his eyes. I can almost retrieve him from nothingness. Sometimes the connections are extended, linking me to a manuscript or printing press; the familiarity takes root. While I'm reading a book, I put it on top of a small bookcase next to where my head lies on the pillow. Before I close my eyes, I look at it. The closeness keeps me company, as if I'm lying beside a companion.

A march

From Anshas to Marsa Matrouh, it's about six hundred kilometers: four hundred on the agricultural road and approximately two hundred through the desert. We went out of the commando training base, the first time I'd been in the company of Colonel Ibrahim al-Rifaei. He said that going on the march with them would be a prelude to accompanying them on combat operations. He said they walked long distances here, so that longer distances behind the lines wouldn't tax them. He asked me if I'd ever walked such a distance before. I bowed my head, thinking. I recalled a trip to Luxor and Aswan with the scout troop, where we hadn't walked more than ten kilometers at a time. I said, "No."

We passed Tanta. We crossed the Kafr al-Zayyat Bridge. They allowed me to wear camouflage uniform and equipped me with a backpack that contained everything I needed, except water. Drinking water was stored in a flask covered with yellow fabric, while each individual's ration for bathing was distributed before first light.

I summoned my energy. Fatigue overcame me, but I was embarrassed to show it in front of them. Being in a group helped; all the more when the members were so exceptional. At times I felt better, and I almost jumped for joy when I realized that I was one of them. Ibrahim al-Rifaei took special care of me, and asked about me twice. He told his second, Lieutenant Colonel Aali, "He's a civilian . . . "

Before we reached Alexandria, the order was given to halt. Conditions required a return to Anshas in trucks and Jeeps. This was repeated on two subsequent marches. Later—before October—I asked Ibrahim al-Rifaei to explain. He looked at me. He was of the type that didn't say much, so I considered what he said to be tantamount to an unexpected confession.

He said that if he announced that the march was from Anshas to Alexandria, everyone would summon up just enough energy for what was announced. But when they were told it was further, they would have twice the energy. Reaching Alexandria was only a stage among stages that hadn't yet ended.

He said that his experience—especially in the desert—confirmed what his first teachers had said: within each person lies boundless energy, if only he's resolute and has the will.

An engraving

I didn't know it would be the last time.

I stand in front of the dome of al-Mansur Qalawun. I catch sight of *Amm* Mustafa coming from Nahhasin, heading to Khurunfish, to Amir al-Goyoush Street, where he lives. He's led by a young man, perhaps his son, perhaps a grandson, or someone to whom he's related. He wears his yellow *gallabiya* that is almost light brown. His hair is partly gray—not pure white.

His strides are short, feeble; he moves forward bent over, and he sits bent over. I only see him bending over.

That was the first and last time I saw him on the street: I'd only known him to sit in front of the small room in the Silahdar Complex, next to the Khan al-Khalili Association headquarters, where I worked for two years. On a stool. At a table on which lay a disc of black tar, on which the piece to be engraved was fastened: a round or rectangular tray of whatever size, or a silver box, or gold. Dark black bitumen was melted and, when soft, a piece of brass or silver was placed on it; each became an extension of the other. At this point, the engraving began. People call bitumen "tar" when it covers the roads. But in the Khan, they don't give it that name; in order to give it a positive association, they call it "whitening." It's because it's connected to work, their livelihood. Just as people say the "terrible disease" or, if they go further, will say "cancer"—in English—as if using another language ensured that one would avoid it. *Amm* Mustafa once said that he actually saw it as white—not as black!

I always arrived after *Amm* Mustafa and left before he did. Because of that, I would only see him sitting, engraving, and talking as he bent over, holding the small mallet in one hand and, in the other, a sharp-edged chisel that engraved those lines, round and straight, on the empty surface. His eyes were on the piece, but if he lifted them, he didn't stop. I thought that the times he arrived at work and left were connected to the daylight, but in the final years it was the same, even though everything was growing dark before him, the result of his nerves weakening as he grew older. This is one of those things medicine can't help. Praise God for everything—his boys got an education and graduated from universities, and the girl is as well looked after as can be. *Amm* Mustafa said little and had an unassuming presence. I could count the words I exchanged with him. I used to like seeing him at work, how he remained bent over for long hours, the engraving flowing from his fingers. His designs were known in the market and among collectors. For those not in the know, all products seem similar. But the one who looks closely—who is familiar—sees the difference between precise work and *bazaari*, or vulgar work. The informed observer can tell *Amm* Mustafa's work from that of al-Zayni, and the great Munirgi. There were four remaining engraving masters: each of them had his own style and spirit. The oldest by far was *Amm* Mustafa: if not for his graciousness and modesty, he would have said that the other three were his students, but he never did.

But what's certain is that he came to the Silahdar Complex as a small child. I never asked him if his father was an engraver or if he'd brought him as an apprentice, as many from the area did. They turned their children over to the master engravers just to master a craft, unpaid. With time, each of them progressed. Mustafa was among those who succeeded, but he didn't change his trade. Some of those who began with him went on to become well-known merchants in the Khan. He only knew engraving. He spoke highly of the great master Snaybar, who'd taught him the basics, who'd led him to the sources. There's no mosque in Cairo that he hadn't sought out. He would lie on his back for hours in order to absorb the carvings on the ceiling, the walls and the minbars. He would look at doors for a long time, at entrances—with time, his brain teemed with all the shapes and designs. He didn't study patterns drawn on tracing paper, like the modernizers or art students. The important thing was the starting point: he might begin in the middle of a piece or one of its corners. His starting point was a secret—even those closest to him didn't know, nor those on the market today who continue the tradition of engraving. He taught them that each of them should have a logic, a starting point. It may be a circle, a triangle, a square, after which the creation beings. The shapes flow from this—balanced, intertwined. Arranging them across a circular or rectangular surface is not easy for those not in the know. There has to be a system. And because he didn't work according to a prior design, no piece that emerged from his hands looked like another—they were unique. Anyone could observe him for hours as he bent over, indifferent to what was going on around him. Yet no one saw him at the moment he began. *Amm* Ibrahim—who rented the room from him in his last years—said that he thought of it like a man being alone with his lady for the first time, in complete isolation. His words were few, and limited. I always wanted to hear him say "creation." I didn't ask him outright, but I would go about it in a roundabout way, in conversation, so that he would say it. I would see it as a sign, a gesture to the concealed.

When I visited him with Janka the Bulgarian, she stood observing him, dazzled. She decided to buy one of his engravings, a brass tray, and asked him to sign it on the back. He looked pleased, telling me that the lady valued his work and that this was only the second time that he'd been asked for his signature. He looked up at me, saying that the first was fifty years ago, when all the work was in gold and silver—brass wasn't widespread until things became difficult for many, and the market grew poor. The person who'd asked him to sign his name was kind and nice and looked like me. I repeated, "He looked like me, *Amm* Mustafa?" He nodded his head emphatically. I realized that I hadn't ever asked him for his signature, even though I'd bought several pieces from him. In order to conceal my embarrassment, I asked him if engraving in silver differed from that in brass. He continued hammering at the yellow surface, creating the shapes. He would continue in this way after his sight went completely. He had no need for a ray of light in order to see the lines—they flowed from his hands, from within him, arranging themselves. He told me that engraving was engraving—for him there was no difference between silver and brass. Even if he were to engrave the air, he would embody precision and care. Long ago he used to engrave gold—it's precisely the engraving that he does on brass now.

He said, sure and emphatic, "Engraving is from me, and to me . . . "

Praise

Praise God for everything, for every circumstance, for every situation in which I've been. Gratitude and thanks to him, for the breaths still come one after another and my existence is uninterrupted. My senses are able to differentiate between darkness and light, between the wicked and the vile, are able to read the lines and probe the secrets of words. And to listen to "the night and all that it enshroudeth" (Qur'an 84:17) and to the teeming day, to the sounds of the universe: the repetition and the trilling, the cooing of a pigeon and a dove, the braying of a donkey, the neighing of a horse, the sound of a migrating bird—one passing, one staying—and the roar of thunder, the falling of a downpour, the flow of water in a stream, the rustle of a flower as it blossoms at dawn, and the mysterious echoes—whose explanation preoccupied me—that come from the depths of the vast universe whose beginning we will not know and which we will never grasp in its entirety. The same goes for the howl of those winds, the source of which baffles me: where did it begin, and where will it end? I often praise him for the lingering tones of Sheikh Muhammad Rifat's voice, especially during his recitation of

"By the glorious morning light
And by the night when it's still
Thy Lord hath not forsaken thee, nor is He displeased"
(Qur'an 93:1–3)

In that recitation lies an essence and precise meaning that it's not possible to understand fully. Praise is required for my understanding of the clamor of humanity that issues from both near and far.

Gratitude and thanks that my ability to distinguish between the trace and the original still survives. The ability to tell the difference between colors: this is white, that is black, and between the two is gray. All colors need white, while it does not need them. Other colors come from black, while it does not come from them. There's no limit to the variety of its tones and its gradation, negatively or positively. How great my joy at being able to see yellow, red, and blue and what results from mixing them, at being able to see the differences between the moments of dusk, the consummations of twilight, and "the night and all it enshroudeth" (Qur'an 84:17).

It's thanks to his grace that I'mstill able to distinguish between wicked and good, between good on the one hand and better, more beautiful, and purer on the other, even when it occasionally disappears into the shadows, vanishes into the dark. The desire to comprehend is stronger, to understand is firmer. I realize I'm growing weak, beginning to lean, but the goodwill that I feel toward all of creation is enough for me. The feeling of getting closer to the secret, like the brush of the wind, the embrace of the palm's shadows, gazing at the edges of branches that reach for the sky, understanding the curves that lead away, the corners that divide and the entrances that inspire—preparing for what comes after, the mysteries of passages, the musings of bridges. My gazing at the vast horizon, just as it is, inspires in me the same nostalgia for what I don't know. Likewise my attempts to understand the movements of the waves and the secret of the blue of the sea—to understand its sounds, to arrive at an understanding of the relationship between above and below, between first and last, between place and time. I thank God often for the ability to come and go, for having tasted the secret of "the fig and the olive / By Mount Sinai / By this secure city of Mecca" (Qur'an 95:1–3).[9]

Fuul

Before and after, the matter seems similar—even if, at its heart, it's not.

Before the surgery, I used to go off to beloved places, and to faces that remained from times gone by, just as I did with food—but what limited my enthusiasm was sticking to a strict diet in order to lose weight. Things change after the surgery, especially when the doctor treating me advises me

---

9   Here, the author invokes sacred references. The surah refers to God's creation of humankind "in the best of moulds, but that man is capable of the utmost degradation unless he has faith and leads a good life." "By" indicates an oath.

that I can eat what I wish for a period of forty days—with no restrictions of any kind—but at the end of the period, I have to return to my diet.

The first thing I want is *fuul midammis*, fava beans in oil. But . . . where will I find it in these distant, frozen lands? Not only are we in the United States but in a far-off city, all organized around the hospital. But the people seem to have studied everything to do with patients from the East, especially Egypt, a number of whose sons work as successful physicians here. In the hotel, there's a restaurant that serves breakfast. A fava bean dish is available. It's true that it costs seven dollars, but it's available and there's a demand for it.

Fava beans are not just beans but an ancient time—or intertwining times, consecutive, belonging to me. They were found in foods discovered in Tutankhamen's tomb, now displayed in the Egyptian Museum. The bean goes through many stages. I don't know how many centuries it took humanity to plant a bean and harvest it, then dry it, cover it in holes underground totally sealed off from any air or light, and then cook it on a low flame—as low as possible—until the beans become soft and take on the consistency of butter. My relatives are in the trade: they know its varieties and sources. The centers where it's prepared are in the big cities. Every public bath has an oven beside it, a quiet furnace that uses refuse for fuel. It used to be clay pipes that passed through it, carrying water to the bath. The clay pots containing the beans are placed carefully on the fire. Later, the clay pots were replaced by copper ones, then aluminum. Of course, this affects the flavor, but who takes any notice? On the slow continuous low flame, the beans cook quietly, expectantly. I'm partial to fava beans with oil—any oil. I prefer the beans mashed, perhaps because the first that I had were like that—*fuul* from Abu Hagar, who disappeared suddenly at the beginning of the sixties. My father mourned him after close to half a century of him being at the same place at the entrance of Umm al-Ghulam. People sought him out one morning and found no trace of him—neither of him nor his cart, as if he'd never existed. Some whispered that he'd been detained for political reasons, and others said that someone in power had got angry at him and arranged to get rid of him. *Osta* Sayyid the barber said that he went back to his town, east of the Nile in Assiut, to meet his Maker, after the hidden call alerted him that his time was near. The last possibility was the one my father thought most likely. He was sad for him, praising his name, and praying for mercy for him.

The flavor is not complete without *baladi* bread, whether soft or hard: this is what I can't find in the hospital restaurant. There's a harmony between the fava bean and the bread, as if the two are twins. It's preferable to scoop up *fuul* with bread, not a knife and fork. Among the preferred accompaniments are pickled onion and lemon and heirloom eggplant, coated in garlic and cilantro. If I mention pickles, the only thing that comes to me is al-Bulaqi and his thick, black hair. Despite the importance of pickles, they're only a supplement, additional, not sought out for their own sake. They're a prop, an aid—just like tahini sauce, which the Alexandrians add.

Despite my connection to *fuul*, an aversion came between us when they forced it on us in prison—three meals of it a day. But what *fuul* was it? I don't know where the Prisons Department got these large, coarse beans, filled with weevils, with thick skins that had to be removed. We would mash them with great difficulty. No matter what we ate with them, they would defy being mashed and chewed. After I got out, I stopped eating them for breakfast for a short time, before reverting again out of desire, but my preference for them transferred to dinner: they became my favorite evening meal. It became a vital component of my life—not just for its own sake but for what it was associated with. For this reason, whenever my existence is threatened, I fall back on it and depend on it.

A list

I'm staying in Abydos. Tranquility and a distant dread envelop me, surrounding me without weighing me down. A small hotel. From the balcony, I can see the great temple. It's impossible to know it by standing in front of it or even by looking from above. Gradually, I approach it.

Here, I become one with myself. Even my friends from the area understand; not one of them annoys me by starting up a conversation. They content themselves with a brief greeting. The town stands at the edge, just like the village in which I came into the world, to the north, some sixty kilometers away. Both locations face west. I wake up early, before sunrise. I take my time looking around the nine sacred chapels, but what I stand in front of each time is that wall.

A short passage to the east. It curves to the west, where it descends to the lake, to which water still runs. The Osirian Temple is the most sacred site of ancient Egypt; but that's another story. The wall lies to the west, where Sethi I stands, holding an incense burner. In front of him is his son, who will become Ramses II and who will add to the building his father began. He points to lines of royal cartouches: seventy-six *shinn* frames, each enclosing the *rinn*, the name. Seventy-six kings, the first of which is Menes, who we know united the two kingdoms. But from other lists in Karnak, and some papyrus scrolls, we know he eliminated a number of those associated with periods of great upheaval. There's Hatshepsut, who seized power; Akhenaten, the first to create a rift with the established beliefs; Smenkhkare, Tutankhamen, and Ay: the latter a priest, a murderer, and a usurper. What could be said about each of them is vast, but that would be to stray from the point.

Seventy-six names: all that remains of their eras and what they contained. If each of those pharaohs had lived for a typical length of time, the total period would be no less than 1,500 years, that is to say, three-quarters of what now separates us from the prophet, the Messiah, on whom we depend as a basis for our calendar and for a beginning. Eras that follow each other, just like the sequence of lines. Within the frames, their positions differ. The frames were intended to protect the names, to protect their owners, the kings, the demigods. It's about 3,500 years since those lines—a long journey across time. But . . . until when?

A chime

The building overlooks Bab al-Louq Square, on the corner of Falaki Street. It didn't occur to me that one day I would go there. For me, it's associated with the shop for repairing rare antique rugs. Inside would sit a man, advanced in age, almost blind, although his hand would quickly and skillfully work the needle and thread. At three o'clock in the afternoon, I climb the stairs. My friend, whom I'd got to know in the café, is in front of me. I knew he worked in the Finance Ministry, but until that day I'd no notion of the nature of his work: an office specializing in the estates of those who have no offspring, inventorying their possessions, recording them, and disposing of them after a predetermined time, when it would be declared that no party was entitled to what the deceased had left behind.

My friend is accompanied by two men. We stop before a locked door on the top floor. One of them steps forward and opens the door. When I go through it, the odor of someone who was here comes to me. A particular odor: a mixture of the smell of the one who was, and the fragrance of the place. It fills the air, putrid and stagnant, suspended for a while. I know it will pass quickly, now that the person has left, but I contemplate the years during which it has lasted.

Old furniture—stylish, chosen with care. In the entrance, a mirror in a wooden frame, decorated with boldly colored flowers—yellow, red, green. Small flowers of Slavic origin: I saw similar ones in a Caucasian fabric and in wooden vessels produced on the banks of the Volga. On the right and left side of the mirror are two small shelves; on each is a porcelain vase of ancient Greek style, with two harps drawn on each vase. On the floor is a small carpet, its colors natural and without dye—white, dark brown, light brown, and black.

A medium-sized, rectangular reception room. A long sofa, a comfortable chair, both of them light blue, pale, perhaps due to age. Everything suggests antiquity—the furniture, the furnishings. On a chair, a woman's *gallabiya*. On the floor, one woolen sock, folded, not discarded. On the right, a table with a rectangular radio on it. The top of the radio is curved, its face is divided into two halves: at the bottom is the dial, with the frequencies and names of the stations in English, and behind it is the tuning needle. The knobs jut out—three and three, with a small divider between. The top is covered in a yellow fabric that looks like straw. The circular speaker looks like a shadow.

I follow my friend, who starts instructing the others to note down the contents. First the large items, then the medium-sized ones, followed by the smallest: pieces of furniture, electrical appliances. He exchanges rapid words with them, making observations. After a few minutes, his words become fewer. We look at each other. We become quiet as we grow aware of more details, especially as the smell grows stronger the longer we stay. It persists, uninterrupted, as if its source were still there. As it increases, the air becomes deeper, as if it would no longer accept anything else, wouldn't even allow sound to travel from one person to another. My friend and his two colleagues become engrossed in cataloging—examining and describing what they find. What's important now is to record. The evaluation would come later. After this, one room—only one, with a small corridor leading to it, facing the bathroom and the toilet. On the glass shelf, tubes of toothpaste and small bottles. A cup from which a toothbrush peeks out, perhaps three, four. The bed is wide and luxurious, and antique—heavy, made of solid wood, wood within wood. The cover has been pushed aside, unmade; the pillow is tattered. There are only three photos that are visible to someone lying on the bed. Each in a silver frame. An officer wearing a hat I've not seen before. He's looking steadily—stern, with a high collar around his neck. A foreign-looking girl, turning to look at the viewer; her eyes are wide, her lips parted slightly—the beginning of a smile. The third is of another girl. Both the girls are under ten years old, but this latter one is different, slimmer, her hair arranged in a thick braid, in profile.

Which one was she?

I don't know.

That one or this, I don't know. No inclination to wonder out loud. Clothes peek out of one side of the wardrobe. One of the doors is ajar. It seems that she was large—the clothes are loose. She appears to me, either lying down with her eyes closed in bed, with a buried pain in her features, her head drooping onto her chest, not falling forward, or sitting on the sofa in the room—or her features get mixed up with a face I saw years ago, in an old house in Zaher which belonged to a lady from Alexandria, and another, of Greek origin, who used to manage a restaurant that no longer exists, near Cinema Miami. I don't know her name and I didn't ask anyone. All my friend said was that she was Armenian and had lived alone for decades. Fortunately, she was able to call the porter for help and had passed away in front of him. He tried to save her but wasn't able to do anything. If it hadn't been for him, no one would have known about her death until after her smell had spread.

It grows heavy in the air until I'm almost able to see her. I've never known anything like this before—that a smell could embody to this degree the features of the person from whom it emanated. As it continues to penetrate, the silence deepens.

A chime.

Two chimes.

A porcelain clock in the shape of a bird's nest, hanging on the wall facing the bed—precisely in the middle of the room. From a circular window, a little nightingale emerges, a miniature. It lets out a chirp that lasts for a few seconds, then it withdraws and the window closes. The chimes and the chirp echo in the silence, weighing heavily until we're unable to speak. My friend looks at me, questioning. I answer him with a look, repeating: did I actually hear the chime?

A journey

I ask about them. My wife says, "Muhammad went out with Magda to get a breath of fresh air. She's been working on her paper since yesterday."

I fall silent. I see them in some place. They're sitting at a table or walking in the garden of the club. I wonder: next year—where will they be? Where will any of us be? The pace quickens for me, the days pass. I'm standing at the beginning of something invisible. I can't make it out. A boat—an unknown means of transport. I'm looking at a marina still shrouded in secrecy.

In recent weeks—or rather months—the feelings of love between us have grown stronger. There have been no arguments with my son or my daughter. We don't speak much, but we say a lot with our looks; we communicate by our silence. I feel for any ill that might befall them when they end up alone! My son is preparing to travel to that cold, distant country where he will settle for several years. His sister will become a voice on the phone, trying to reassure him in every situation. We're with her now, but what will happen after we've gone? Why didn't we have a third child, a boy or a girl who would be a companion to them both? I start to think about that unknown brother who didn't arrive. Our parents were braver than we'd been: if they'd checked their finances, we wouldn't exist. My son looks at me at length, silently. I recall his tenderness after he left. I fear even a moment of suffering that my daughter might experience. Our mutual understanding, the silence that speaks, resembles those brief moments that precede leaving on a journey . . .

Her physique

A terrace—long, somewhat wide. The tables and chairs are lined up. Being March, the breeze is still thin and gentle. I sit, tired, looking off into the extended space, facing the hotel in which I'm staying. The hotel is on the other side of the motorway but seems unreachable—getting to it from here requires taking roads and crossing a bridge, mastered only by those who have lived here for years and who drive, or by taxi drivers. Most of them here are Indians or Pakistanis. I speak to them in English. Various nationalities. The waiter is Lebanese. I can distinguish the Syrian dialect from the Palestinian now: there's a kind of pronunciation that only someone familiar with the people would be aware of. Through my travels, I've become knowledgeable. I go back to looking at the massive hotel—a black glass facade. All alike—from the outside I can't make out my room.

"Is there any tobacco?"

"From Iran . . . yes . . . "

"One tea, no sugar, and a shisha with Iranian tobacco."

I quit smoking eight years ago. The doctor's decision. I stick to it, but when I'm traveling and the shisha is available, I order it. I run my lips over the mouthpiece—I don't inhale any smoke. I recall the smell of tobacco, an element from memory. Especially when I'm alone. Now, most of the cafés serve the honey-flavored tobacco—*maassil*—not just in Cairo but here in Dubai as well. An Iranian waiter in another café tells me that the older people, the old-timers, are the ones who order tobacco. Young men and women smoke *maassil*; their demand for it is ferocious.

Yaah . . . how did I not see them?

Did they both arrive after I sat down? Did they pass in front of me as I closed my eyes? If I'd come when they were already seated at their table, I must have been looking the other way. How did I not see them? They're directly in front of me, only two tables away. They must have arrived before me. The young man, his broad, solid back toward me, is feeding her. As he holds out the spoon, she touches it gently, her eyes on him, wide and gazing, brimming with an incendiary desire, as if kissing an extension of his fingers, slowly sipping and swallowing the contents. She looks desirous of him, for him, her entire being oriented toward him. He seems rebuked—distressed, isolated, withdrawn. But desire fills him too. He extends his hand, stroking her bare arm as she leans closer toward him, then he stops.

I'm able to see the hotel, turn my head toward the building and keep them in my field of vision. I notice her lithe physique as her left side is facing me. As for him, I see only his back, his stoop.

She's wearing a gray, sleeveless sweater. The hem ends near the downward slope of her supple arm: when she leans forward, it moves up and the gap between the top of her pants and the edge of her blouse widens, highlighting what shows of her body which is light colored, almost blond. She moves toward her friend, revealing her skimpy underwear.

What a display!

The waiter comes over. Carefully, he places the shisha, with its feminine form, on my right, with the tea and a bottle of mineral water. I look at the bowl of the shisha: tobacco, shredded and twisted in clumps, a brown-yellow color. How many bowls like this have I smoked in Cairo's cafés—in Fishawi Café, in the Cultural Club in the Bab al-Louq area, in Ahmad Said Café and Farouq Café in Alexandria—at all times, night and day, dawn and afternoon. That day, when the doctor asked me to quit, I said I would head to the Ahmad Said Café where I only ever go alone. I like its airiness and the old-fashioned arrangement of its furnishings. I would have one more smoke and then quit forever. The doctor looked at me from underneath his glasses and said, "You can do it."

Then he said, "I trust you." Then, "If you cheat, you'll only be harming yourself."

Her mouth parts in a broad smile, as if it were a sign and a summation of the clear city sky—perhaps of the freedom that I feel and of a horizon open to the sea and to the people. She isn't so much looking at her friend as feeling him with her eyes, touching him occasionally with her fingers. Instead of responding in kind, he pulls away. I don't know the nature of their relationship: perhaps he's her fiancé, or they're newlyweds, or he's a friend or a passing acquaintance. It doesn't concern me. What concerns me is her continuous display, her full figure, her harmonious, well-proportioned form.

I notice another young man coming over, holding a brazier. He arranges the burning coals with care at the edge of the crown of tobacco. I watch his skillful fingers. I don't start a conversation, I don't ask about his home country, about the background to his skillful arranging of the coals. I hurry him away in order to leave myself free for this feminine display: her advances are continuous, suggestive. He gives only a cautious response, like someone performing a duty rather than a true emotion. I run my lips over the mouthpiece of the shisha. The smell of the cured tobacco is piercing. I'm careful not to exhale the smoke from where it lies inside me, as it will constrict my chest: when I walk through the shopping mall, I receive signals from within that no one else would be aware of.

Her lips part. There's an agreement between her lips and her eyes. The mouth is always an invitation, especially when the lips part: a child asking for food, a woman quenching her desire. However, this friend of ours remains deaf to her messages. He smiles without smiling, just as I'm smoking without smoking. In every action, this is how I am now! Whenever we used to see a beautiful woman with a man, we would whisper to each other if we were sitting close to them, or speak openly if they were passing by and moving on, our voices rising as we criticized him, pointing out his flaws. Each of us thought he was the more suited, the most entitled. I smile to myself. That was back then, long ago.

Yaah . . .

Her buttocks part from the seat. Her body faces his. The pants pull further away, and her body is glowing, but I don't pause at her visible cleft—I contemplate her posture. I remember a white marble statue that captivated me once, during my first visit to the Rodin Museum in Paris—it's as if she'd emerged from it, as an expression of it. As she resumes the way she was sitting, she focuses her gaze on me. So . . . she's aware, she realizes where I am, but she shows only a hidden readiness and continues with her seduction.

I'm taken by her lithe physique—its softness, its balanced proportions, some parts more prominent than others, a heavenly body spinning on its own axis and revolving around her friend who remains withdrawn from her. Is he truly like this? Or, under the influence of a primordial rivalry, is this only how I see it?

I look at the tobacco; its fragrance began with the touch of the flame, but it doesn't glow and the smoke doesn't flow across the coils. I don't take the smoke into my chest. The fragrance is enough for me. I go back to trying to take in this presence. If only she'd appeared before me twenty or thirty years earlier, my soul would have blazed and my body would have simmered. I would have exhausted my imagination, stripping her naked, imagining positions that no one had ever set eyes on before. I would have plunged into the deep, ever deeper . . .

I look in their direction. In this light, under that pure blue, accompanied by the gentle breeze, I observe them together. If not for the risk of a misunderstanding, I would go over and wish them the sweetest of happiness, congratulating him on what she gives to life, on the beauty of her bounty . . .

Feebleness

I'm forced to slow my pace. I take my time, listening to a hidden rhythm that flows inside me, that is new to me, warning me that I'm reaching a point I haven't reached before. It warns me to see, to look at myself, to take note of the change in my being. There are fleeting, decisive moments to which we usually pay no attention—but I did. Perhaps because I've been listening for so long now to what arises from inside me. There's something that is slowing my pace, reducing my longing.

I'm standing, trying to trace the other who emerged from me, who left me for a destination that is difficult for me to locate—to no place, no domain. My other, who was with me for so long, pushing me, urging me to lengthen my stride, to be more vigorous, to surpass others in zeal. A long time passes before we realize that we've moved from one phase to another, that what we've been approaching, what we've been eager to arrive at—to attain—is no longer the same. At times the edges get lost, but I remember those milestones. Among them is the moment I reached puberty—the pleasure of the first orgasm, never to be repeated, neither as a response to my imagination, nor during an interaction with a woman in reality, nor during sleep that teemed with mysterious phantoms. The pleasure has never recurred: that spurt that surged from deep inside me, ejaculating from "between my loins and ribs" (Qur'an 86:7)—a flourishing torrent accompanied by an inexplicable pain. Perhaps all the times that I made love later were a kind of longing to repeat that first time. Someone who should know once told me that a person who is about to die ejaculates, as if bidding farewell—with some of his seed—to external existence. Who knows if the pleasure of the first time is repeated in that final moment?

Among the moments of my first-ever journey: my realization that a life separate from my family was beginning, that we were in the process of being dispersed. I recall the moment the train pulled away, going south, as I set out on my first mission. That fleeting moment is near, distinct, despite its quietness, its distance. Now, as I walk around the wide, multistory mall, the entire space is air-conditioned, the shopfronts are magnificent, the windows offer well-known products with endless advertisements, both heard and seen. I stop unexpectedly. A faint flutter—I can pinpoint it in my chest, but it spreads through me. I slow down, fearful of falling over or losing consciousness. To lose consciousness was the worst thing I could imagine during my travels away from home. I remember a display of Middle Eastern sweets that leads to a wide balcony where I can rest before resuming my walk back to the hotel. I set out: with my first footstep, the certainty increases that I've lost someone who used to give me support. With each step, he grows further from me . . .

Nebula

At times I look at those I can't see; at times I talk to those who don't exist, whom I can't identify, a defined space from which they look out at me. They have no features that can be described, no way of telling this one from that. Sometimes I think they are many when they are one. At times I have the illusion that I'm speaking to someone: he has features I would recognize if I were to study them at length. But, as I examine them, I don't find what I thought I was about to confirm. I find only an empty space of pure blue if I'm facing a sea or a clear sky, or plunging into a cluster of clouds that I'm watching from the small window of the plane, through which those nomads swimming in the air and I are interconnected, their limbs and features intermingling. Sometimes, they become fused with patches of cloud, or shades of twilight, or moments before dusk, or crowns of palms and outlines of trees, or when I'm alone in a café that I've sought out from habit or am just passing by.

Their apparitions don't come to me when I have company. They appear only when I'm ready. It begins within me; only I'm aware of it.

229

Traces may appear in my features, in my stare, or when I screw up my eyes, purse my lips, or twiddle my thumbs. At this point, they begin to flood in. They're closest when I'm alone, detached from what's around me, self absorbed even if I'm in a group—especially when I'm sitting and listening to music at a concert that touches the deepest layers within me or listening to old songs that frame times gone by. The dialogue begins at the moment I'm completely silent—another message from within that I don't grant permission or give any signal to. It takes me by surprise, unknown and mysterious, and at this point the unspoken dialogue begins, right in front of me, between someone I can't identify and those I'm incapable of knowing. Little by little, my physical presence vanishes. The give and take between what emanates from within me and what comes to me from outside. As my unheard cry rises, my presence grows faint. I become transparent, lighter, my features become blurred through that argument between me and those whom I haven't met and whose origins I haven't figured out. Things become confused and difficult: the questions become answers, the answers become questions. As for all those emotions that I cataloged through the voyage of my days, they become like wisps floating in my nebula . . .

An eclipse

The newspapers hadn't published a word about it, nor the radio or television news, even though I was expecting it and was eager to observe it—not because I'm an astronomer but because I'm an interested observer for reasons I've described here and others I haven't.

I knew the moment it would start. Precisely at the nineteenth hour, fifty minutes, and eight seconds. It would enter the umbra at exactly the twentieth hour, forty-eight minutes, and two seconds. I knew the time it would enter the total eclipse, and the moment it would leave it, as well as leaving the umbra and penumbra. The end would be at precisely the twenty-fifth hour, nine minutes, and five seconds. I knew the time of the full moon was the twenty-second hour and thirty-three minutes.

Each year, I receive numerous calendars as gifts. I give them out to those who are dear to me; I keep only one, that of the Institute for Astronomical Observation. Each day has a page, with the Arabic, Western, and Coptic dates, as well as the prayer times. It's superior to any other calendar because at the bottom of the page it records the movement of the stars. Each day, I look at it in order to find out the news of the planets and the stars. From it, I learned of the eclipse on the fourth of May. A Tuesday.

I go out to the small balcony from which I look out at the open sky. I've been out there on many nights as Mars approached the earth—an event that will be repeated only after thousands of years. It was destined that I would witness it. Tonight, a full eclipse will begin and end. A total eclipse happens only with the full moon. According to the experts, for the shadow to be complete and block the light entirely, it must illuminate the orb to the furthest extent and it must be fully round. The precise timing is measured in fractions of a second because the full moon isn't actually full, except for fractions of a second. Before then, it's incomplete, and afterward it has waned. But the only ones who realize are the ones who look closely, the experts. For the observer who's not in the know, he thinks it's complete while it's not; he sees it as a full moon while the truth is different.

Here it is—it has begun to enter the umbra. The illuminated orb wanes, eroding noticeably. The roundness is not the same, each must take from the other. What seems to be a dense shadow is only the shadow of the earth. The planet, in the path of its orbit, comes between the sunlight and the surface of the moon. The incidental darkness begins—each swims in its orbit. What if something goes wrong, goes awry? Someone I trust told me that it's possible. So then . . . why? And how? And when?

When faced with what we can't control, we're reduced to questioning—silently or out loud. With the length of time that I've kept up my constant gaze, I've almost become a part of the event of the two spheres combining, each of them taking something—as the shadow merges with the vanishing light so that deep color, mixed with red, appears. It's the opposite of those nights during which the moon appears as a crescent, newborn or larger, when we see a part of the sphere but can't see the rest of the outline. Total darkness, but in this incidental state the outline is not hidden. With the growing shadow, the invisible edges of the moon appear, as this exceptional color—produced by this merging—becomes more distinct.

I know that the earth revolves on its axis, but from time to time I think about the succession of night and day as an indication of that rotation. As the shadow begins to creep across, as it advances and then begins its anticipated retreat, I'm conscious of the movement of two planets in space. In the emptiness, the approach of the circle of shadow and the decrease in the circle of light signify a reciprocal movement, arriving at an exceptional alignment that is repeated only at intervals determined by . . . what? A trajectory, the completion of a rotation, or something unknown?

My breaths slow down as the darkness becomes complete. The total eclipse. The red, mixed with the dark, becomes distinct. It's the shadow of the planet on whose surface I exist.

At the same time, those who came before me rest under the earth, with all the countless living things that accompanied them, that filled the world with their clatter and clamor. All that preceded me is within that shadow, there—as is my existence at that moment. I'm merely a part of this circular shadow. I'm there, and here as well. I'm not there because I'm here; I'm here because I'm there. Of this, I'm certain: the shadow contains me, and I contain it.

Which one am I joining? The one I'm standing on or the one I'm reflecting?

Architecture

The last thing to remain of man is architecture. A building may contain a code, a message that goes from one era to another, from epoch to epoch. You may find someone to decipher it, or it may disappear without making a connection . . .

What is before and after

Marking boundaries was very important to my Egyptian ancestors: agricultural boundaries, irrigation boundaries, construction boundaries. They didn't just mark the boundaries of places—they also marked off times. The ways of marking off places that have come down to us make sense to me, but I don't understand the method concerning time. The first is concrete, tangible; the second is abstract—relative, imagined. The ancients determined time by looking at the rotation of the planets. They thought of the present as a gauge of what preceded it and what came after—past and present. But for me both are relative; when I think about it, I say that "now" doesn't exist. There's no "now." Just by uttering "now," it has slipped away, gone—with only a signal, it has gone. Yesterday and tomorrow—both are imagined. Where is yesterday and where is tomorrow? Both are imagined: "afterward" and "beforehand." Why do we assume the forward progression of time? Why doesn't it move in an opposite way, especially if it has a beginning? It proceeds toward its diminution, to an end. So then . . . is the past not before us, do we not turn toward it, ascending to it? Then the future would be in what has elapsed, being closer to the beginning. As for what will come, it's closer to the end. Will a person not meet his end at some point hidden in what will come? Will this planet not perish at a particular point that we can measure with instruments? Will all of creation not be transformed, and what has elapsed will equal what's to come? So then . . . are destinies not oriented toward the past? Will they not unite with the all-encompassing past, where every living thing will end up? As everything in existence unites with the past, it becomes nothing, only nothingness— where what was and what will be are one.

The earth's womb

On this trip, I realize what has been hidden from me in previous times.

As I approach the entrance to the Valley of the Kings, I stop. The valley parts like a reclining woman, her thighs and her calves are the two sides of the valley. They meet to form the pyramid-shaped hill which rises from them like a young breast, erect. I think of those who were guided to this place that was meant to remain peaceful and hidden, far from any intrusion. The parting and small pyramid carved by nature were a crucial part, but the eternal resting places attempted to make that link with the human dimension.

The entrances are similar: some openings are rectangular, others are circular or irregular in shape, just like vaginas. None is identical to another. The opening leads to a passage, sloping downward or upward—so narrow that one must crouch down to go through it or be forced to crawl on all fours. Whether the distance is long or short, the passage leads to the burial chamber, oval in shape—oval, just like the uterus. The ultimate shape of the universe is oval and not round. Is the egg a sign? And is the womb a symbol? When a person expires, he returns to the great womb, to the earth. He seeks shelter and unites with her. But in a noble effort to understand, he shapes his final resting place in the shape of a womb, with the coffin, the burial room, the carvings, paintings, and symbols, the ceiling strewn with stars and painted with the signs of the zodiac. Meanwhile, the goddess Nut reclines from the furthest eastern point to the furthest west. From her vagina, the sun is being born. On the walls are the eternal Fields of Yaru, with the details of the crossing from one hour to another in the eternal night. The inside lid of the coffin is carved with the image of the goddess Nut, sheltering the deceased, the traveler through infinity. On the base is the image of Geb, ruler of the earth. The sides illustrate the traveler on his journey. No matter how small the space, all the distances are foreshortened: the foreshortening of space, of time, of meanings, and the foreshortening of the universe in the earth's womb, foreshortening itself.

The first

I bend down, examining that first ejaculation again. Such first moments containing beginnings are very rare. They quickly break away from whatever precedes and follows. There it is, and I stare. The moment I reached puberty, the first ejaculation, my first acquaintance with that mysterious pleasure, then unfamiliar to me, like a hidden power bearing me, all of me, to a place that couldn't be seen, that I didn't know, inflicting an intense sharpness, accompanied by a stab from the furthest depths. A pain? Perhaps. A uniqueness I'd never known before, nor since; a first pleasure that hasn't recurred. Since that time, I've pursued it without ever attaining it. To this day, it hasn't recurred, although what I've learned leads me to think it might. It happened that a friend of mine died in a hotel. They found him while he was on a trip. He was lying on his back, staring upward. A heart attack. I don't know who it was that told me that the last thing a man does when he dies a natural death is to ejaculate. Aside from the reasons for the sudden death, the last thing he experiences is that pleasure, that hidden essence. It has a sweet taste, but it's a rare sweetness, the source of which lies within the body, not outside it. I'm certain that the final pleasure will resemble the first, paralleling it: the first time is the opening of the bracket, the last is its closing. I'm certain that if I have the opportunity to enjoy the last one, it will be a recollection of the first—the introduction and the finale together.

A butterfly

I stop and watch in silence. It lands on the edge of the balcony, a butterfly of deep green—I've never seen such a hue. Although I say "butterfly," I've never seen anything like it before, it's like something between a butterfly and a larger insect. I gaze at it and something occurs to me for the first time. Something that links me and it and flows between us. My son looks at me. He doesn't ask anything, as he watches me and sees the state I'm in.

I recall a distant moment. I'm a child, sitting on the ground beside my mother. I ask her about the strange expression on her face, why she's staring at a butterfly that has landed. I can't remember the color—it's gone.

"What's wrong, Mama?"

She gestures with her hand, without turning to me.

"Be quiet . . . it's your grandmother's soul."

Later, she explained to me that after death the soul is reborn in numerous forms—as a bird, as a butterfly, hovering around those who seek it.

It draws nourishment from them and departs. Words to describe my surroundings disappear—the nearby street, the visible trees, the wall— although I become aware of my son insisting:

"What's wrong, Father?"

A beginning

Between the bed and the wardrobe. A confined space. I'm sitting with my head bowed in the small room overlooking the alley, one day in 1959. I don't know what day of the week or month, or what time of year. Suddenly, what was obscured from me stirs—desire, longing, yearning, an energy that defies categorization or identification—to compose, to set down a tale that I heard in detail from my father, to narrate in writing: of a poor man who pretended to stagger around drunkenly in order to steal a loaf of bread. But the people were alerted and captured the thief. Between the onset of desire—the flow of the energy—and the enactment is a short time. And since I began, I've never stopped . . .

—※—

Why do people fear death, even though death is necessary in order for there to be life? If those who preceded us hadn't died, we wouldn't have come to be and wouldn't be followed by those after us. Why then, this fear of the conclusion?

—※—

From the window of the train I look out at the trees—palms, roads, villages, cities, smooth deserts, everything that passes by. I wonder: Who is passing the other? Am I passing through all of this, or is it passing through me? Who gives rise to the other: I, by seeing things, or do things see me? Who sees whom? Do the cities and the villages see me, or is it I who sees the cities, the villages, the people, and the humanity?

—※—

Why does the newborn infant cry the instant he appears?

—※—

Does time have a beginning?

—∾—

Why is there comfort only after a succession of profound sighs?

—∾—

Among humankind's attempts to understand the origin of everything, there's the theory that the universe in which we live began at the moment of a massive explosion, followed by a constant expansion that continues until today and which may reach a point at which it begins to recede. In the beginning, the elements had a high density. With the explosion began time and place. And since what we know of the laws of existence confirms that matter can neither be destroyed nor created, am I entitled to ask about the dense beginning of my own cosmic atoms and their location? How did they look and what forms did they take during the expansion of the universe, until the time came in which I took shape, in which I lived and wrote? Then, will I return just as I began? How will I end? As the universe contracts, where will the parts of me go? Will they be compressed, compacted, or will they be dispersed after the receptacle that contains me has decomposed, after it has dissipated into I don't know what? How will it be?

—∾—

I lean forward, staring into the mirror.

Those are my features. I know them perfectly. I recognize them. These are the traces of my passions: my descents into the abyss, my defeats, the glimmers of my hopes, the misfortunes of my yearning, my lack of vigor, the urgings of my youthful passions, the domains of my nostalgia.

All this looks back at me from my reflection—so who sees whom?

2003–2004

Glossary of Arabic terms and people

Terms

adwar: (plural of *dawr*, also spelled *dur*) a vocal genre that developed in Egypt during the nineteenth century (see Habib Hassan Touma, *The Music of the Arabs*, trans. Laurie Schwarts (Portland, OR: Amadeus, 2003)).

amm: literally, "uncle," but used as a form of address. It's less formal than "sir"—along the lines of "chief" or "boss."

balouza: dessert made with milk, starch, and fruit with a consistency like gelatin.

darabukkah: (also rendered as *darbuka*; also known as *tabla*) a goblet drum played with both hands (see Touma, Music of the Arabs).

darb: a feature of Cairo's medieval layout, linking two larger streets.

fatta: a dish made with stewed bread, rice, and tomato sauce topped with chunks of meat.

gallabiya: a full-length, loose traditional gown worn by men and women.

ghutra: (also called *kuffiya* or *hatta*) a traditional Arab headdress.

hajj/hagg: the word refers to the Muslim pilgrimage to Mecca, as well as to males who have made the pilgrimage. In standard Arabic, the word is hajj; in Egyptian colloquial, it's pronounced *hagg*, as the titles of those who made the pilgrimage are rendered in this book.

harissa: a traditional dessert made of semolina, also known as *basbousa* or namoura.

iqal: (also pronounced *agal* or *igal*) a cord wound around the *ghutra* to hold it in place.

ishtingil: a soft, rolled pastry, like a petit pain, usually stuffed with cheese.

iwan: an open-ended, vaulted reception area (*The Encyclopaedia of Islam*, 2nd ed.)

kahk: cookies that are baked during religious holidays such as Eid al-Fitr, at the end of Ramadan, and Easter. They can be covered with powdered sugar and are often filled with nuts or dates.

keddah: a unit of measurement equivalent to about two liters.

Kerman: a style of Persian rugs.

kunafa: (also spelled *kanafe*, *knafeh*) a dessert filled with cheese soaked in syrup. It can be garnished with nuts and cream and often has a distinctive orange color.

maallim: a casual form of address, along the lines of "boss" or "chief" in Egyptian dialect.

maqam: (plural, *maqamat*) a mode of Arabic music in which melody adheres to notes of specific scales (see Scott Marcus, *Music in Egypt* (New York and Oxford: Oxford University Press, 2007)).

molasses tobacco: known as *maassil*, it's treated with molasses and other flavors. The literal meaning of the name is "honeyed" and is meant to be smoked in a water pipe.

molokhiya: a traditional soup made of jute leaves, for which it's named; served with rice and meat, most often chicken or lamb.

muwashahat: (plural of *muwashah*, also spelled *muwashshah*) a genre of Arabian vocal art music based on the poetic form of the same name and that originates in medieval Andalusia (see Touma, *Music of the Arabs*.

osta: much like *maallim* (see above), a casual form of address in the Egyptian dialect, similar to "boss" or "chief."

oud: a short-necked lute.

rimsh al-ayn: literally, "eyelash," referring to a light fabric.

roumi: a hard, salty cheese made of cow's milk.

Sitt: a title meaning "Lady," used as a respectful address for women or venerated figures like Mary or Fatima.

smeet: also known as *samid* (semolina), this refers to round bread popular in Turkey and the Middle East, often sprinkled with semolina or other seeds.

tambour: (also spelled *tanbour*) a long-necked lute.

taqatiq: (plural of *taqtuqa*) a genre of vocal music originating in the music of nineteenth-century women performers, later incorporated into performances by male and female singers (see Marcus, *Music in Egypt*).

thomn: the word means "eighth," referring to a particular area, based on previous administrative divisions of the city.

People

al-Hamra: translating to "The Red," she is a figure to whom the author repeatedly refers in the third volume *(Streaks of Red)* in the series "Composition Books," of which this memoir is a part. She serves as both his first love and the ideal of womanhood.

Qadi Ayyad: venerated as one of the seven patron-saints of Marrakesh, he is also known as Abu al-Fadl Ayyad ibn Musa ibn Ayyad al-Yahsubi al-Sabti (d. 1149): one of the great religious figures of Islamic Spain, Cadi Ayyad University in Marrakesh, Morocco, is named after him.

al-Sheikh al-Akbar: one of the greatest Sufis in Islam and the most prolific of Sufi writers, Muhyi al-Din Ibn al-Arabi, or Ibn Arabi (d. 1240), is referred to as "al-Sheikh al-Akbar," or "the greatest teacher." (*The Encyclopaedia of Islam*, 2nd ed.).